W9-CPO-829

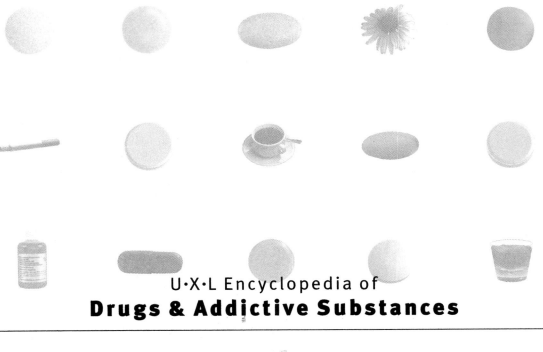

U·X·L Encyclopedia of
Drugs & Addictive Substances

U·X·L Encyclopedia of
Drugs & Addictive Substances

Volume 1:
2C-B (Nexus) to Benzylpiperazine/Trifluoromethyl-phenylpiperazine

Barbara C. Bigelow, MAT

Kathleen J. Edgar, Project Editor

U·X·L

An imprint of Thomson Gale, a part of The Thomson Corporation

THOMSON
™
GALE

Detroit • New York • San Francisco • San Diego • New Haven, Conn. • Waterville, Maine • London • Munich

THOMSON
™
GALE

U·X·L Encyclopedia of Drugs & Addictive Substances

Barbara C. Bigelow, MAT

Project Editor
Kathleen J. Edgar

Editorial
Stephanie Cook, Madeline Harris, Melissa Hill, Kristine Krapp, Paul Lewon, Elizabeth Manar, Heather Price

Rights and Acquisitions
Ron Montgomery, Shalice Shaw-Caldwell

Imaging and Multimedia
Leitha Etheridge-Sims, Lezlie Light, Dan Newell, Christine O'Bryan

Product Design
Pamela A. E. Galbreath, Tracy Rowens

Composition
Evi Seoud, Mary Beth Trimper

Manufacturing
Rita Wimberely

LIBRARY OF CONGRESS CATALOGING-IN-PUBLICATION DATA

Bigelow, Barbara C.
  UXL encyclopedia of drugs & addictive substances / Barbara C. Bigelow, Kathleen J. Edgar.
    p. cm.
  Includes bibliographical references and index.
  ISBN 1-4144-0444-1 (set hardcover : alk. paper) – ISBN 1-4144-0445-X (volume 1) – ISBN 1-4144-0446-8 (volume 2) – ISBN 1-4144-0447-6 (volume 3) – ISBN 1-4144-0448-4 (volume 4) – ISBN 1-4144-0449-2 (volume 5)
  1. Drugs–Encyclopedias, Juvenile. 2. Drugs of abuse–Encyclopedias, Juvenile. 3. Substance abuse–Encyclopedias, Juvenile. I. Title: Encyclopedia of drugs & addictive substances. II. Title: UXL encyclopedia of drugs and addictive substances. III. Edgar, Kathleen J. IV. Title.
  RM301.17.B54 2006
  615'.1'03–dc22
                                                                    2005017640p

This title is also available as an e-book.
ISBN: 1414406193 (set).
Contact your Gale sales representative for ordering information.

Printed in the United States of America
10 9 8 7 6 5 4 3 2 1

Table of Contents

Volume 3

Volume 4

Volume 5

45-minute psychosis *see* **Dimethyltryptamine (DMT)**
714s *see* **Methaqualone**

A

A-bomb *see* **Marijuana**
A2 *see* **Benzylpiperazine/Trifluoromethyl-phenylpiperazine**
Abyssinian tea *see* ***Catha Edulis***
Acapulco gold *see* **Marijuana**
Ace *see* **Marijuana**
Acid *see* **LSD (Lysergic Acid Diethylamide)**
ADAM *see* **Designer Drugs** and **Ecstasy (MDMA)**
African black *see* **Marijuana**
African salad *see* ***Catha Edulis***
Afro *see* **2C-B (Nexus)** and **Designer Drugs**
Ah-pen-yen *see* **Opium**
AIP *see* **Heroin**
Air blast *see* **Inhalants**
Allium sativum see **Herbal Drugs**
Amp *see* **Amphetamines**
Amys *see* **Amyl Nitrite, Inhalants,** and **Tranquilizers**
Andro *see* **Steroids**
Angel dust *see* **Designer Drugs** and **PCP (Phencyclidine)**
Antifreeze *see* **Heroin**
Antipsychotics *see* **Tranquilizers**
Anxiolytics *see* **Tranquilizers**
Apache *see* **Fentanyl**
Aries *see* **Heroin**
Aunt Hazel *see* **Heroin**
Aunt Mary *see* **Marijuana**
Aunti *see* **Opium**
Aunti Emma *see* **Opium**

B

Backbreaker *see* **LSD (Lysergic Acid Diethylamide)**
Balloons *see* **Inhalants** and **Nitrous Oxide**
Bang *see* **Inhalants**

Barbs *see* **Barbiturates** and **Tranquilizers**
Barr *see* **Codeine**
Battery acid *see* **LSD (Lysergic Acid Diethylamide)**
Batu *see* **Methamphetamine**
Bees *see* **2C-B (Nexus)** and **Designer Drugs**
Bennies *see* **Amphetamines**
Benzos *see* **Benzodiazepines** and **Tranquilizers**
Bhang *see* **Marijuana**
Bidis *see* **Nicotine**
Big chief *see* **Mescaline**
Big d *see* **Hydromorphone**
Big H *see* **Heroin**
Big Harry *see* **Heroin**
Big O *see* **Opium**
Black *see* **Opium**
Black hash *see* **Opium**
Black pearl *see* **Heroin**
Black pill *see* **Opium**
Black Russian *see* **Opium**
Black stuff *see* **Opium**
Black tar *see* **Heroin**
Blanche *see* **Marijuana**
Blind squid *see* **Ketamine**
Block *see* **Opium**
Blotter *see* **LSD (Lysergic Acid Diethylamide)**
Blow *see* **Cocaine**
Blue cap *see* **Mescaline**
Blue dolls *see* **Barbiturates**
Blue Nitro *see* **GBL**
Blues *see* **Barbiturates** and **Tranquilizers**
Blunt *see* **Marijuana**
Boat *see* **PCP (Phencyclidine)**
Bonita *see* **Heroin**
Boo *see* **Marijuana**
Boom *see* **Marijuana**
Boomers *see* **LSD (Lysergic Acid Diethylamide)** and **Psilocybin**
Booty juice *see* **Ecstasy (MDMA)**
Booze *see* **Alcohol**
Bozo *see* **Heroin**
Brain damage *see* **Heroin**
Brew *see* **Alcohol**
Brick gum *see* **Heroin**
Bromo *see* **2C-B (Nexus)** and **Designer Drugs**
Brown acid *see* **LSD (Lysergic Acid Diethylamide)**
Brown sugar *see* **Heroin**

Buddha *see* **Opium**

Bull dog *see* **Heroin**

Bundle *see* **Heroin**

Bush *see* **Marijuana**

Bushman's tea *see* ***Catha Edulis*** and **Dimethyltryptamine (DMT)**

Butterbur *see* **Herbal Drugs**

Buttons *see* **Mescaline** and **Methaqualone**

Buzz bombs *see* **Inhalants** and **Nitrous Oxide**

BZDs *see* **Tranquilizers**

BZP *see* **Benzylpiperazine/Trifluoromethyl-phenylpiperazine**

C

C *see* **Cocaine**

Cactus buttons *see* **Mescaline**

Cactus head *see* **Mescaline**

Cadillac *see* **Designer Drugs**

Camellia sinensis see **Herbal Drugs**

Caps *see* **Psilocybin**

Cartridges *see* **Nitrous Oxide**

Cat valium *see* **Designer Drugs** and **Ketamine**

Chalk *see* **Designer Drugs** and **Methamphetamine**

Chamaemelum nobile see **Herbal Drugs**

Chamomile *see* **Herbal Drugs**

Chandoo/Chandu *see* **Opium**

Charas *see* **Marijuana**

Charley *see* **Heroin**

Chat *see* ***Catha Edulis***

Cherry meth *see* **Designer Drugs** and **GHB**

Chew *see* **Nicotine**

Chewing tobacco *see* **Nicotine**

Chicken powder *see* **PMA and PMMA**

Chicken yellow *see* **PMA and PMMA**

Chief *see* **Mescaline**

China girl *see* **Fentanyl**

China town *see* **Fentanyl**

China white *see* **Fentanyl** and **Heroin**

Chinese molasses *see* **Opium**

Chinese tobacco *see* **Opium**

Chronic *see* **Marijuana**

Cid *see* **LSD (Lysergic Acid Diethylamide)**

Cigarettes *see* **Nicotine**

Cigars *see* **Nicotine**

Circles *see* **Rohypnol**

Cloud-9 *see* **2C-B (Nexus)** and **Designer Drugs**

Coffin nails *see* **Nicotine**
Coke *see* **Cocaine**
Comfrey *see* **Herbal Drugs**
Contact lenses *see* **LSD (Lysergic Acid Diethylamide)**
Copilots *see* **Dextroamphetamine**
Coties *see* **Codeine**
Crack cocaine *see* **Cocaine**
Crank *see* **Designer Drugs** and **Methamphetamine**
Crystal *see* **Designer Drugs** and **Methamphetamine**
Crystal meth *see* **Designer Drugs** and **Methamphetamine**
Cubes *see* **Psilocybin**

D

D-ball *see* **Steroids**
D-bol *see* **Steroids**
D's *see* **Hydromorphone**
Dagga *see* **Marijuana**
Dance fever *see* **Fentanyl**
Death *see* **PMA and PMMA**
Deca *see* **Steroids**
Deca-D *see* **Steroids**
Delantz *see* **Hydromorphone**
Delaud *see* **Hydromorphone**
Delida *see* **Hydromorphone**
Demmies *see* **Meperidine**
Depo-T *see* **Steroids**
DET *see* **Dimethyltryptamine (DMT)**
Dex *see* **Dextromethorphan**
Dexies *see* **Dextroamphetamines**
Diesel *see* **Heroin**
Dietary supplements *see* **Creatine**
Dillies *see* **Hydromorphone**
Disco biscuit *see* **Designer Drugs**
Disco biscuits *see* **Ecstasy** and **Methaqualone**
Discorama *see* **Inhalants**
Diviner's sage *see* ***Salvia Divinorum***
DM *see* **Dextromethorphan**
Dollies *see* **Methadone**
Dolls *see* **Barbiturates** and **Methadone**
Dope *see* **Marijuana**
Dopium *see* **Opium**
Dors and fours *see* **Codeine**
Doses *see* **LSD (Lysergic Acid Diethylamide)**
Dots *see* **LSD (Lysergic Acid Diethylamide)**

Double-stacked *see* **PMA and PMMA**

Dover's deck *see* **Opium**

Down *see* **Codeine**

Downers *see* **Barbiturates, Benzodiazepines, Over-the-Counter Drugs,** and **Tranquilizers**

Drank *see* **Codeine**

Dream gun *see* **Opium**

Dream stick *see* **Opium**

Dreams *see* **Opium**

Drex *see* **Dextromethorphan**

Drug store heroin *see* **Hydromorphone**

Dust *see* **Designer Drugs, Hydromorphone,** and **PCP (Phencyclidine)**

DXM *see* **Dextromethorphan**

E

E *see* **Designer Drugs** and **Ecstasy (MDMA)**

Easing powder *see* **Opium**

Easy lay *see* **GHB**

Echinacea *see* **Herbal Drugs**

Echinacea purpurea see **Herbal Drugs**

Elderberry *see* **Herbal Drugs**

Electric kool-aid *see* **LSD (Lysergic Acid Diethylamide)**

Elephant *see* **PCP (Phencyclidine)**

Embalming fluid *see* **Designer Drugs**

Empathy *see* **Ecstasy (MDMA)**

Ephedra *see* **Herbal Drugs**

Ephedra sinica see **Herbal Drugs**

Essence *see* **Ecstasy (MDMA)**

Eve *see* **2C-B (Nexus)** and **Designer Drugs**

F

Fags *see* **Nicotine**

Fantasia *see* **Dimethyltryptamine (DMT)**

Fi-do-nie *see* **Opium**

Firewater *see* **GBL**

Fizzies *see* **Methadone**

Footballs *see* **Hydromorphone**

Forget-me pill *see* **Rohypnol**

Foxy *see* **Dimethyltryptamine (DMT)**

Foxy methoxy *see* **Dimethyltryptamine (DMT)**

Friend *see* **Fentanyl**

Fry *see* **Designer Drugs** and **Marijuana**

Fry sticks *see* **Marijuana**
Fungus *see* **Psilocybin**

G

G *see* **GHB**
G-riffick *see* **GHB**
G3 *see* **GBL**
Gamma G *see* **GBL**
Gamma X *see* **GBL**
Gangster *see* **Marijuana**
Ganja *see* **Marijuana**
Garlic *see* **Herbal Drugs**
Gas *see* **Inhalants**
Gat *see* ***Catha Edulis***
Gear *see* **Steroids**
Gee *see* **Opium**
Georgia home boy *see* **Designer Drugs** and **GHB**
GH Revitalizer *see* **GBL**
Ginkgo *see* **Herbal Drugs**
Ginkgo biloba *see* **Herbal Drugs**
Ginseng *see* **Herbal Drugs**
Glass *see* **Designer Drugs** and **Methamphetamine**
Glue *see* **Inhalants**
Go-pills *see* **Dextroamphetamine**
God's medicine *see* **Opium**
Gondola *see* **Opium**
Goodfellas *see* **Fentanyl**
Goofballs *see* **Tranquilizers**
Goop *see* **Designer Drugs**
Goric *see* **Opium**
Grass *see* **Marijuana**
Great bear *see* **Fentanyl**
Great tobacco *see* **Opium**
Green tea *see* **Herbal Drugs**
Grievous bodily harm *see* **Designer Drugs** and **GHB**
Gum *see* **Opium**
Guma *see* **Opium**

H

H *see* **Heroin**
Happy pills *see* **Antidepressants** and **Tranquilizers**
Harry *see* **Heroin**
Hash *see* **Marijuana**

Hash oil *see* **Marijuana**

He-man *see* **Fentanyl**

Herb *see* **Marijuana**

Herbal ecstasy *see* ***Salvia Divinorum*** and **Benzylpiperazine/
    Trifluoromethyl-phenylpiperazine**

Herbal speed *see* **Benzylpiperazine/Trifluoromethyl-phenylpiperazine**

Hierba Maria *see* ***Salvia Divinorum***

Hillbilly heroin *see* **Oxycodone**

Hippie crack *see* **Inhalants** and **Nitrous Oxide**

Hippy flip *see* **Psilocybin**

Hog *see* **PCP (Phencyclidine)**

Honey oil *see* **Inhalants** and **Ketamine**

Hooch *see* **Alcohol**

Hop/Hops *see* **Opium**

Huff *see* **Inhalants**

Hug drug *see* **Designer Drugs** and **Ecstasy (MDMA)**

Hypericum perforatum see **Herbal Drugs**

I

Ice *see* **Designer Drugs** and **Methamphetamine**

Indian snakeroot *see* **Tranquilizers**

Invigorate *see* **GBL**

J

Jackpot *see* **Fentanyl**

Jet *see* **Designer Drugs** and **Ketamine**

Joint *see* **Marijuana**

Jolt *see* **GBL**

Joy plant *see* **Opium**

Juice *see* **Hydromorphone** and **Steroids**

Junk *see* **Steroids**

K

K *see* **Designer Drugs** and **Ketamine**

Karo *see* **Codeine**

Kat *see* ***Catha Edulis***

Kava *see* **Herbal Drugs**

Kef *see* **Marijuana**

Ket *see* **Designer Drugs** and **Ketamine**

Khat *see* ***Catha Edulis***

Kick *see* **Inhalants**

Kief *see* **Marijuana**

Kif *see* **Marijuana**

Killer *see* **PMA and PMMA**

Killer joints *see* **PCP (Phencyclidine)**

Killer weed *see* **PCP (Phencyclidine)**

Killers *see* **Oxycodone**

King ivory *see* **Fentanyl**

Kit kat *see* **Ketamine**

Kreteks *see* **Nicotine**

L

La rocha *see* **Rohypnol**

Laughing gas *see* **Inhalants** and **Nitrous Oxide**

Lean *see* **Codeine**

Leaves of Mary *see* **Salvia Divinorum**

Legal E *see* **Benzylpiperazine/Trifluoromethyl-phenylpiperazine**

Legal X *see* **Benzylpiperazine/Trifluoromethyl-phenylpiperazine**

Liberty caps *see* **Psilocybin**

Liquid E *see* **GHB**

Liquid ecstasy *see* **GHB**

Liquid gold *see* **Amyl Nitrite**

Liquid X *see* **GHB**

Little d *see* **Hydromorphone**

Locker room *see* **Amyl Nitrite** and **Inhalants**

Looney tunes *see* **LSD (Lysergic Acid Diethylamide)**

Lords *see* **Hydromorphone**

Love drug *see* **Methaqualone**

Lovelies *see* **PCP (Phencyclidine)**

Lucy in the sky with diamonds *see* **LSD (Lysergic Acid Diethylamide)**

Ludes *see* **Methaqualone** and **Tranquilizers**

Lunch money *see* **Rohypnol**

M

M *see* **Morphine**

Ma huang see **Ephedra**

Magic mushrooms *see* **Psilocybin**

Mahuang see **Ephedra**

Mandies *see* **Methaqualone**

Mandrakes *see* **Methaqualone**

Mandrax *see* **Methaqualone**

Manteca *see* **Heroin**

Mary Jane *see* **Marijuana**

Matricaria recutita see **Herbal Drugs**

Max *see* **Designer Drugs**
Medusa *see* **Inhalants**
Mel *see* **Melatonin**
Melliquid *see* **Melatonin**
Mellow tonin *see* **Melatonin**
Mentha pulegium *see* **Herbal Drugs**
Mesc *see* **Mescaline**
Mescal *see* **Mescaline**
Meth *see* **Designer Drugs** and **Methamphetamine**
Mexican brown *see* **Fentanyl**
Mexican mint *see* ***Salvia Divinorum***
Mexican mud *see* **Heroin**
Mexican mushrooms *see* **Psilocybin**
Mexican Valium *see* **Rohypnol**
Microdots *see* **LSD (Lysergic Acid Diethylamide)**
Midnight oil *see* **Opium**
Mind erasers *see* **Rohypnol**
Miraa *see* ***Catha Edulis***
Miss Emma *see* **Morphine**
Mitsubishi *see* **PMA and PMMA**
Mitsubishi double-stack *see* **PMA and PMMA**
MLT *see* **Melatonin**
Monkey *see* **Morphine**
Moon *see* **Mescaline**
Moon gas *see* **Inhalants**
Moonshine *see* **Alcohol**
Mormon tea *see* **Ephedra**
Morph *see* **Morphine**
Mud *see* **Heroin**
Murder 8 *see* **Fentanyl**
Mushies *see* **Psilocybin**
Mushrooms *see* **Psilocybin**
MX missile *see* **Psilocybin**

N

Neuroleptics *see* **Tranquilizers**
Nexus *see* **2C-B (Nexus)** and **Designer Drugs**
Nice and easy *see* **Heroin**
Nickel *see* **Marijuana**
Nitrous *see* **Nitrous Oxide**
Nods *see* **Codeine**
Noise *see* **Heroin**
Nose candy *see* **Cocaine**
Number 4 *see* **Heroin**

Number 8 *see* **Heroin**
Nurse *see* **Heroin**

O

O *see* **Opium**
O.P. *see* **Opium**
Oat *see* *Catha Edulis*
OCs *see* **Oxycodone**
Oil *see* **Marijuana**
Old man *see* **Marijuana**
Ope *see* **Opium**
Oxies *see* **Oxycodone**
Oxycons *see* **Oxycodone**
Oz *see* **Inhalants**
Ozone *see* **PCP (Phencyclidine)**

P

P-dope *see* **Fentanyl**
P-funk *see* **Fentanyl**
Panax ginseng *see* **Herbal Drugs**
Panes *see* **LSD (Lysergic Acid Diethylamide)**
Party pill *see* **Benzylpiperazine/Trifluoromethyl-phenylpiperazine**
Pastora *see* *Salvia Divinorum*
PCE *see* **PCP (Phencyclidine)**
Pearls *see* **Amyl Nitrite** and **Inhalants**
Peg *see* **Heroin**
Pen yan *see* **Opium**
Pennyroyal *see* **Herbal Drugs**
Pep pills *see* **Amphetamines** and **Dextroamphetamine**
Perc-o-pop *see* **Fentanyl**
Percs *see* **Oxycodone**
Perks *see* **Oxycodone**
Persian white *see* **Fentanyl**
Petasites hybridus *see* **Herbal Drugs**
Pin gon *see* **Opium**
Pin yen *see* **Opium**
Pink spoons *see* **Oxycodone**
Piper methysticum *see* **Herbal Drugs**
Piperazine *see* **Benzylpiperazine/Trifluoromethyl-phenylpiperazine**
Poison *see* **Fentanyl**
Poor man's cocaine *see* **Methamphetamine**
Poor man's heroin *see* **Oxycodone**
Poor man's pot *see* **Inhalants**

Poppers *see* **Amyl Nitrite** and **Inhalants**
Pot *see* **Marijuana**
Powder *see* **Cocaine**
Pox *see* **Opium**
Psilcydes *see* **Psilocybin**
Psychedelic mushrooms *see* **Psilocybin**
Purple haze *see* **LSD (Lysergic Acid Diethylamide)**
Purple hearts *see* **Barbiturates**
Purple passion *see* **Psilocybin**

Q

Qaadka *see* ***Catha Edulis***
Qat *see* ***Catha Edulis***
Quaalude *see* **Methaqualone**
Quads *see* **Methaqualone**
Quat *see* ***Catha Edulis***
Quay *see* **Methaqualone**

R

R-2 *see* **Rohypnol**
R-ball *see* **Ritalin and Other Methylphenidates**
Ragers *see* **Steroids**
Rainbows *see* **Barbiturates** and **Tranquilizers**
Rauwolfia *see* **Tranquilizers**
Rave *see* **Ecstasy (MDMA)**
ReActive *see* **GBL**
Red birds *see* **Barbiturates**
Red death *see* **PMA and PMMA**
Red devils *see* **Barbiturates, Dextromethorphan, Over-the-Counter Drugs,** and **Tranquilizers**
Red mitsubishi *see* **PMA and PMMA**
Reds *see* **Barbiturates**
Reefer *see* **Marijuana**
REMForce *see* **GBL**
RenewTrient *see* **GBL**
Rest-eze *see* **GBL**
Revivarant *see* **GBL**
Rib *see* **Rohypnol**
Ro *see* **Rohypnol**
Roach *see* **Marijuana**
Roaches *see* **Rohypnol**
Roachies *see* **Rohypnol**
Roapies *see* **Rohypnol**

Robo *see* **Dextromethorphan**
Robo-tripping *see* **Dextromethorphan**
Roche *see* **Rohypnol**
Rock *see* **Cocaine**
Rocket fuel *see* **PCP (Phencyclidine)**
Roids *see* **Steroids**
Roll *see* **Ecstasy (MDMA)**
Roofies *see* **Rohypnol**
Rope *see* **Rohypnol**
Rophies *see* **Rohypnol**
Rophy *see* **Rohypnol**
Ruffies *see* **Rohypnol**
Ruffles *see* **Rohypnol**
Rush *see* **Amyl Nitrite** and **Inhalants**

S

Salty dog *see* **GHB**
Salty water *see* **GHB**
Salvia *see* ***Salvia Divinorum***
Sambucus nigra *see* **Herbal Drugs**
Sauce *see* **Alcohol**
Saw palmetto *see* **Herbal Drugs**
Schoolboy *see* **Codeine**
Scooby snacks *see* **Ecstasy (MDMA)**
Scoop *see* **GHB**
Sedative-hypnotics *see* **Tranquilizers**
Semilla de la Virgen *see* ***Salvia Divinorum***
Sensi *see* **Marijuana**
Serenoa repens *see* **Herbal Drugs**
Shabu *see* **Methamphetamine**
Shays *see* **Rohypnol**
Shepherdess *see* ***Salvia Divinorum***
Sherm *see* **PCP (Phencyclidine)**
Shermans *see* **PCP (Phencyclidine)**
Sh#t *see* **Heroin**
Shoot the breeze *see* **Inhalants**
Shrooms *see* **Psilocybin**
Sillies *see* **Psilocybin**
Silly putty *see* **Psilocybin**
Simple Simon *see* **Psilocybin**
Sinsemilla *see* **Marijuana**
Ska Maria Pastora *see* ***Salvia Divinorum***
Skag *see* **Heroin**
Skee *see* **Opium**

Skittles *see* **Dextromethorphan** and **Over-the-Counter Drugs**
Skunk *see* **Marijuana**
Sleeping pills *see* **Barbiturates**
Smack *see* **Heroin** and **Hydromorphone**
Smoke *see* **Marijuana**
Smokes *see* **Nicotine**
Snappers *see* **Amyl Nitrite** and **Inhalants**
Sniff *see* **Inhalants**
Snow *see* **Cocaine**
Snuff *see* **Nicotine**
Soap *see* **Designer Drugs** and **GHB**
Somniset *see* **Melatonin**
Sopors *see* **Tranquilizers**
Special K *see* **Designer Drugs** and **Ketamine**
Speed *see* **Adderall, Amphetamines, Designer Drugs, Dextroampheta-
    mine,** and **Methamphetamine**
Spirits *see* **Alcohol**
Spit *see* **Nicotine**
Splif *see* **Marijuana**
St. John's wort *see* **Herbal Drugs**
Stacy *see* **Designer Drugs**
Stuff *see* **Heroin** and **Steroids**
Stupefi *see* **Rohypnol**
Suds *see* **Alcohol**
Sunshine *see* **LSD (Lysergic Acid Diethylamide)**
Supergrass *see* **PCP (Phencyclidine)**
Superweed *see* **PCP (Phencyclidine)**
Supps *see* **Creatine**
Symphytum officinale see **Herbal Drugs**
Synthetic heroin *see* **Fentanyl**
Syrup *see* **Codeine**

T

T-threes *see* **Codeine**
Tango & Cash *see* **Fentanyl**
Tar *see* **Marijuana**
Texas shoeshine *see* **Inhalants**
TFMPP *see* **Benzylpiperazine/Trifluoromethyl-phenylpiperazine**
Thai sticks *see* **Marijuana**
Thrust *see* **Amyl Nitrite** and **Inhalants**
Tic tac *see* **PCP (Phencyclidine)**
Tina *see* **Methamphetamine**
TNT *see* **Fentanyl**
Toilet water *see* **Inhalants**

Tombstone *see* **Fentanyl**
Toonies *see* **2C-B (Nexus)** and **Designer Drugs**
Tootsie roll *see* **Heroin**
Topi *see* **Mescaline**
Toxy *see* **Opium**
Toys *see* **Opium**
Tranks *see* **Benzodiazepines** and **Tranquilizers**
Tranx *see* **Tranquilizers**
Trash *see* **Methamphetamine**
Triple-C *see* **Dextromethorphan** and **Over-the-Counter Drugs**
Tschat *see* ***Catha Edulis***
Tussin *see* **Dextromethorphan**

U

Uppers *see* **Adderall, Amphetamines, Dextroamphetamine,** and **Over-the-Counter Drugs**
Utopia *see* **2C-B (Nexus)** and **Designer Drugs**

V

V35 *see* **GBL**
Valerian *see* **Herbal Drugs** and **Tranquilizers**
Valeriana officinalis see **Herbal Drugs**
Velvet *see* **Dextromethorphan**
Venus *see* **2C-B (Nexus)** and **Designer Drugs**
Verve *see* **GBL**
Vino *see* **Alcohol**
Virgin Mary's herb *see* ***Salvia Divinorum***
Virgin's seed *see* ***Salvia Divinorum***
Vitamin D *see* **Dextromethorphan**
Vitamin K *see* **Designer Drugs** and **Ketamine**
Vitamin R *see* **Ritalin and Other Methylphenidates**

W

Wack *see* **PCP (Phencyclidine)**
Water pills *see* **Diuretics**
Weed *see* **Marijuana**
West Coast *see* **Ritalin and Other Methylphenidates**
Wets *see* **PCP (Phencyclidine)**
When-shee *see* **Opium**
Whip-its *see* **Nitrous Oxide**
Whippets *see* **Inhalants** and **Nitrous Oxide**

Whippits *see* **Nitrous Oxide**
White mitsubishi *see* **PMA and PMMA**
White stuff *see* **Heroin** and **Morphine**
Whiteout *see* **Inhalants**
Windowpanes *see* **LSD (Lysergic Acid Diethylamide)**
Wolfies *see* **Rohypnol**

X

X *see* **Designer Drugs** and **Ecstasy (MDMA)**
XTC *see* **Designer Drugs** and **Ecstasy (MDMA)**

Y

Ya ba see **Methamphetamine**
Yellow jackets *see* **Barbiturates** and **Tranquilizers**
Yellow sunshine *see* **LSD (Lysergic Acid Diethylamide)**
Yellows *see* **Barbiturates**

Z

Ze *see* **Opium**
Zen *see* **LSD (Lysergic Acid Diethylamide)**
Zero *see* **Opium**
Zip *see* **Methamphetamine**
Zonked *see* **GHB**

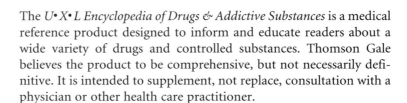

The *U•X•L Encyclopedia of Drugs & Addictive Substances* is a medical reference product designed to inform and educate readers about a wide variety of drugs and controlled substances. Thomson Gale believes the product to be comprehensive, but not necessarily definitive. It is intended to supplement, not replace, consultation with a physician or other health care practitioner.

Although Thomson Gale has made substantial efforts to provide information that is accurate, comprehensive, and up-to-date, Thomson Gale makes no representations or warranties of any kind, including without limitation, warranties of merchantability or fitness for a particular purpose, nor does it guarantee the accuracy, comprehensiveness, or timeliness of the information contained in this product. Readers should be aware that the universe of medical knowledge is constantly growing and changing, and that differences of medical opinion exist among authorities. Readers are also advised to seek professional diagnosis and treatment of any possible substance abuse problem, and to discuss information obtained from this book with their health care provider.

Preface

Education is the most powerful tool an individual can have when facing decisions about drug use. The *U•X•L Encyclopedia of Drugs & Addictive Substances* puts clear, comprehensive, and current information on fifty-two drugs at readers' fingertips. The set was designed with middle-school students in mind but can serve as a useful resource for readers of all ages. Each of the entries in this five-volume encyclopedia offers insights into the history, usage trends, and effects of a specific drug or addictive substance.

What Does "Addiction" Mean?

According to the National Institute on Drug Abuse's *NIDA InfoFacts: Understanding Drug Abuse and Addiction,* dated March 2005, drug addiction is more than just "a lot of drug use." The term "addiction" is described as:

- an overpowering desire, craving, or need to take a certain drug
- a willingness to obtain the drug by any means
- a tendency to keep increasing the dose that is consumed
- a psychological and/or physical dependence on the effects of the drug
- an inability to stop using the drug without treatment
- an illness that has harmful effects on the individual and on society.

What Can Readers Expect to Find in This Encyclopedia?

Every entry in the *U•X•L Encyclopedia of Drugs & Addictive Substances* has been painstakingly researched and is based on data from the latest government and university studies on the use and abuse of drugs and other addictive substances. In fact, the results of certain studies were first released to the public while this project was being researched. We are pleased to be able to pass along to readers some of the most up-to-date information on drug use available as this project went to press.

Please note that every effort has been made to secure the most recent information available. Readers should bear in mind that many major studies take years to conduct. Also, several additional years may pass before the data from these studies are made available to the public. As such, in some cases, the most recent information available in 2005 dated from 2001 or 2002. We've presented older statistics as well if they are of particular interest and no more recent data exist.

Some of the substances profiled in the *U•X•L Encyclopedia of Drugs & Addictive Substances* are legal. Examples of legal—but nevertheless addictive—substances are caffeine, nicotine, and certain over-the-counter medications. Many other substances described in this set are illicit, or illegal. Drugs that fall into this category include cocaine, ecstasy (MDMA), and heroin, among many others.

One of the leading concerns of the late 1990s and early 2000s was the spike in methamphetamine abuse. Methamphetamine, or "meth," is a highly addictive drug that can kill. It is interesting to note that methamphetamine is available by prescription for a limited number of medical uses. However, the bulk of the illicit meth that is sold on the streets is smuggled in from Mexico or manufactured by so-called "bathtub chemists" in the United States. This nickname is given to amateur drug makers working in illegal, makeshift labs. These drug makers are out to make a quick buck. They produce their drugs as cheaply as possible, often adding other dangerous substances or filler ingredients to their homemade concoctions. The risks involved in making and taking laboratory-produced mind-altering substances are discussed at length in this encyclopedia.

The Coining of a Brand-New Term: "Generation Rx"

Among the most notable trends in drug use during the first five years of the twenty-first century was the growing abuse of two types of substances: 1) inhalants, including glue, nitrous oxide, and spray paint, and 2) prescription drugs, especially painkillers and stimulants. Drugs such as oxycodone (OxyContin), Adderall, and methylphenidate (Ritalin) have been approved by the U.S. Food and Drug Administration (FDA) for legitimate uses when prescribed by a physician. Increasingly, however, these drugs have made their way from home medicine cabinets to schools and dance clubs. Because of the sizable increase in prescription drug abuse among young people, the term "Generation Rx" is frequently used to describe the teens of the early 2000s.

The magnitude of inhalant and prescription drug abuse problems first became apparent with the release of the 2004 Monitoring the Future (MTF) study results. MTF is a survey of drug use and attitudes conducted by the University of Michigan with funds from the National Institute on Drug Abuse (NIDA). In late April of 2005, the Partnership for a Drug-Free America released its 2004 Partnership Attitude Tracking Study (PATS). At that time, the extent of

Vicodin abuse, in particular, became apparent. Vicodin is the brand name of the prescription painkiller hydrocodone. To ensure that information on this growing Vicodin trend was available to readers of this encyclopedia, we have included an informative sidebar and other information on the drug within the Meperidine entry. Please consult the master index for a complete list of pages that address the topic of Vicodin.

Format

The *U•X•L Encyclopedia of Drugs & Addictive Substances* is arranged alphabetically by drug name over five volumes. Each entry follows a standard format and includes the following sections:

- What Kind of Drug Is It?
- Overview
- What Is It Made Of?
- How Is It Taken?
- Are There Any Medical Reasons for Taking This Substance?
- Usage Trends
- Effects on the Body
- Reactions with Other Drugs or Substances
- Treatment for Habitual Users
- Consequences
- The Law
- For More Information

Each entry also includes the official drug name, a list of street or alternative names for the drug, and the drug's classification according to the U.S. government's Controlled Substances Act (1970). Important glossary terms are highlighted in the text in small caps with the definitions of the words appearing in the margin.

Features

All entries contain informative sidebars on historical, social, legal, and/or statistical aspects of the drugs. This encyclopedia contains nearly 200 sidebars. In addition, the encyclopedia features more than 300 graphics, including black and white photos, maps, tables, and other illustrations.

The *U•X•L Encyclopedia of Drugs & Addictive Substances* also includes:

- Alternative Drug Names guide. As most students recognize drugs by their common rather than official names, this guide to street and other alternative names points students to the correct entry name.

- Chronology. This section presents important historical moments in the history of drugs, from the discovery of dried peyote buttons in c. 5000 BCE to the withdrawal of the prescription drug Palladone in 2005.
- Words to Know. This master glossary defines difficult terms to help students with words that are unfamiliar to them.
- Color insert. Included in each volume, the insert visually informs readers about various drug topics discussed in the set, such as natural sources of drugs, herbal and dietary supplements, older illicit drugs, prescription drugs, public service announcement posters, and the rave culture.
- Highlights of the U.S. Controlled Substances Act (CSA) of 1970. This section discusses the various drug schedules created by the U.S. government and what they mean.
- Where to Learn More. This bibliography presents important sources (books, periodicals, Web sites, and organizations) where more information on drugs and addictive substances can be obtained.
- Cumulative Index. The master index points readers to topics covered in all five volumes of the encyclopedia.

Special Thanks

Various individuals are to be thanked for aiding in the creation of the *U•X•L Encyclopedia of Drugs & Addictive Substances*. These include the following writers and editors: Pamela Willwerth Aue, Denise Evans, Joan Goldsworthy, Margaret Haerens, Anne Johnson, Jane Kelly Kosek, Mya Nelson, Diane Sawinski, and Les Stone.

In addition, special thanks go out to the project's advisory board members. Thomson Gale would like to express its appreciation to the following board members for their time and valuable contributions:

- Carol M. Keeler, Media Specialist, Detroit Country Day Upper School, Beverly Hills, Michigan
- Nina Levine, Library Media Specialist, Blue Mountain Middle School, Cortlandt Manor, New York
- Toni Thole, Health Educator, Vicksburg Middle School, Vicksburg, Michigan
- Susan Vanneman, NBPTS, Robin Mickle Middle School, Lincoln Public Schools, Lincoln, Nebraska

Comments and Suggestions

We welcome your comments on the *U•X•L Encyclopedia of Drugs & Addictive Substances* and suggestions for other topics to consider. Please write: Editors, *U·X·L Encyclopedia of Drugs & Addictive Substances,* Thomson Gale, 27500 Drake Rd., Farmington Hills, MI 48331-3535; call toll free: 1-800-877-4253; fax to 248-699-8097; or send e-mail via http://www.gale.com.

Chronology

c. 5000 BCE Dried peyote buttons dating from this era are later found in Shumla Cave, Texas.

c. 4000 BCE Opium poppies are cultivated in the Fertile Crescent (now Iran and Iraq) by the ancient cultures of Mesopotamia.

1552 BCE An ancient Egyptian papyrus text from the city of Thebes lists 700 uses for opium.

c. 1300 BCE A Peruvian carving depicting a San Pedro cactus, a source of mescaline, is made on stone tablets.

c. 700 BCE Archaeological tablets record that Persians and Assyrians used cannabis as a drug.

c. 199 Galen (129–c. 199), a medical authority during late Antiquity and the Middle Ages, creates a philosophy of medicine, anatomy, and physiology that remains virtually unchallenged until the sixteenth and seventeenth centuries.

c. 200 Chinese surgeons boil hemp in wine to produce an anesthetic called *ma fei san.*

c. 400 Hemp is cultivated in Europe and in England.

600-900 Arabic traders introduce opium to China.

1000 In Coahuila, Mexico, corpses are buried with beaded necklaces of dried peyote buttons.

c. 1200 Peoples of pre-Hispanic America throughout the Inca Empire (1200–1553) chew coca leaves for their stimulating effects and view the plant as a divine gift of the Sun God.

c. 1300 Arabs develop the technique of roasting coffee beans (native to the Kaffa region of Ethiopia), and cultivation for medicinal purposes begins.

c. 1350 Germany bans the sale of alcohol on Sundays and other religious holidays.

c. 1500 Following the Spanish conquest of the Aztecs, unsuccessful attempts are made to prohibit the use of the "magic mushroom" (*Psilocybe* mushrooms) in Central America.

c. 1500 With the rise of national navies during the sixteenth century, hemp farming is encouraged in England and continental Europe to meet the demand for rope and naval rigging.

1524 Paracelsus (1493–1541), Swiss physician and alchemist, mixes opium with alcohol and names the resulting product laudanum.

1556 Andre Thevet brings tobacco seeds to France from Brazil, thus introducing tobacco to Western Europe. Jean Nico suggests that tobacco has medicinal properties in 1559 at the French court, and the plant is renamed nicotina in his honor. By 1565, tobacco seeds are brought to England, where smoking is later made popular by Sir Walter Raleigh.

1612 Tobacco cultivation begins in America and soon becomes a major New World crop. Exports to England begin in 1613, with the first shipment by John Rolfe.

1640 First distillery is established in the United States.

1772 Nitrous oxide is discovered by British scientist, theologian, and philosopher Joseph Priestly (1733–1804).

1775 William Withering, a British physician with a strong interest in botany, introduces the drug digitalis (Foxglove *Digitalis purpurea*) into common medical practice for the treatment of dropsy. Dropsy is a now-obsolete term for edema (fluid retention or swelling) due to heart failure.

1798 Government legislation is passed to establish hospitals in the United States devoted to the care of ill sailors. This initiative leads to the establishment of a Hygenic Laboratory that eventually grows to become the National Institutes of Health.

1799 Chinese emperor Kia King's ban on opium fails to stop the profitable British monopoly over the opium trade.

1799 British scientist Humphry Davy (1778–1829) suggests nitrous oxide can be used to reduce pain during surgery.

c. 1800 Records show that chloral hydrate is used in the "Mickey Finn" cocktail—a drink used to knock people out. The Mickey Finn was used by people wanting to abduct or lure sailors to serve on ships bound for sea.

1803 German scientist Friedrich Sertürner isolates morphine as the most active ingredient in the opium poppy.

1824 Performances in London of "M. Henry's Mechanical and Chemical Demonstrations" show the effects of nitrous oxide on audience volunteers.

1827 Caffeine from tea, originally named "theine," is isolated.

1828 Nicotine ($C_{10}H_{14}N_2$, beta-pyridyl-alpha-N methylpyrrolidine), a highly poisonous alkaloid, is first isolated from tobacco.

1829 Salicin, the precursor of aspirin, is purified from the bark of the willow tree.

1832 French chemist Michel-Eugène Chevreul (1786–1889) isolates creatine from muscle tissue.

1832 Pierre-Jean Robiquet (1780–1840) discovers codeine. Codeine is an alkaloid found in opium that is now used in prescription pain relievers and cough medicines.

1837 Edinburgh chemist and physician William Gregory discovers a more efficient method to isolate and purify morphine.

1839 The First Opium War begins between Britain and China. The conflict lasts until 1842. Imperial Chinese commissioner Lin Tse-Hsu seizes or destroys vast amounts of opium, including stocks owned by British traders. The Chinese pay compensation of more than 21 million silver dollars, and Hong Kong is ceded to Britain under the Treaty of Nanking.

1841 The anesthetic properties of ether are first used by Dr. Crawford W. Long as he surgically removes two tumors from the neck of an anesthetized patient.

1844 The first recorded use of nitrous oxide in U.S. dentistry occurs and involves Quincy Colton, a former medical student, and dentist Horace Wells.

1848 The hypodermic needle is invented, allowing for quicker delivery of morphine to the brain.

1856 The Second Opium War begins between Britain and China. The conflict lasts until 1860. Also known as the Arrow War, or the Anglo-French War in China, the war breaks out after a British-flagged ship, the *Arrow*, is impounded by China. France joins Britain in the war after the murder of a French missionary. China is again defeated and made to pay another large compensation. Under the Treaty of Tientsin, opium is again legalized.

1860 German chemist, Albert Niemann, separates cocaine from the coca leaf.

1861–1865 Morphine gains wide medical use during the American Civil War. Many injured soldiers return from the war as morphine addicts. Morphine addiction becomes known as the "soldiers' disease."

1862 The Department of Agriculture establishes the Bureau of Chemistry, the forerunner of the U.S. Food and Drug Administration (FDA).

1863 German chemist Adolf von Baeyer (1835–1917) discovers barbituric acid.

1864 Amyl nitrite is first synthesized. During the last decades of the twentieth century, amyl nitrite and similar compounds (e.g., butyl, isobutyl, isoamyl, isopropyl, and cyclohexyl nitrates and nitrites) become the chemical basis of "poppers."

1864 German scientists Joseph von Mering (1849-1908) and Nobel prizewinner Emil Hermann Fischer (1852-1919) synthesize the first barbiturate.

1867 Thomas Lauder Brunton (1844–1916), a medical student in Scotland, discovers that amyl nitrite relieves angina by increasing blood flow to the heart. A few years later, nitroglycerine is discovered to have a similar dilating effect. Although both can still be prescribed for angina, nitroglycerine became more commonly prescribed because it is more easily administered and has fewer side effects.

1871 Companies in both the United States and the United Kingdom succeed in producing compressed and liquid nitrous oxide in cylinders.

1874 British chemist Alder Wright uses morphine to create diacetyl-morphine (heroin), in an effort to produce a less addictive painkiller.

1879 The Memphis, Tennessee, public health agency targets opium dens by making it illegal to sell, own, or borrow "opium or any deleterious drug." Critics point out that it is unfair to deny opium to Chinese immigrants while allowing white citizens to freely purchase morphine. In fact, people could legally inhale, drink, or inject morphine at that time. It wasn't until 1909 that federal law outlawed smoking or possessing opium.

1882 Production of the drug barbital begins, and doctors start using the barbiturate in various treatments.

1887 Amphetamines are first synthesized.

1889 French-born scientist Charles Edouard Brown-Sequard (1817–1894) reports that he has injected himself with a compound taken from the testicles of dogs. He says the compound made him feel stronger and more energetic.

1891 *The British Medical Journal* reports that Indian hemp was frequently prescribed for "a form of insanity peculiar to women."

1893 The first diet pills (e.g., thyroid extracts) are marketed in United States.

1895 Heinrich Dreser, working for the Bayer Company in Germany, produces a drug he thinks is as effective as morphine in reducing pain, but without its harmful side effects. Bayer began mass production of diacetylmorphine, and in 1898 begins marketing the new drug under the brand name "Heroin" as a cough sedative.

1896 More than 300 opium "dens" are in operation in New York City alone.

1897 German chemist Arthur Heffter identifies mescaline as the chemical responsible for peyote's hallucinogenic effects.

1898 German chemical company Bayer aggressively markets heroin as a cough cure for the rampant disease of the time, tuberculosis.

1901 Jokichi Takamine (1854–1922), Japanese American chemist, and T. B. Aldrich first isolate epinephrine from the adrenal gland. Later known by the trade name Adrenalin, it is eventually identified as a neurotransmitter.

1903 Barbiturate-containing Veronal is marketed as a sleeping pill.

1903 Barbiturates (a class of drugs with more effective sedative-hypnotic effects) replace the use of most sedative bromides.

1903 To determine the safety of additives and preservatives in foods and medicines, the U.S. government establishes a "poison squad," a group of young men who volunteer to eat foods treated with chemicals such as borax, formaldehyde, and benzoic acid. The poison squad was established by Dr. Harvey W. Wiley (1844–1930), head of the U.S. Bureau of Chemistry, the precursor to the FDA.

1906 The U.S. Congress passes the Pure Food and Drug Act.

1909 Congressional legislation stops U.S. imports of smokable opium or opium derivatives except for medicinal purposes.

1910 Britain signs an agreement with China to dismantle the opium trade. However, the profits made from its cultivation, manufacture, and sale are so enormous that no serious interruption occurs until World War II (1939–1945) closes supply routes throughout Asia.

1912 Casimir Funk (1884–1967), Polish American biochemist, coins the term "vitamine." Because the dietary substances he discovers are in the amine group, he calls all of them "life-amines" (using the Latin word *vita* for "life").

1912 Ecstasy, 3,4-Methylenedioxymethamphetamine (MDMA), is developed in Germany.

1912 Phenobarbital is introduced under the trade name Luminal.

1912 The U.S. Public Health Service is established.

1912 The U.S. Congress enacts the Shirley Amendment that prohibits false therapeutic claims in advertising or labeling medicines.

1913 The U.S. Congress passes the Gould Amendment requiring accurate and clear labeling of weights, measures, and numbers on food packages.

1914 The Harrison Narcotic Act bans opiates and cocaine in the United States. Their use as local anesthetics remains legal, however.

1916 Oxycodone is first developed in Germany and marketed under the brand name Eukodal.

1918 The Native American Church (NAC) is founded and combines Christian practices with the use of peyote rituals. Ultimately, the U.S. government exempts the NAC from its ban on peyote if the drug is used as part of a bona fide religious ceremony. This point remains a center of legal controversy in states that want to limit peyote use or outlaw it completely.

1919 The Eighteenth Amendment to the U.S. Constitution (ratified on January 29, 1919) begins the era of Prohibition in the United States. It prohibits the sale and consumption of alcohol in the nation.

1919 Methamphetamine is first manufactured in Japan.

1925 The League of Nations adopts strict rules governing the international heroin trade.

1926 Phencyclidine (PCP) is first synthesized.

1927 Albert Szent-Györgyi (1893–1986), Hungarian American physicist, discovers ascorbic acid, or vitamin C, while studying oxidation in plants.

1929 Scottish biochemist Alexander Fleming (1881–1955) discovers penicillin. He observes that the mold *Penicillium notatum* inhibits the growth of some bacteria. This is the first antibiotic, and it opens a new era of "wonder drugs" to combat infection and disease.

1930 The U.S. Food, Drug, and Insecticide Administration is renamed the U.S. Food and Drug Administration (FDA).

1932 Pharmaceutical manufacturer Smith, Kline and French introduces Benzedrine, an over-the-counter amphetamine-based inhaler for relieving nasal congestion.

1933 The Twenty-first Amendment to the U.S. Constitution repeals the Eighteenth Amendment and makes it legal to sell and consume alcohol in United States again.

1935 The Federal Bureau of Narcotics, forerunner of the modern Drug Enforcement Administration (DEA), begins a campaign that portrays marijuana as a drug that leads users to addiction, violence, and insanity. The government produces films such as *Marihuana* (1935), *Reefer Madness* (1936), and *Assassin of Youth* (1937).

1935 The first Alcoholics Anonymous (AA) group is formed in Akron, Ohio.

1935 Testosterone is first isolated in the laboratory.

1936 The U.S. government begins to open a series of facilities to help deal with the rising number of opiate addicts in the nation.

1937 Amphetamine is used to treat a condition known as minimal brain dysfunction, a disorder later renamed attention-deficit/hyperactivity disorder (ADHD).

1937 Diethylene glycol, an elixir of sulfanilamide, kills 107 people, including many children. The mass poisoning highlights the need for additional legislation regarding drug safety.

1937 The Marijuana Tax Act effectively makes it a crime to use or possess the drug, even for medical reasons.

1938 The Federal Food, Drug, and Cosmetics Act gives regulatory powers to the FDA. It also requires that new drugs be clinically tested and proven safe.

1938 Meperidine is synthesized. Other synthetic opioids soon follow.

1938 Swiss chemist Albert Hofmann (1906–) at Sandoz Laboratories synthesizes LSD. After initially testing it on animals, Hofmann accidentally ingests some of the drug in 1943, revealing LSD's hallucinogenic properties.

1938 The Wheeler-Lea Act empowers the U.S. Federal Trade Commission to oversee non-prescription drug advertising otherwise regulated by the FDA.

1939 Ernest Chain (1906–1979) and H. W. Florey (1898–1968) refine the purification of penicillin, allowing the mass production of the antibiotic.

1939 Methadone, a synthetic opioid narcotic, is created in Germany. Originally named Amidon, early methadone was used mainly as a pain reliever.

1942 The Opium Poppy Control Act outlaws possession of opium poppies in United States.

1944 To combat battle fatigue during World War II, nearly 200 million amphetamine tablets are issued to American soldiers stationed in Great Britain during the war.

1944 The U.S. Public Health Service Act is passed.

1945 After World War II, anabolic-androgenic steroids (AASs) are given to many starving concentration camp survivors to help them add skeletal muscle and build up body weight.

1948 A U.S. Supreme Court ruling allows the FDA to investigate drug sales at the pharmacy level.

1948 The World Health Organization (WHO) is formed. The WHO subsequently becomes the principal international organization managing public health related issues on a global scale. Headquartered in Geneva, Switzerland, the WHO becomes, by 2002, an organization of more than 190 member countries. The organization contributes to international public health in areas including disease prevention and control, promotion of good health, addressing disease outbreaks, initiatives to eliminate diseases (e.g., vaccination programs), and development of treatment and prevention standards.

1949 The FDA publishes a "black book" guide about the toxicity of chemicals in food.

1950 A U.S. Court of Appeals rules that drug labels must include intended regular uses of the drug.

1951 The U.S. Durham-Humphrey Amendment defines conditions under which drugs require medical supervision and further requires that prescriptions be written only by a licensed practitioner.

1952 The tranquilizer Reserpine rapidly begins replacing induced insulin shock therapy (injecting patients with insulin until their blood sugar levels fall so low that they become comatose), electroconvulsive (ECT) therapy (inducing seizures by passing an electric current through the brain), and lobotomy (making an incision in the lobe of the brain) as treatments for certain types of mental illness.

1953 British novelist Aldous Huxley (1894–1963) publishes *The Doors of Perception*, a book in which he recounts his experiences with peyote.

1953 Jonas Salk (1915–1995) begins testing a polio vaccine comprised of a mixture of killed viruses.

1953 Narcotics Anonymous (NA) is founded.

1953 The U.S. Federal Security Agency becomes the Department of Health, Education, and Welfare (HEW).

1954 Veterinarians begin using piperazines, which are designed to rid the lower intestinal tract of parasitic worms.

1955 Scientists in India first synthesize methaqualone.

1956 The American Medical Association defines alcoholism as a disease.

1956 Dimethyltriptamine (DMT) is recognized as being hallucinogenic.

1957 Researchers John Baer, Karl Beyer, James Sprague, and Frederick Novello formulate the drug chlorothiazide, the first of the thiazide diuretics. This groundbreaking discovery marks a new era in medicine as the first safe and effective long-term treatment for chronic hypertension and heart failure.

1958 Aaron B. Lerner isolates melatonin from the pineal gland.

1958 The FDA publishes a list of substances generally recognized as safe.

1958 The Parke-Davis pharmaceutical company synthesizes and patents PCP. After testing, Parke-Davis sells the drug as a general anesthetic called Sernyl.

1958 The U.S. government passes food additives amendments that require manufacturers to establish safety and to eliminate additives demonstrated to cause cancer.

1959 Fentanyl, first synthesized in Belgium by Janssen Parmaceutica, is used as a pain management drug.

1960 The FDA requires warnings on labels of potentially hazardous household chemicals.

1960 Gamma butyrolactone (GBL) is first synthesized.

1960 GBH, a fast-acting central nervous system depressant, is developed as an alternative anesthetic (painkiller) for use in surgery because of its ability to induce sleep and reversible coma.

1961 Commencing a two-year study, Harvard professor Timothy Leary attempts to reform criminals at the Massachusetts Correctional Institute. The inmates are given doses of psilocybin and psychological therapy. Ultimately, the psilocybin-subjected inmates have the same rate of return to prison as the inmates who were not part of the study. In addition to this, they have more parole violations than the general parolees.

1961 Ketamine (originally CI581) is discovered by Calvin Stevens of Wayne State University in Detroit, Michigan.

1962 The American Medical Association publishes a public warning in its journal *JAMA* regarding the increasingly widespread use of LSD for recreational purposes.

1962 Thalidomide, a sleeping pill also used to combat morning sickness in pregnant women, is discovered to be the cause of widespread and similar birth defects in babies born in Great

Britain and western Europe. Earlier, Dr. Frances Kelsey of the FDA had refused to approve the drug for use in the United States pending further research. Due to her steadfast refusal, countless birth defects are prevented in the United States.

1962 The U.S. Congress passes the Kefauver-Harris Drug Amendments that shift the burden of proof of clinical safety to drug manufacturers. For the first time, drug manufacturers have to prove their products are safe and effective before they can be sold.

1964 The first Surgeon General's Report on Smoking and Health is released. The U.S. government first acknowledges and publicizes that cigarette smoking is a leading cause of cancer, bronchitis, and emphysema.

1965 At the height of tobacco use in the United States, surveys show 52 percent of adult men and 32 percent of adult women use tobacco products.

1965 Because of disturbing side effects including horrible nightmares, delusions, hallucinations, agitation, delirium, disorientation, and difficulty speaking, PCP use on humans is stopped in the United States. PCP continued to be sold as a veterinary anesthetic under the brand name Sernylan.

1965 The manufacture of LSD becomes illegal in the United States. A year later it is made illegal in the United Kingdom. The FDA subsequently classifies LSD as a Schedule I drug in 1970.

1965 The U.S. Congress passes the Drug Abuse Control Amendments—legislation that forms the FDA Bureau of Drug Abuse Control and gives the FDA tighter regulatory control over amphetamines, barbiturates, and other prescription drugs with high abuse potential.

1966 The FDA and the National Academy of Sciences begin investigation of the effectiveness of drugs previously approved because they were thought to be safe.

1966 The U.S. Narcotic Addiction Rehabilitation Act gives federal financial assistance to states and local authorities to develop a local system of drug treatment programs. Methadone clinic treatment programs begin to rise dramatically.

1967 A "Love-In" in honor of LSD is staged at Golden Gate Park in San Francisco, California. Before LSD was made illegal, more than 40,000 patients were treated with LSD as part of psychiatric therapy.

1967 News accounts depict illicit use of PCP, then sometimes known as the "Peace Pill," in the Haight-Ashbury district of San Francisco during the "Summer of Love." PCP reemerges in the early 1970s as a liquid, crystalline powder, and tablet.

1968 Psilocybin and *Psilocybe* mushrooms are made illegal in United States.

1970 The U.S. Congress passes the Controlled Substance Act (CSA). It puts strict controls on the production, import, and prescription of amphetamines. Many amphetamine forms, particularly diet pills, are removed from the over-the-counter market.

1970 Ketamine is used as a battlefield anesthetic agent during the Vietnam war (1954–1975).

1970 The U.S. Comprehensive Drug Abuse Prevention and Control Act classifies drugs in five categories based on the effect of the drug, its medical use, and potential for abuse.

1970 Widespread use of peyote is halted by the Comprehensive Drug Abuse Prevention and Control Act of 1970. During the 1950s and 1960s, peyote was legal throughout most of the United States. During the peak of the psychedelic era, dried peyote cactus buttons were readily available through mail-order catalogs.

1971 Cigarette advertising is banned from television and radio. The nonsmokers' rights movement begins.

1971 The United Kingdom passes the Misuse of Drugs Act.

1974 2C-B is first produced by American chemist and pharmacologist Alexander Shulgin.

1974 The first hospice facility opens in the United States.

1975 Anabolic-androgenic steroids (AASs) are added to the International Olympic Committee's list of banned substances.

1975 Rohypnol, developed by the pharmaceutical firm of Hoffmann-La Roche, is first sold in Switzerland as a sleeping aid for the treatment of insomnia. Reports begin surfacing that Rohypnol is abused as a recreational or "party" drug, often in combination with alcohol and/or other drugs. It also becomes known as a date rape drug.

1976 The FBI warns that "crack" cocaine use and cocaine addiction are on the rise in the United States.

1976 Oxycodone is approved by the FDA. Various formulations follow, including drugs that combine oxycodone with either aspirin or acetaminophen.

1976 The U.S. Congress passes the Proxmire Amendments to stop the FDA from regulating vitamin and mineral supplements as drugs based on their potency or strength. This legislation also prohibits the FDA from regulating the potency of vitamin and mineral supplements.

1978 The American Indian Religious Freedom Act is passed and protects the religious traditions of Native Americans, including the use of peyote.

1978 Because of escalating reports of abuse, PCP is withdrawn completely from the U.S. market. Since 1978, no legal therapeutic use of PCP exists.

1980 The FDA proposes removing caffeine from its Generally Recognized as Safe list. Subsequently, the FDA concludes in 1992 that, after reviewing the scientific literature, no harm is posed by a person's intake of up to 100 milligrams (mg) of caffeine per day.

1980 World Health Organization (WHO) classifies khat as a drug of abuse that may produce mild to moderate psychological dependency.

1981 Alprazolam (Xanax) is introduced and subsequently becomes the most widely prescribed benzodiazepine.

1982 The FDA issues regulations for tamper-resistant packaging after seven people die in Chicago from ingesting Tylenol capsules laced with cyanide. The following year, the federal Anti-Tampering Act is passed, making it a crime to tamper with packaged consumer products.

1983 The U.S. Congress passes the Orphan Drug Act, which allows the FDA to research and market drugs necessary for treating rare diseases.

1984 Methaqualone (Quaalude, Sopor), a nonbarbiturate hypnotic that is said to give a heroin-like high without drowsiness, is banned in the United States.

1984 Nicotine gum is introduced.

1985 The FDA approves synthetic THC, or dronabinol (Marinol), to help cancer patients undergoing chemotherapy.

1985 Ecstasy (MDMA) becomes illegal in the United States.

1985 The United Kingdom passes the Intoxicating Substances (Supply) Act, making it an offense to supply a product that will be abused. Subsequent legislation, the Cigarette Lighter Refill (safety) Regulations, passed in 1999, regulates the sale of purified liquefied petroleum gas, mainly butane. Butane is the substance most often involved in inhalant deaths in the United Kingdom.

1986 The United Kingdom passes the Medicines Act.

1986 The U.S. Congress passes the Anti-Drug Abuse Act. This federal law includes mandatory minimum sentences for first-time offenders with harsher penalties for possession of crack cocaine than powder cocaine.

1986 The U.S. Surgeon General's report focuses on the hazards of environmental tobacco smoke to nonsmokers.

1987 The legal drinking age is raised to 21 years in United States.

1988 Canadian sprinter Ben Johnson (1961–) tests positive for anabolic-androgenic steroids (AASs) at the Seoul Olympic games and forfeits his gold medal to the second-place finisher, American Carl Lewis (1961–).

1990 The FDA bans the use of GHB, a drug related to GBL, a central nervous system depressant with sedative-hypnotic and hallucinogenic properties.

1990 The U.S. Supreme Court decision in *Employment Division v. Smith* says that the religious use of peyote by Native Americans is not protected by the First Amendment.

1991 Anabolic-androgenic steroids (AASs) are listed as Schedule III drugs in accord with the U.S. Controlled Substances Act (CSA).

1991 Nicotine skin patches are introduced.

1992 The Karolinska Institute publishes a study that finds subjects who take creatine supplements can experience a significant increase in total muscle creatine content. Creatine is thrust onto the global athletic scene as British sprinters Linford Christie and Sally Gunnel win Olympic gold in Barcelona after reportedly training with the aid of creatine supplementation. Subsequently, a lack of well-designed clinical studies of creatine's long-term effects combined with loose regulatory standards for creatine supplement products causes some athletic associations, including the U.S. Olympic Committee (USOC), to caution against its use without banning it outright.

1993 2C-B becomes widely known as a "rave" drug in United States.

1993 The first news accounts that cite the use of Rohypnol as a "date rape" drug are published. Rohypnol becomes one of more than 20 drugs that law enforcement officials assert are used in committing sexual assaults.

1993 The U.S. Religious Freedom Restoration Act and the American Indian Religious Freedom Act Amendments (AIRFA) restore the rights of Native Americans to use peyote in religious ceremonies.

1994 Cigarette industry secrets are revealed causing a storm of controversy. The list of some 700 potential additives shows 13 additives that are not allowed to be used in food.

1994 The U.S. Congress passes the Dietary Supplement Health and Education Act (DSHEA) in an effort to standardize the manufacture, labeling, composition, and safety of botanicals, herbs, and nutritional supplements. It expressly defines a dietary supplement as a vitamin, a mineral, an herb or other botanical, an amino acid, or any other "dietary substance." The law prohibits claims that herbs can treat diseases or disorders, but it allows more general health claims about the effect of herbs on the "structure or function" of the body or about the "well-being" they induce. Under the Act, supplement manufacturers are allowed to market and sell products without federal regulation. As a result, the FDA bears the burden of having to prove an herbal is unsafe before it can restrict its use.

1995 2C-B is classified as a Schedule I drug under the U.S. Controlled Substances Act (CSA).

1995 A study published by the *British Journal of Urology* asserts that khat (*Catha edulis*) chewing inhibits urine flow, constricts blood vessels, and promotes erectile dysfunction.

1995 A study by the Rand Corporation finds that every dollar spent in drug treatment saves society seven dollars in crime, policing, incarceration, and health services.

1995 The National Household Survey on Drug Abuse finds inhalants to be the second most commonly abused illicit drug by American youth ages 12–17 years, after marijuana.

1996 Anabolic-androgenic steroids (AASs) and other performance-enhancing drugs are added to the United Kingdom Misuse of Drugs Act.

1996 Nicotine nasal spray is introduced.

1996 The U.S. Drug-Induced Rape Prevention and Punishment Act makes it a felony to give an unsuspecting person a drug with the intent of committing violence, including rape. The law also imposes penalties of large fines and prison sentences of up to 20 years for importing or distributing more than one gram of date-rape drugs.

1997 2C-B is banned in Great Britain.

1997 The FDA proposes new rules regarding some ephedra dietary supplements and seeks to regulate certain products containing the drug. The FDA claims that certain ephedrine alkaloids resemble amphetamine, which stimulates the heart and nervous system. Congress rejects the FDA's attempt to subject ephedra products to regulation. In 2000, an ephedra study published in the *New England Journal of Medicine* shows a link between heart attacks, strokes, seizures, and mental side effects (including anxiety, tremulousness, and personality changes) with ephedra intake. Other possible mental side effects associated with ephedra are depression and paranoid psychosis.

1997 The FDA investigates the link between heart valve disease in patients using the Fen-Phen drug combination for weight loss. The FDA notes that the Fen-Phen treatment had not received FDA approval.

1997 The Institute of Medicine (IOM), a branch of the National Academy of Sciences, publishes the report *Marijuana: Assessing the Science Base*, which concludes that cannabinoids show significant promise as analgesics, appetite stimulants, and antiemetics. It states that further research into producing such medicines was warranted.

1997 Oregon voters approve the Death with Dignity Act, allowing terminally ill people to receive prescriptions for lethal doses of drugs to end their lives.

1997 Rohypnol is banned in the United States.

1997 The *Journal of the American Medical Association (JAMA)* publishes a study indicating that ginkgo dietary supplements might be useful in treating Alzheimer's disease, sparking additional research interest.

1997 The National Institutes of Health (NIH) estimate that approximately 600,000 people in the United States are opiate-dependent, meaning they use an opiate drug daily or on a frequent basis.

1998 A study at the Psychiatric University Hospital in Zurich, Switzerland, demonstrates that psilocybin produces a psychosis-like syndrome in healthy humans that is similar to early schizophrenia.

1998 Amendments made to the U.S. Higher Education Act make anyone convicted of a drug offense ineligible for federal student loans for one year up to an indefinite period of time. Such convictions may also render students ineligible for state aid.

1998 The nicotine inhaler (Nicotrol Inhaler) is introduced.

1998 The tobacco industry settles lengthy lawsuits by making a historic agreement with the States' Attorneys General called the Master Settlement Agreement (MSA). In exchange for protection from further lawsuits, the industry agrees to additional advertising restrictions and to reimburse the states billions of dollars over 25 years to pay for smoking-related illnesses.

1998 The U.S. Drug Free Communities Act offers federal money to communities to help educate citizens on the dangers on methamphetamine use and production.

1998 The U.S. Speed Trafficking Life in Prison Act increases penalties for the production, distribution, and use of methamphetamine.

1999 The Drug Enforcement Administration (DEA) lists GBL as a scheduled (controlled) substance.

1999 The FDA lists ketamine as a Schedule III drug.

1999 National Household Survey on Drug Abuse (NHSDA) estimates that a third of the American population (then an estimated 72 million people) had tried marijuana at least once.

1999 DEA agents seize 30 gallons (113.5 liters) of a dimethyltriptamine (DMT) tea called "hoasca" from the office of the O Centro Espirita Beneficiente Uniao do Vegetal (UDV), a New Mexico-based religious organization with approximately 500 members. The organization subsequently sued the U.S. Government, alleging a violation of their constitutional right of freedom of religion.

2000 The *Journal of Pharmacy and Pharmacology* concludes that khat (*Catha edulis*), like amphetamines and ibuprofen, can relieve pain.

2000 The National Cancer Institute (NCI) estimates that 3,000 lung cancer deaths, and as many as 40,000 cardiac deaths per year among adult nonsmokers in the United States can be attributed to passive smoke or environmental tobacco smoke (ETS).

2000 The U.S. Congress considers but does not pass the Pain Relief Promotion Act, which would have amended the Controlled Substances Act to say that relieving pain or discomfort—within the context of professional medicine—is a legitimate use of controlled substances. The bill died in the Senate.

2000 The U.S. Congress Ecstasy Anti-proliferation Act increases federal sentencing guidelines for trafficking and possessing with intent to sell ecstasy (MDMA). It drastically increases jail terms for fewer numbers of pills in personal possession.

2000 The U.S. Congress passes a transportation spending bill that includes creating a national standard for drunk driving for adults at a 0.08 percent blood alcohol concentration (BAC) level. States are required to adopt this stricter standard by 2004 or face penalties. By 2001, more than half the states adopt this stricter standard.

2000 U.S. President William J. Clinton (1946–) signs the Hillory J. Farias and Samantha Reid Date-Rape Drug Prohibition Act into law.

2001 The *American Journal of Psychiatry* publishes studies providing evidence that methamphetamine can cause brain damage that results in slower motor and cognitive functioning—even in users who take the drug for less than a year.

2001 *International Journal of Cancer* researchers assert that khat (*Catha edulis*) chewing, especially when accompanied by alcohol and tobacco consumption, may cause cancer.

2001 National Football League (NFL) joins the National Collegiate Athletic Association (NCAA) and the International Olympic Committee (IOC) in issuing a ban on ephedrine use. The NFL ban on ephedrine prohibits NFL players and teams from endorsing products containing ephedrine or companies that sell or distribute those products.

2001 National Institute of Drug Abuse (NIDA) research reveals that children exposed to cocaine prior to birth sustained long-lasting brain changes. Eight years after birth, children exposed to cocaine prior to birth had detectable brain chemistry differences.

2001 A thoroughbred race horse wins a race at Suffolk Downs in Massachusetts but then tests positive for BZP (also known as Equine Ecstasy).

2001 The U.S. Supreme Court rules (unanimously) in *United States vs. Oakland Cannabis Buyers' Cooperative* that the cooperatives permitted under California law to sell medical marijuana to patients who had a physician's approval to use the drug were unconstitutional under federal law.

2002 Companies begin developing drink coasters and other detection kits that allow consumers to test whether drinks have been drugged. If date-rape drugs are present, a strip on the testing kit changes color when a drop of the tampered drink is placed on it.

2002 A Florida physician is convicted of manslaughter for prescribing OxyContin to four patients who died after overdosing on the powerful opiate. News reports allege that he is the first doctor ever convicted in the death of patients whose deaths were related to OxyContin use.

2002 Health Canada, the Canadian health regulatory agency, requests a voluntary recall of products containing both natural and chemical ephedra.

2002 The U.S. military's use of go-pills (dextroamphetamine) comes under fire after two U.S. Air Force pilots are involved in a friendly fire incident in Afghanistan. Four Canadian soldiers are killed and eight wounded when one of the American pilots bombs them from his F-16 after mistaking them for the enemy.

2002 In the aftermath of the September 11, 2001, terrorist attacks on the United States, the U.S. government dramatically increases funding to stockpile drugs and other agents that can be used to counter a bioterror attack.

2002 Several states, including Connecticut and Minnesota, pass laws that ban teachers from recommending psychotropic drugs, especially Ritalin, to parents.

2002 A U.S. federal district court judge rejects a U.S. Justice Department attempt to overturn Oregon's physician-assisted suicide law. The Justice Department had claimed that the state law violated the federal Controlled Substances Act.

2002-2003 During the severe acute respiratory syndrome (SARS) scare, many people visit Chinese herbalists to purchase a mixture of herbs to help protect them from the disease.

2003 More than 2,200 pounds (998 kilograms) of khat are seized at the Dublin Airport in Ireland. The bundles were being sent to New York from London.

2003 The FDA approves the use of Prozac in depressed children as young as seven years old.

2003 The U.S. government implements the Reducing Americans' Vulnerability to Ecstasy Act.

2003 Steve Bechler, a pitcher with the Baltimore Orioles, collapses during a preseason workout in Florida and dies the next day. His death is linked to the use of ephedra.

2003 More than 3,500 children in the United States are involved in meth lab incidents during the year.

2004 Australian police begin stopping motorists randomly to conduct saliva tests to check for various illegal drugs, including marijuana and amphetamines.

2004 Adderall XR is approved by the FDA for use by adults with ADHD.

2004 The FDA announces that "black box" labeling of antidepressants will become mandatory.

2004 The federal court case regarding the O Centro Espirita Beneficiente Uniao do Vegetal religious sect concludes with the group winning the right to use an hallucinogenic tea in its religious services.

2004 The FDA bans the use of ephedra in the United States following reports of more than 150 deaths linked to the supplement.

2004 The Warner Bros. movie *Scooby-Doo 2: Monsters Unleashed* contains a scene showing Shaggy taking a hit of nitrous oxide off a whipped cream can. The scene angers many parents who have lost children due to inhalant abuse.

2004-2005 BZP is still being sold over-the-counter in New Zealand as an herbal party pill. In 2005, the DEA officially classifies BZP as a Schedule I drug in the United States.

2004-2005 After the fall of the Taliban government in Afghanistan in late 2001, opium poppy production begins to soar by 2004. Street heroin becomes purer and available in larger quantities. Prices reach a twenty-year low.

2005 Baseball players and managers are called to testify before Congress about steroid use in the Major Leagues.

2005 The Partnership for a Drug-Free America releases a study showing that prescription drug abuse among teens is growing rapidly. Teens are dubbed "Generation Rx."

2005 The U.S. Supreme Court agrees to hear a case involving Oregon's physician-assisted suicide law.

2005 Utah-based Nutraceutical International successfully challenges the FDA ban on ephedra in federal court. U.S. judge Tena Campbell rules that the FDA has failed to prove that the company's ephedra-based product is unsafe.

2005 The FDA launches a pilot program using high-tech radio frequency identification (RFID) tags to track the movement of bottles of the most addictive prescription painkillers.

2005 The Canadian government joins several European nations (most notably the Netherlands) in a pilot program to give free heroin to heroin addicts to help them stabilize their lives, eventually overcome addiction, and prevent them from contracting diseases by sharing dirty needles.

2005 The U.S. Supreme Court rules against the use of medical marijuana. At the time of the ruling, ten states allow medical marijuana to be used by cancer, AIDS, and other patients suffering severe pain when prescribed by a physician.

2005 The FDA issues a public health advisory about the use of fentanyl skin patches after receiving reports that people have died or experienced serious side effects after overdosing on the drug.

2005 The new opiate drug Palladone is pulled off the market for further research by its maker, Purdue Pharma.

2005 Oregon lawmakers vote to make over-the-counter cold and allergy remedies containing pseudoephedrine available by prescription only beginning in mid-2006. The move is taken to make it harder for illegal methamphetamine "cooks" to obtain the ingredient. A dozen other states move the product "behind the counter."

A

acetaminophen: Pronounced uh-SEE-tuh-MINN-uh fenn; a non-aspirin pain reliever, such as Tylenol.

acetylcholine: Pronounced uh-settle-KOH-leen; a neurotransmitter that forms from a substance called choline, which is released by the liver.

acquired immunodeficiency syndrome (AIDS): An infectious disease that destroys the body's immune system, leading to illness and death.

active ingredient: The chemical or substance in a compound known or believed to have a therapeutic, or healing, effect.

adenosine triphosphate (ATP): An important energy-carrying chemical, created with the assistance of creatine.

adrenaline: Pronounced uh-DREN-uh-linn; a natural stimulant produced by the human body; also known as epinephrine (epp-ih-NEFF-run).

adverse reactions: Side effects, or negative health consequences, reported after taking a certain substance.

aerobic exercises: Exercises performed to increase heart health and stamina, such as jogging, biking, and swimming, usually lasting between twenty minutes and an hour.

aerosol: Gas used to propel, or shoot out, liquid substances from a pressurized can.

alchemists: Those who study or practice medieval chemical science aimed at discovering a cure for all illnesses.

alcoholism: A disease that results in habitual, uncontrolled alcohol abuse; alcoholism can shorten a person's life by damaging the brain, liver, and heart.

alkaloid: A nitrogen-containing substance found in plants.

Alzheimer's disease: A brain disease that usually strikes older individuals and results in memory loss, impaired thinking, and personality changes; symptoms worsen over time.

amines: Organic (or carbon-containing) chemical substances made from ammonia.

amino acids: Any of a group of chemical compounds that form the basis for proteins.

ammonia: A strong-smelling colorless gas made of nitrogen and hydrogen; often used as a cleaning agent in its liquid form.

amnesia: The loss of memory.

amphetamines: Pronounced am-FETT-uh-meens; stimulant drugs that increase mental alertness, reduce appetite, and help keep users awake.

anabolic agents: Substances that promote muscle growth.

anaerobic exercise: Short, strenuous exercises that require sudden bursts of strength, such as weight lifting and batting a baseball.

analgesics: Pain relievers or the qualities of pain relief.

analogs: Drugs created in a laboratory, having a slightly different chemical composition than a pharmaceutical, yet having the same effects on the brain as the pharmaceutical.

anemia: A blood condition that results in the decreased ability of the blood to transport enough oxygen throughout the body.

anesthesiologists: Medical doctors trained to use medications to sedate a surgery patient.

anesthetic: A substance used to deaden pain.

angina pectoris: Pronounced an-JINE-uh peck-TOR-ess; a feeling of suffocation and pain around the heart that occurs when the blood supply to the heart is not adequate.

anhedonia: Pronounced ann-heh-DOE-nee-uh; the inability to experience pleasure from normally enjoyable life events.

anorectics: Pronounced ah-nuh-RECK-ticks; diet pills that cause a loss of appetite; they were developed to replace amphetamines.

anorexia: Pronounced ah-nuh-REK-see-uh; a severe eating disorder characterized by an intense fear of gaining weight, a refusal to eat, a distorted sense of self-image, and excessive weight loss.

antagonist: Pronounced ann-TAG-uh-nist; a drug that opposes the action of another drug.

anthelmintic: Pronounced ant-hel-MINN-tick; a substance that helps destroy and expel parasitic worms, especially worms located in the intestines.

antidote: A remedy to reverse the effects of a poison.

antihistamines: Drugs that block *histamine,* a chemical that causes nasal congestion related to allergies.

antioxidant: A chemical that neutralizes free radicals (chemicals with an unpaired electron) that can damage other cells.

antitussants: Pronounced an-ty-TUH-sihvs; medicines that quiet coughs.

anxiety: A feeling of being extremely overwhelmed, restless, fearful, and worried.

anxiety disorders: A group of mental disorders or conditions characterized in part by extreme restlessness, uncontrollable feelings of fear, excessive worrying, and panic attacks.

aphrodisiac: Pronounced aff-roh-DEE-zee-ack; a drug or other substance that excites or increases sexual desire.

arthritis: Painful swelling of joints caused by abnormal bone growth or wear and tear on the joint.

asphyxiation: Death or unconsciousness caused by one of three things: 1) a lack of adequate oxygen, 2) the inhalation of physically harmful substances, or 3) the obstruction of normal breathing.

asthma: Pronounced AZ-muh; a lung disorder that interferes with normal breathing.

ataxia: Pronounced uh-TAKS-ee-uh; loss of control of muscle coordination.

attention-deficit/hyperactivity disorder (ADHD): A disorder characterized by impulsive behavior, difficulty concentrating, and hyperactivity that interferes with social and academic functioning.

autism: Pronounced AW-tizm; a psychological disorder, usually diagnosed in children, that affects emotional development, social interactions, and the ability to communicate effectively.

***ayahuasca*:** One of several teas of South American origin used in religious ceremonies, known to contain dimethyltryptamine (DMT); also a plant.

B

barbiturates: Pronounced bar-BIH-chuh-rits; drugs that act as depressants and are used as sedatives or sleeping pills; also referred to as "downers."

bathtub chemists: Inexperienced and illegal drug makers who concoct homemade drugs; also referred to as "kitchen chemists" or "underground chemists."

behavior modification: A type of therapy that changes behavior by substituting desired responses for undesired ones.

benzodiazepines: A type of drug used to treat anxiety.

binge drinking: Consuming a lot of alcohol in a short period of time.

bipolar disorder: A psychological disorder that causes alternating periods of depression and extreme elevation of mood.

black market: The illegal sale or trade of goods; drug dealers are said to carry out their business on the "black market."

boils: Large pimples that are inflamed and filled with pus.

bone marrow: Soft tissue in the center of bones where blood cell formation occurs.

bronchitis: An illness that affects the bronchial tubes in the lungs, leading to shortness of breath and coughing.

bronchodilator: A drug that relaxes breathing muscles, allowing air to flow more easily through the tubes that lead to the lungs.

bufotenine: The component of venom from the toad genus *Bufo* that contains dimethyltryptamine (DMT).

bulimia: Pronounced bull-EEM-eeh-yuh; an eating disorder that involves long periods of bingeing on food, followed by self-induced vomiting and abuse of laxatives.

C

cancer: Out-of-control cell growth leading to tumors in the body's organs or tissues.

cannabinoids: Chemical compounds found in cannabis plants and in small amounts in the brains of humans and animals.

carbon monoxide: A poisonous gas with no odor; carbon monoxide is released when cigarettes burn.

carcinogens: Chemicals that can cause cancer in the body.

cardiovascular illnesses: Illnesses involving the heart and blood vessels.

carries: Doses of methadone given to users to take home for another day.

chemotherapy: A medically supervised regimen of drugs used to kill cancer cells in the body. The drugs have potential side effects including nausea, vomiting, and other reactions.

cholesterol: Pronounced kuh-LESS-tuhr-ol; an essential substance made of carbon, hydrogen, and oxygen that is found in animal cells and body fluids; in high amounts, it may be deposited in blood vessels, resulting in dangerous blockages of blood flow.

cirrhosis: Pronounced sir-OH-sis; destruction of the liver, possibly leading to death.

clinical trials: Scientific experiments that test the effect of a drug in humans.

club drugs: Mostly synthetic, illegal substances found at raves and nightclubs, including the drugs ecstasy, GHB, ketamine, LSD, methamphetamines, PCP, and Rohypnol.

coca paste: An impure freebase made from coca leaves and used mainly in South America; coca paste is smoked and is highly addictive.

cocaethylene: A substance formed by the body when cocaine and alcohol are consumed together; it increases the chances of serious adverse reactions or sudden death from cocaine.

cognitive behavioral therapy (CBT): A type of therapy that helps people recognize and change negative patterns of thinking and behavior.

coma: A state of unconsciousness from which a person cannot be aroused by noise or other stimuli.

congestive heart failure (CHF): Inability of the heart to circulate, or pump, the blood throughout the body with sufficient force.

constipation: An inability to have a bowel movement.

control group: In a drug test, the group that does *not* receive the drug being tested.

controlled substance analog: Any chemical compound that acts on the body the same way a controlled substance does.

coroner: An official who investigates unexplained deaths.

corticosteroids: Pronounced kor-tih-koh-STEH-roydz; medications widely prescribed to treat inflammation.

crack cocaine: A highly addictive, smokable freebase cocaine made by combining powder cocaine with water and sodium bicarbonate.

cravings: Overwhelming urges to do something, such as take an illegal drug.

Crohn's disease: A serious disease of the intestines that causes inflammation, along with severe pain, diarrhea, nausea, and sometimes extreme weight loss.

cutting: Adding other ingredients to a powdered drug to stretch the drug for more sales.

cyanide: A poisonous chemical compound that shuts down the respiratory system, quickly killing people who have been exposed to it.

cyanosis: Bluish or purplish skin caused by a lack of oxygen in the blood.

D

decongestant: A drug that relieves nasal congestion.

dehydration: An abnormally low amount of fluid in the body.

delirium: A mental disturbance marked by confusion, hallucinations, and difficulty focusing attention and communicating.

delusions: False, unshakable beliefs indicating severe mental difficulties; "delusional" refers to the inability to distinguish between what is real and what seems to be real.

dementia: Pronounced dih-MENN-shuh; a brain disorder that causes a reduction in a person's intellectual functioning, most often affecting memory, concentration, and decision-making skills.

dependent: When a user has a physical or psychological need to take a certain substance in order to function.

depressants: Substances that slow down the activity of an organism or one of its parts.

depression: A mood disorder that causes people to have feelings of hopelessness, loss of pleasure, self-blame, and sometimes suicidal thoughts.

designer drugs: Harmful and addictive substances that are manufactured illegally in homemade labs.

detoxification: Often abbreviated as detox; a difficult process by which substance abusers stop taking those substances and rid their bodies of the toxins that accumulated during the time they consumed such substances.

diabetes: A serious disorder that causes problems with the normal breakdown of sugars in the body.

dietary supplements: Products including vitamins, herbal extractions, and synthetic amino acids sold for specific uses such as weight loss, muscle building, or prevention of disease.

dilate: Expand or open up.

dissociation: A psychological syndrome in which the mind seems detached from the body; sometimes referred to as an "out of body" experience.

dissociative anesthetics: Pronounced dih-SOH-shee-uh-tiv ANN-ess-THET-iks; drugs that cause users to feel as if their minds are separated from their bodies.

diuretic: Pronounced die-er-EH-tik; substances that reduce bodily fluids by increasing the production of urine.

divination: The mystical experience of seeing into the future, witnessing a hidden truth, or gaining a deep insight.

doctor shopping: A practice in which an individual continually switches physicians so that he or she can get enough of a prescription drug to feed an addiction; this makes it difficult for physicians to track whether the patient has already been prescribed the same drug by another physician.

dopamine: Pronounced DOPE-uh-meen; a combination of carbon, hydrogen, nitrogen, and oxygen that acts as a neurotransmitter in the brain.

dysphoria: Pronounced diss-FOR-ee-yuh; an abnormal feeling of anxiety, discontent, or discomfort; the opposite of euphoria.

E

edema: Pronounced ih-DEEM-uh; water buildup in the body's tissues that causes swelling.

electrolytes: Charged atoms such as sodium, potassium, chloride, calcium, and magnesium that conduct electrical impulses in the body, and therefore are essential in nerve, muscle, and heart function.

elixirs: Pronounced ih-LIK-suhrs; medicines made of drugs in a sweetened alcohol solution.

emaciated: Pronounced ee-MASE-ee-ate-ed; very thin and sickly looking.

endocrine system: The bodily system made of glands that secrete hormones into the bloodstream to control certain bodily functions.

endogenous: Pronounced en-DAH-juh-nuss; produced within the body.

endorphins: A group of naturally occurring substances in the body that relieve pain and promote a sense of well-being.

enkephalins: Pronounced en-KEFF-uh-linz; naturally occurring brain chemicals that produce drowsiness and dull pain.

enzymes: Substances that speed up chemical reactions in the body.

ephedrine: Pronounced ih-FEH-drinn; a chemical substance that eases breathing problems.

epilepsy: A disorder involving the misfiring of electrical impulses in the brain, sometimes resulting in seizures and loss of consciousness.

epinephrine: Pronounced epp-ih-NEFF-run; a hormone that increases heart rate and breathing; also called adrenaline.

ergot: Pronounced URH-got; a fungus that grows on grains, particularly rye, and contains lysergic acid, a chemical used to make LSD.

esophagus: The muscular tube connecting the mouth to the stomach.

essential amino acid: An amino acid that is only found in food; amino acids make up proteins.

estrogen: A hormone responsible for female reproductive traits.

ethanol: The colorless flammable liquid in alcoholic drinks; ethanol is the substance that gets people drunk.

ether: A flammable liquid used as an anesthetic.

euphoria: Pronounced yu-FOR-ee-yuh; a state of extreme happiness and enhanced well-being; the opposite of dysphoria.

expectorant: A cough remedy used to bring up mucus from the throat or bronchial tubes; expectorants cause users to spit up thick secretions from their clogged breathing passages.

F

fetal alcohol effects (FAE): The presence of some—but not all—of the symptoms of fetal alcohol syndrome (FAS).

fetal alcohol syndrome (FAS): A pattern of birth defects, learning deficits, and behavioral problems affecting the children of mothers who drank heavily while pregnant.

fix: A slang term referring to a dose of a drug that the user highly craves or desires.

forensics: The scientific analysis of physical evidence.

freebase: Term referring to the three highly addictive forms of cocaine that can be smoked: 1) coca paste, which is made from processed coca leaves, 2) freebase, which is made with powder cocaine, ammonia, and ether, and 3) crack, which is made with powder cocaine and sodium bicarbonate.

fry sticks: Marijuana cigarettes laced with formaldehyde, a chemical used to keep dead tissues from decaying.

G

general anesthetic: Anesthetics that cause a loss of sensation in the entire body, rather than just a specific body part, and bring on a loss of consciousness.

glaucoma: An eye disease that causes increased pressure within the eyeball and can lead to blindness.

glycerin: A syrupy form of alcohol.

Golden Triangle: The highlands of Southeast Asia, including parts of Burma, Laos, Vietnam, and Thailand, where opium poppies are grown illegally.

gynecomastia: Pronounced GY-nuh-koh-MASS-tee-uh; the formation of female-type breasts on a male body.

H

hallucinations: Visions or other perceptions of things that are not really present.

hallucinogen: A substance that brings on hallucinations, which alter the user's perception of reality.

hangover: An uncomfortable set of physical symptoms caused by drinking too much alcohol; symptoms include headache, upset stomach, and trembling feelings and are caused by an expansion of blood vessels in the brain.

hashish: Concentrated, solidified cannabis resin.

heat exhaustion: A condition that results from physical exertion in extreme heat; symptoms range from clammy and cool skin, tiredness, nausea, weakness, confusion, and vision problems to a possible loss of consciousness.

heat stroke: A condition resulting from longtime exposure to high temperatures; symptoms include an inability to sweat, a very high body temperature, and, eventually, passing out.

hemp: Cannabis plant matter used to make fibers.

hepatitis: A group of viruses that infect the liver and cause damage to that organ.

herniated disk: A rupture of a spinal disk that puts painful pressure on nerves in the spinal column.

high: Drug-induced feelings ranging from excitement and joy to extreme grogginess.

hippocampus: A part of the brain that is involved in learning and memory.

histamines: Pronounced HISS-tuh-meenz: chemicals released by the body during an allergic reaction; they cause: 1) an increase in gastric secretions, 2) the dilation, or opening up of capillaries, 3) constriction of the muscles around the airway, and 4) a decrease in blood pressure.

hormone: (from the Greek word *hormo,* meaning "to set in motion") a chemical messenger that is formed in the body and transported by the blood to a certain target area, where it affects the activity of cells.

hospice: A special clinic for dying patients where emphasis is placed on comfort and emotional support.

huffing: Inhaling through the mouth, often from an inhalant-soaked cloth.

hydrocarbon: A compound containing only two elements: carbon and hydrogen; hydrocarbons are found in petroleum and natural gas.

hydrochloride: A chemical compound composed of the elements hydrogen and chlorine, often in the form of a crystallized salt.

hyperkalemia: A dangerous build-up of excess potassium in the body.

hypertension: Long-term elevation of blood pressure.

hyperthermia: A dangerous rise in body temperature.

hypogonadism: Pronounced high-poh-GO-nad-izm; a lack of activity in the male testicles, which can be caused by low testosterone levels.

hypokalemia: A loss of potassium in the body.

hyponatremia: Pronounced HY-poh-nuh-TREE-mee-uh; a potentially fatal condition brought on by drinking too much water; can cause swelling of the brain or sodium imbalance in the blood and kidneys.

hypothalamus: A region of the brain that secretes hormones.

hypoxia: A dangerous condition brought on by an inadequate amount of oxygen circulating throughout the body.

I

illicit: Unlawful.

impulsive behavior: (sometimes called impulsivity) Acting quickly, often without thinking about the consequences of one's actions.

incontinence: The loss of bladder and/or bowel control.

infertility: The inability to have children.

inflammation: A physical reaction to injury, infection, or exposure to an allergen characterized by redness, pain or swelling.

ingest: To take in for digestion.

inhalant: A chemical that gives off fumes or vapors that are sniffed, or breathed in.

inhibitions: Inner thoughts that keep people from engaging in certain activities.

insomnia: Difficulty falling asleep or an inability to sleep.

intermediaries: Chemical compounds that are intended for use in the manufacture of more complex substances.

intoxicating: Causing drunkenness, but not necessarily from alcohol; the loss of physical or mental control due to the use of any drug is termed "intoxication."

intramuscular: Injected into a muscle.

intravenous: Injected into a vein.

intubation: Putting a plastic tube into the lungs through the nose and throat, thus opening the airway of a person unable to breathe independently.

K

kidney: The body's urine-producing organ.

L

laxatives: Drugs that help produce bowel movements.

levomethorphan: A synthetic substance that mimics the behavior of opiates such as heroin, morphine, or codeine; levomethorphan is the parent drug of dextromethorphan.

lipase: A substance that speeds up the breakdown of fats in the body.

local anesthetic: A painkiller applied directly to the skin or mucus membranes.

loop of Henle: The U-shaped part of the nephron (tiny filtering unit of the kidney) where reabsorption processes take place.

M

mania: A mental disorder characterized by intense anxiety, aggression, and delusions.

menopause: A hormonal process associated with aging in females that results in an inability to become pregnant; also known as the "change of life."

menstrual cycle: Commonly referred to as a woman's "period"; the monthly discharge of blood and other secretions from the uterus of nonpregnant females.

metabolism: The process by which food is converted to energy that the body uses to function.

methylation: Pronounced meh-thuh-LAY-shun; the process of synthesizing or transforming codeine from morphine.

microgram: A millionth of a gram; there are 28 grams in 1 ounce.

miscarry: When a pregnancy ends abruptly because a woman is physically unable to carry the fetus (unborn baby) until it is able to survive on its own.

morphine: An addictive opiate that is used to kill pain and bring on relaxation and sleep.

mucus: A secretion released by the body to prevent germs and allergens from entering the bloodstream.

multiple sclerosis: A progressive illness that affects muscle tissue, leading to pain and inability to control body movements.

muscle dysmorphia: Pronounced muh-SUL diss-MORE-fee-uh; a mental disorder leading to a desire for larger and larger muscles.

mycologist: A person who studies mushrooms.

N

narcolepsy: A sleep disorder characterized by daytime tiredness and sudden attacks of sleep.

narcotic: A painkiller that may become habit-forming; in a broader sense, any illegally purchased drug.

nausea: Upset stomach, sometimes with vomiting.

nephrons: Tiny working units of the kidney; each kidney has more than a million nephrons.

neurological: Related to the body's nervous system.

neuron: A cell in the central nervous system that carries nerve impulses.

neurotransmitter: A substance that helps spread nerve impulses from one nerve cell to another.

nitrite: A negatively charged molecule of nitrogen and oxygen.

nitroglycerin: A heavy, oily, highly explosive liquid that—when used in very small doctor-prescribed amounts—relieves the pain of angina pectoris in heart patients.

nitrous oxide: A gas given to surgical patients to induce sleep.

norepinephrine: Pronounced nor-epp-ih-NEFF-run; a natural stimulant produced by the human body.

noxious: Physically harmful.

nurse anesthetist: (full title is certified registered nurse anesthetist, or CRNA) Nurses who receive special training in the administration of anesthesia.

O

obsessive-compulsive disorder (OCD): An anxiety disorder that causes people to dwell on unwanted thoughts, act on unusual urges, and perform repetitive rituals such as frequent hand washing.

obstetrician: A physician specializing in the birthing process.

opiate: Any drug derived from the opium poppy or synthetically produced to mimic the effects of the opium poppy; opiates tend to decrease restlessness, bring on sleep, and relieve pain.

opioid: A substance created in a laboratory to mimic the effects of naturally occurring opiates such as heroin and morphine.

opium dens: Darkly lit establishments, often in the Chinatown section of big cities, where people went to smoke opium; many dens had beds, boards, or sofas upon which people could recline while experiencing the effects of the drug.

organic: A term used to describe chemical compounds that contain carbon.

osteoporosis: A loss in bone density resulting in thinned and fragile bones.

ovulation: The release of an egg from an ovary.

P

panic attacks: Unexpected episodes of severe anxiety that can cause physical symptoms such as shortness of breath, dizziness, sweating, and shaking.

paranoia: Abnormal feelings of suspicion and fear.

parasitic infections: Infection with parasites, which are organisms that must live with, in, or on other organisms to survive.

Parkinson's disease: An incurable nervous disorder that worsens with time and occurs most often after the age of fifty; it is generally caused by a loss of dopamine-producing brain cells; symptoms include overall weakness, partial paralysis of the face, trembling hands, and a slowed, shuffling walk.

passive smoking: Inhaling smoke from someone else's burning cigarette.

pesticide: A chemical agent designed to kill insects, plants, or animals that threaten gardens, crops, or farm animals.

phenethylamine: A type of alkaloid, or nitrogen-containing molecule.

phenylketonuria: Pronounced fenn-uhl-keet-uh-NORR-ee-yuh; an inherited disorder that interferes with the breakdown of a certain protein called phenylalanine (fenn-uhl-AL-uh-neen). Phenylalanine is found in milk, eggs, and other foods. Without treatment, this protein builds up in the bloodstream and causes brain damage.

phlegm: Pronounced FLEM; thick, germ-filled mucus secreted by the respiratory system.

phobias: Extreme and often unexplainable fears of certain objects or situations.

piperazines: Pronounced pih-PAIR-uh-zeens; chemical compounds made of carbon, hydrogen, and nitrogen that are used medically to destroy worms and other parasites in humans and animals.

placebo: Pronounced pluh-SEE-boh; a "sugar pill" or "dummy pill" that contains no medicine.

placebo effect: A psychological effect noted by researchers in which patients' conditions improve if they *believe* they are taking a medication that will relieve their symptoms.

pneumonia: A disease of the lung, usually brought on by infection, that causes inflammation of the lung tissue, fluid buildup inside the lungs, lowered oxygen levels in the blood, and difficulty breathing.

postmortem examinations: Examining the body after death; also called an autopsy.

postpartum depression: A form of depression that affects more than one in ten new mothers; symptoms include sadness, anxiety, irritability, tiredness, interrupted sleep, a loss of enjoyment or desire to do anything, and guilt over not being able to care properly for their babies.

post-traumatic stress disorder (PTSD): An illness that can occur after experiencing or witnessing life-threatening events, such as serious accidents, violent assaults, or terrorist attacks; symptoms include reliving the experience through nightmares and flashbacks, having problems sleeping, and feeling detached from reality.

potent: Powerful.

powder cocaine: (cocaine hydrochloride) an addictive psychoactive substance derived from coca leaves; it is either snorted into the nose or mixed with water and injected into the veins.

premenstrual syndrome: Symptoms that occur in some women about a week before the start of their monthly period and may include irritability, fatigue, depression, and abdominal bloating.

propellant: A gas that pushes out the contents of a bottle, can, or cylinder.

prostate: A male reproductive gland.

pseudoephedrine: Pronounced SUE-doh-ih-FEH-drinn; a chemical similar to ephedrine that is used to relieve nasal congestion.

psychedelic: The ability to produce hallucinations or other altered mental states.

psychoactive: Mind-altering; a psychoactive substance alters the user's mental state or changes one's behavior.

psychological addiction or psychological dependence: The belief that a person needs to take a certain substance in order to function, whether that person really does or not.

psychosis: Pronounced sy-KOH-sis; a severe mental disorder that often causes hallucinations and makes it difficult for people to distinguish what is real from what is imagined.

psychostimulant: Pronounced SY-koh-STIM-yew-lent; a stimulant that acts on the brain.

psychotherapy: The treatment of emotional problems by a trained therapist using a variety of techniques to improve a patient's outlook on life.

psychotic behavior: A dangerous loss of contact with reality, sometimes leading to violence against self or others.

psychotropic: Having an effect on the mind.

pulmonary hypertension: A life-threatening condition of continuous high blood pressure in the blood vessels that supply the lungs.

Q

quarantined: Isolated in order to prevent the spread of disease.

R

raves: Overnight dance parties that typically involve huge crowds of people, loud techno music, and illegal drug use.

receptors: Group of cells that receive stimuli.

recreational drug use: Using a drug solely to achieve a high, not to treat a medical condition.

respiratory depression: A slowed breathing rate; severe cases can cause a person to slip into a coma or even stop breathing entirely.

retina: A sensory membrane in the eye.

rhabdomyolysis: Pronounced rabb-doh-my-OLL-uh-sis; destruction of muscle tissue leading to paralysis.

rush: A feeling of euphoria or extreme happiness and well-being.

S

schizophrenia: A mental disease characterized by a withdrawal from reality and other intellectual and emotional disturbances.

screw music: An engineered music inspired by codeine use that uses existing songs but slows them down and makes certain segments repetitive.

secondhand smoke: The smoke from a cigarette user and breathed in by someone nearby.

sedation: Drowsiness or lowered levels of activity brought on by a drug.

sedative: A drug used to treat anxiety and calm people down.

sedative-hypnotic agents: Drugs that depress or slow down the body.

self-mutilation: Deliberately cutting or injuring oneself in some way.

senility: Pronounced suh-NILL-ih-tee; a condition associated with old age; symptoms include a decrease in the ability to think clearly and make decisions.

serotonin: A combination of carbon, hydrogen, nitrogen, and oxygen; it is found in the brain, blood, and stomach lining and acts as a neurotransmitter and blood vessel regulator.

shaman: Spiritual leader who cures the sick and uncovers hidden truths.

sinsemilla: Literally, "without seeds"; buds from female marijuana plants carrying the highest concentration of THC.

sodium bicarbonate: A fizzy, liquid, over-the-counter antacid taken by mouth to relieve upset stomachs.

sodium pentathol: A drug given to surgical patients to induce sleep, usually administered by injection.

solvent: A substance, usually liquid, that dissolves another substance.

speed: The street name for amphetamines.

speedball: A combination of cocaine (a stimulant) and heroin (a depressant); this combination increases the chances of serious adverse reactions and can be more toxic than either drug alone.

steroids: Drugs that mimic the actions of testosterone, a hormone found in greater quantities in males than in females, and help build muscle mass and strength.

stimulant: A substance that increases the activity of a living organism or one of its parts.

stroke: A loss of feeling, consciousness, or movement caused by the breaking or blocking of a blood vessel in the brain.

sudden sniffing death (SSD) syndrome: Death that occurs very quickly after inhaled fumes take the place of oxygen in the lungs; SSD is most often caused by butane, propane, and aerosol abuse.

suffocate: Unable to breathe; death caused by a blockage of air to the lungs.

sulfuric acid: A strong and oily compound made of hydrogen, sulfur, and oxygen; it is capable of eating away at other substances.

suppository: Medicine that is delivered through the anus.

sympathomimetics: Pronounced SIMM-path-oh-muh-MEH-ticks; medications similar to amphetamines but less powerful and with less potential for addiction.

synapses: Junctions between two nerve cells where signals pass.

synthetic: Made in a laboratory.

T

tactile: Pronounced TAK-tuhl; relating to the sense of touch.

testicular atrophy: Pronounced tess-TIK-you-lar AH-truh-fee; the shrinking of the male testicles, which sometimes results from overdoses of testosterone or anabolic-androgenic steroids.

testosterone: Pronounced tess-TOS-tuhr-own; a hormone—found in greater quantities in males than in females—that is responsible for male traits and the male sex drive.

THC: The main active ingredient in cannabis.

thebaine: pronounced thee-BAIN; one of the active alkaloids in opium, used to create synthetic painkillers.

theobromine: Pronounced THEE-uh-BROH-meen; a xanthine found in cacao (kah-KOW) beans (the source of chocolate).

theophylline: Pronounced thee-AFF-uh-lun; a xanthine found in tea leaves.

thyroid: An important gland, or group of cells, in the body that secretes chemical messengers called hormones; these hormones control metabolism, the process by which food is converted to energy that the body uses to function.

tics: Repetitive, involuntary jerky movements, eye blinking, or vocal sounds that patients cannot suppress on their own.

tinctures: Combinations of an active drug and a liquid alcohol.

tolerance: A condition in which higher and higher doses of a drug are needed to produce the original effect or high experienced.

toluene: Pronounced TOL-yuh-ween; a household and industrial solvent common in many inhaled substances, including model airplane glue, spray paint, correction fluid, paint thinners, and paint removers.

Tourette's syndrome: A severe tic disorder that causes distress and significant impairment to those affected by it.

toxic: Harmful, poisonous, or capable of causing death.

trafficking: Making, selling, or distributing a controlled drug.

trance: A sleep-like state in which important body functions slow down.

tranquilizers: Drugs such as Valium and Librium that treat anxiety; also called benzodiazepines (pronounced ben-zoh-die-AZ-uh-peens).

traumatic: Dangerous, life-threatening, and difficult to forget.

trip: An intense and usually very visual experience produced by an hallucinogenic drug.

tuberculosis: Pronounced tuh-burk-yuh-LOH-siss; a highly contagious disease of the lungs.

tryptamine compound: A crystalline compound of carbon, hydrogen, and nitrogen that is made in plant and animal tissues.

U

ulcers: The breakdown of mucus membranes, usually in the stomach.

V

vapors: Gas or fumes that can be irritating or physically harmful when inhaled.

venom: A liquid poison created by an animal for defense against predators or for killing prey.

W

withdrawal: The process of gradually cutting back on the amount of a drug being taken until it is discontinued entirely; also the accompanying physiological effects of terminating use of an addictive drug.

X

xanthine: Pronounced ZAN-thene; a compound found in animal and plant tissue.

Highlights of the U.S. Controlled Substances Act (CSA) of 1970

The Controlled Substances Act (CSA) is part of a larger piece of legislation called the Comprehensive Drug Abuse Prevention and Control Act of 1970. It provides the legal basis for the U.S. government to fight the ongoing war against drugs.

Under the CSA, all drugs are categorized into one of five "schedules." A substance's scheduling is based on three factors: 1) its medicinal value; 2) its possible harmfulness to human health; and 3) its potential for abuse or addiction. Schedule I is reserved for the most dangerous drugs that have no recognized medical use, while Schedule V is the classification used for the least dangerous drugs.

Schedule I Drugs

- have no known medical use in the United States
- have a very high potential for abuse
- are too dangerous to be used even under medical supervision

Drugs classified as Schedule I include 2C-B (Nexus), dimethyl-tryptamine (DMT), ecstasy (MDMA), GHB, heroin, LSD, mescaline, PMA, and psilocybin.

Schedule II Drugs

- are accepted for medical use in the United States
- may cause severe psychological and/or physical dependence
- have a high potential for abuse

Drugs classified as Schedule II include Adderall, cocaine, hydromorphone, methylphenidates such as Concerta and Ritalin, morphine, and oxycodone.

Schedule III Drugs

- are accepted for medical use in the United States
- may lead to moderate psychological and/or physical dependence
- are less likely to be abused than drugs categorized as Schedule I or Schedule II

Drugs classified as Schedule III include certain barbiturates such as aprobarbital (Alurate), butabarbital (Butisol), and butalbital

(Fiorinal and Fioricet), as well as muscle-building steroids and testosterone.

Schedule IV Drugs

- are accepted for medical use in the United States
- may lead to limited psychological and/or physical dependence
- have a relatively low potential for abuse

Drugs classified as Schedule IV include various benzodiazepines, including alprazolam (Xanax) and diazepam (Valium).

Schedule V Drugs

- are accepted for medical use in the United States
- are less likely to cause psychological and/or physical dependence than drugs in any other Schedule
- have a low potential for abuse

Drugs classified as Schedule V include various over-the-counter medicines that contain codeine.

Source: Compiled by Thomson Gale staff from data reported in "Controlled Substances Act," U.S. Drug Enforcement Administration (DEA), http://www.usdoj.gov/dea/agency/csa.htm (accessed September 4, 2005); and "Controlled Substance Schedules," U.S. Department of Justice, Drug Enforcement Administration (DEA) Office of Diversion Control, http://www.deadiversion.usdoj.gov/schedules/alpha/alphabetical.htm (accessed September 4, 2005).

2C-B (Nexus)

What Kind of Drug Is It?

2C-B is an illegal and dangerous drug that has raised many concerns among medical experts and law enforcement officials worldwide. Its official name, 4-bromo-2,5-dimethoxyphenethylamine, is so difficult to pronounce that it is almost always referred to by its shortened name, 2C-B, or by the street name "nexus." 2C-B is usually sold as a tablet, a capsule, or a white powder. By 2004, however, it began appearing on the streets as both a red pill and an orange powder.

2C-B abuse is most common among teenagers and young adults who attend all-night dance parties, known as RAVES, on a regular basis. It is often taken in combination with other so-called rave or club drugs such as ecstasy (MDMA), GHB, ketamine, LSD (lysergic acid diethylamide), and methamphetamine. (Entries on these drugs are available in this encyclopedia.)

It is important to note that 2C-B is a synthetic drug; in other words, it cannot be grown in a garden or dug up from the ground. This drug is produced solely in illegal labs, has no known medical use, and cannot even be obtained with a doctor's prescription. 2C-B is used for just one reason, and that reason is to get high. It is very similar in chemical makeup to AMPHETAMINES. Amphetamines are stimulants, meaning that they increase the activity of a living organism or one of its parts.

2C-B is a PSYCHOACTIVE SUBSTANCE that affects the behavior and mental state of those who use it. 2C-B is also considered a psychedelic drug and a hallucinogen. Psychedelic drugs and hallucinogens produce HALLUCINATIONS, or strange sights and sounds, in users' heads. In a report filed in late December of 2004, *ABC News* writer Marc Lallanilla called synthetic hallucinogens like 2C-B "a new class of drugs [that are] getting increased attention from police and partiers alike."

Overview

According to the U.S. Department of Justice, the Drug Enforcement Administration (DEA) first came across 2C-B in 1979. The DEA noted in its Drug Intelligence Brief "An Overview of Club

Official Drug Name: 4-bromo-2,5-dimethoxyphenethylamine (BROH-moh dy-meth-OCK-sy-FENN-eh-THY-luh-meen); almost always referred to by the shortened name 2C-B
Also Known As: Afro, bees, bromo, cloud-9, eve, nexus, toonies, utopia, and venus; Nexus is the street name used most frequently for 2C-B
Drug Classifications: Schedule 1, hallucinogen

raves: wild overnight dance parties that typically involve huge crowds of people, loud techno music, and illegal drug use

amphetamines: pronounced am-FETT-uh-meens; stimulant drugs that increase mental alertness, reduce appetite, and help keep users awake

psychoactive substance: a substance that alters the user's mental state or changes behavior

hallucinations: visions or other perceptions of things that are not really present

2C-B Basics

2C-B has been illegal since 1995, when it was classified as a Schedule I drug under the Controlled Substances Act (CSA, 1970). Few state and federal agencies track 2C-B use specifically. Rather, it is lumped in with statistics on club drugs or hallucinogens. 2C-B is often sold and used in combination with other club drugs. It is also sometimes sold as ecstasy (MDMA), especially at raves.

Drugs" (2000) that 2C-B first gained a following among drug users in Germany and Switzerland. However, the drug's effects soon began to "appeal to the U.S. rave culture" as well. These effects include increasing the user's awareness of things seen and heard, "increased sexual desire, and heightened senses of taste and touch."

By 2000, 2C-B had become a considerable concern to U.S. drug officials. At that time, significant seizures of the drug had occurred in nearly twenty states. Among the largest were raids carried out in Richmond, Virginia, and the Washington, D.C., area. By 2002, use of the drug was reported nationwide. Drug officials said they did not expect to see this trend reverse for years.

2C-B's Inventor

American chemist Alexander T. "Sasha" Shulgin (1925–) first produced 2C-B in 1974. Over the next year or so, he and his wife did extensive testing of the drug by using it themselves and recording the results. Shulgin has discovered or synthesized more than 150 drugs, most of them hallucinogens. He has angered U.S. law enforcement agencies for documenting his personal experiences while using drugs. In addition, Shulgin has published the chemical formulas "for almost every mind-bending drug known to humankind," wrote Dennis Romero in the *Los Angeles Times*.

Dr. Shulgin began his controversial career in chemistry in the 1960s. He conducted research at the University of California at San Francisco and worked as a senior research chemist at Dow Chemical. He received a license from the DEA to study seized drugs and "give expert testimony in drug trials," Romero noted. However, this did not "allow him to invent the stuff, though," continued Romero. "A few drugs Shulgin invented, substances with names like STP and 2C-B, escaped to the streets of San Francisco." STP, also called DOM, is another psychedelic hallucinogen.

What Is It Made Of?

Five elements are used to make 2C-B: carbon, hydrogen, nitrogen, oxygen, and bromine. The chemical element bromine is a deep red liquid. It is highly explosive, strong smelling, extremely caustic (burning and corrosive), and poisonous.

Raves are all-night dance parties featuring loud techno music. Illegal drugs, such as 2C-B, are often part of the rave culture. © *Houston Scott/Corbis Sygma.*

Many scientific terms can be applied to 2C-B. First of all, it is considered an ORGANIC chemical compound because it contains carbon. It also falls under the definition of an ALKALOID. The root word PHENETHYLAMINE in 2C-B's official name refers to the phenethylamine group of alkaloids, which also includes ephedrine, methamphetamine, and mescaline. (Entries on ephedra, methamphetamine, and mescaline are available in this encyclopedia.) The chemical properties of 2C-B most closely resemble those of mescaline, a powerful drug that can cause convulsions and is well known for its hallucinogenic properties. According to the DEA, 2C-B is ten times more powerful than the popular club drug ecstasy (MDMA).

How Is It Taken?

2C-B is most often taken by mouth and is available in pill, capsule, or powder form. In powder form, it is usually mixed with

organic: a term used to describe chemical compounds that contain carbon

alkaloids: nitrogen-containing substances found in plants

phenethylamine: a type of alkaloid, or nitrogen-containing molecule

Bromine is one of the chemical elements used to make 2C-B. A deep red liquid, bromine is highly explosive, strong smelling, extremely caustic (burning and corrosive), and poisonous. *Andrew Lambert Photography/Photo Researchers, Inc.*

a drink, but it also can be inhaled through the nose. Users report that snorting 2C-B is painful. The effects of the drug are increased when it is inhaled rather than swallowed.

2C-B is sometimes combined with ecstasy (MDMA) and called a "party pack." Or, it is mixed with LSD and referred to as a "banana split." The average dose of 2C-B sold on the street is 10 to 20 milligrams and costs 10 to 30 dollars each. Because 2C-B is an ILLICIT drug produced only in illegal labs, it is not possible to determine the accuracy of any dose.

Are There Any Medical Reasons for Taking This Substance?

2C-B has no known medical use.

Usage Trends

In the middle and late 1980s, 2C-B became an alternative or replacement for ecstasy (MDMA). Ecstasy was classified as an illegal drug in the United States in 1985. Switching one drug for another without the user's knowledge is a common and very dangerous practice in the world of synthesized drugs. "Drug quality may vary significantly," stated the authors of the Drug Intelligence Brief "An Overview of Club Drugs." "Substitute drugs often are sold when suppliers are unable to provide the drug currently in demand." This increases the likelihood of an overdose in unsuspecting users.

2C-B was not really used as a street drug in its own right until the early 1990s. It was sold in adult book and video stores, drug paraphernalia stores called "head" shops, bars, and nightclubs. Drug enforcement officials noticed the trend in 2C-B abuse and set out to stop it. Even before 2C-B was officially classified as an illegal drug in the United States in 1995, DEA agents closed 2C-B manufacturing laboratories in California and Arizona. In late 2004, 2C-B resurfaced in central New York. *News 10 Now* reporter Sarah Buynovsky referred to it as "a new and dangerous drug." She added that "2C-B is often homemade in labs and [is] difficult to track down."

illicit: unlawful

Illicit drugs like 2C-B are produced in illegal labs. Drugmakers often use abandoned, boarded-up houses as places to create their product.
AP/Wide World Photos.

The 2004 Monitoring the Future (MTF) Study

The results of the 2004 Monitoring the Future (MTF) study, conducted by the University of Michigan (U of M), were released to the public on December 21, 2004. The study is sponsored by research grants from the National Institute on Drug Abuse (NIDA). Since 1991, U of M has tracked patterns of drug use and attitudes toward drugs among students in the eighth, tenth, and twelfth grades. (Prior to that, from 1975 to 1990, the MTF survey was limited to twelfth graders.)

The 2004 MTF survey found that, overall, hallucinogen use among students at all three grade levels was down slightly. Still, the percentage of teens that had tried hallucinogens at least once remained very high—a trend that began in the mid-1980s. 2C-B use is not tracked specifically in the MTF survey, but is grouped in with statistics for "hallucinogens other than LSD." According to MTF charts for 2003 to 2004, about 1.7 percent of tenth and twelfth graders admitted to using hallucinogens at least once a month. About 4 percent of tenth graders and 6 percent of twelfth graders reported hallucinogen use "in the last twelve months."

The perceived availability of hallucinogens (the ease with which seniors said they would be able to get the drugs) was very high as well. About half of those surveyed said it would be "fairly easy" or "very

Who Abuses 2C-B?

Experts in the field of drug research regularly gather information available on certain drugs to create a profile of a typical user. Based on these studies, the typical 2C-B user is usually white but sometimes Hispanic and has a medium to high family income level. The user is roughly eighteen to twenty-six years old, resides in an urban area, and regularly attends all-night dance parties or raves. Use of hallucinogens like 2C-B is reportedly higher among males than females. A user of 2C-B is also very likely to abuse other drugs.

easy" to obtain hallucinogens. It is important to stress, however, that these respondents were not basing their answers specifically on the availability of 2C-B, but on hallucinogens in general.

The MTF survey does not track drug use among people after their high school years. As of 2005, data on 2C-B usage in the general population revealed that "the typical user is a young, white, college-educated and Web-savvy person," noted Lallanilla in his *ABC News* report. A large number of 2C-B users also take other drugs, which increases their risks for physical and mental side effects.

Effects on the Body

The most noticeable physical effects of 2C-B use are anxiety, agitation, facial flushing, sweating, muscle clenching, poor coordination, shaking, chills, tremors, dilated or enlarged pupils, and increased blood pressure and heart rate. Feelings of fear, anger, and distress are often sparked by 2C-B.

Drugs like 2C-B "have law enforcement and health officials concerned because their long-term health effects are virtually unknown," Lallanilla pointed out. 2C-B is capable of producing varying effects in humans based on the dosage taken. In fact, increasing the dose by just a few milligrams can make an enormous difference in what occurs in the user's body.

Although there are reports of negative effects at any dosage, a dose of 2C-B in the 4- to 5-milligram range typically makes users feel calm, relaxed, and more aware of their bodies and their emotions. At slightly higher doses of 8 to 10 milligrams, users usually appear drunk and may experience mild hallucinations.

Effects of Higher Doses

The intensity of the visual effects increases when more 2C-B is taken. Doses of 20 to 40 milligrams reportedly produce very vivid hallucinations. Solid objects appear to crawl and change shape. Geometric patterns can pop up on plain surfaces. Colors become more intense, and moving objects seem to leave trails of color behind them. In addition, music seems to take on a visual dimension, with users experiencing unusual blends of sights and sounds. Doses higher than 40 milligrams can bring on extremely frightening

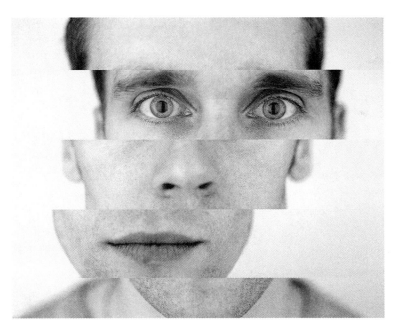

Psychedelic drugs like 2C-B produce hallucinations and distort reality, making it hard for the user to know what is real and what is not.
Gusto/Photo Researchers, Inc.

hallucinations that occur with the eyes open or closed. Users have reported terrifying panic attacks after seeing gruesome 2C-B-induced images. Feelings of anger, PARANOIA, and generalized terror may also occur.

The effects of 2C-B usually become noticeable about fifteen to twenty minutes after the drug is taken. They reach their peak after an hour or so. Typically the effects of the drug do not begin to decrease until three or four hours after ingestion. They can last for up to twelve hours, depending on the strength of the dose taken. Some users have reported having unusual dreams up to three nights after taking 2C-B. Others claim that the mood-altering effects of the drug can remain some five to six days after coming down from an intense 2C-B high.

"Many who try 2C-B find it intensely disagreeable," wrote Paul M. Gahlinger in *Illegal Drugs: A Complete Guide to Their History, Chemistry, Use, and Abuse.* "Diarrhea, cramping, and gas are common, and some have complained of allergic-type reactions with cough and runny nose. Some users feel anxious or have frightening thoughts or visions." 2C-B appears to bind to SEROTONIN receptors in

paranoia: abnormal feelings of suspicion and fear

serotonin: a combination of carbon, hydrogen, nitrogen, and oxygen; it is found in the brain, blood, and stomach lining and acts as a neurotransmitter and blood vessel regulator

Bad Trips

A 2C-B user can have strong feelings of anxiety or fear while "tripping," or experiencing the physical and mental disturbances brought on by the drug. The hallucinatory effects can be intense enough to make users feel that they are losing control or going crazy. When negative feelings dominate the experience, it is commonly called a "bad trip." The reasons for these frightening experiences are not known. Such trips are particularly common among first-time users.

In *A Brief History of Drugs: From the Stone Age to the Stoned Age,* Antonio Escohotado warned that 2C-B "induces terror when overdosed" and has been known to "generate many bad trips." Having a bad trip can cause the user to panic, which can lead to even more dangerous behavior. Sometimes, the fear-provoking effects of 2C-B can last for eight to twelve hours. That is a very long time to be terrified. Medical attention and physical restraint are sometimes required if the user becomes violent.

---

the brain, which is why it has hallucinogenic properties. Serotonin is a NEUROTRANSMITTER or "messenger" substance that carries information throughout the body. When the normal flow of serotonin is interrupted, it becomes difficult for people to distinguish between what is real and what appears to be real. Some people have become terrified of losing their minds or dying while on 2C-B.

Reactions with Other Drugs or Substances

Little is known about 2C-B's effects when taken with alcohol or other drugs. That poses a big problem for paramedics and emergency room doctors and nurses because users typically take 2C-B along with a variety of other dangerous substances. It is much harder to treat a person who has overdosed when a mixture of drugs is involved. 2C-B is frequently used in combination with other illicit club drugs, particularly amphetamines, ecstasy (MDMA), GHB, ketamine, and methamphetamine. Users often say that 2C-B heightens or increases the effects of other drugs.

2C-B is especially dangerous for people with DIABETES, EPILEPSY, or heart problems. It is also dangerous for pregnant women and their unborn children, and for people taking certain types of antidepressants.

neurotransmitter: a substance that helps spread nerve impulses from one nerve cell to another

diabetes: a serious disorder that causes problems with the normal breakdown of sugars in the body

epilepsy: a disorder involving the misfiring of electrical impulses in the brain, sometimes resulting in seizures and loss of consciousness

psychological addiction: the belief that a person needs to take a certain substance in order to function

Treatment for Habitual Users

Frequent use of 2C-B can result in a PSYCHOLOGICAL ADDICTION. Psychological dependence can develop quickly. The treatment program for heavy users of 2C-B is the same as for users of other hallucinogens. A combination of therapy methods is used, including individual counseling, group therapy, and sometimes medication.

Consequences

Studies and surveys conducted in the United States, Canada, and the United Kingdom indicate that 2C-B users are likely to abuse other drugs as well. Taken alone, hallucinogens have a powerful

2C-B is usually sold as a tablet, a capsule, or a white powder. This vial of 2C-B powder contains 22.5 mg of the drug. *Photo by Erowid, © 2001 Erowid.org.*

effect on the brain. They distort the way a person's five senses work, affect the memory, and even change the user's perceptions of time and space. People who use drugs like 2C-B often have a hard time concentrating, communicating, or telling the difference between what is real and what is not. 2C-B is capable of disrupting a person's ability to think, communicate, and act sensibly.

Users of 2C-B will develop a tolerance to the drug over time. If they increase the dose they take, they face a greater risk of having a bad TRIP or disturbing flashbacks of an earlier trip. Since 2C-B is hallucinogenic, it impairs mental functions. This greatly increases the risk of accidents among users and can also lead users to engage in unsafe sex or violent behavior.

The Law

Possession of 2C-B is illegal in the United States, Canada, and the United Kingdom. 2C-B is also considered an illegal substance in Japan and various European countries, including France, the Netherlands, Germany, and Sweden.

One key fact every reader should know about 2C-B is that it is an illicit drug: it cannot, under any circumstances, be used legally. It is considered unsafe even when taken under medical supervision (and it cannot be administered legally by anyone, including physicians).

In the United States, the Controlled Substances Act (CSA) of 1970 called for all federally regulated drug substances to be categorized into one of five schedules. These schedules are based on a substance's medicinal value, possible harmfulness, and potential for abuse and addiction. Schedule I is reserved for the most dangerous

trip: an intense and usually very visual experience produced by an hallucinogenic drug

drugs that have no recognized medical use. 2C-B is a Schedule I drug. "Once a drug has been designated a Schedule I Controlled Substance, it becomes very difficult for researchers to obtain permission to study that drug," explained Gahlinger. That is one of the reasons why "very little is known about . . . 2C-B."

A drug's schedule plays a major role in determining penalties for illegal possession or sale of the drug. In the United States, a person convicted of possessing and/or selling a Schedule I drug such as 2C-B can face a lengthy prison term and hundreds of thousands of dollars in fines. Repeat offenders receive even harsher punishment. The United Kingdom regulates 2C-B under the Medicines Act. In Canada, 2C-B is a scheduled drug under the Controlled Drugs and Substances Act. Japan's Health and Welfare Ministry ruled the drug had no legitimate medical uses and banned it in 1998 under the Narcotics Control Law. In 2000, the World Health Organization (WHO) recommended that 2C-B be placed under international control because its use poses a "substantial" public health and social problem.

For More Information

Books

Escohotado, Antonio. *A Brief History of Drugs: From the Stone Age to the Stoned Age*. Rochester, VT: Park Street Press, 1999.

Gahlinger, Paul M. *Illegal Drugs: A Complete Guide to Their History, Chemistry, Use, and Abuse*. Las Vegas, NV: Sagebrush Press, 2001.

Knowles, Cynthia R. *Up All Night: A Closer Look at Club Drugs and Rave Culture*. North Springfield, VT: Red House Press, 2001.

Periodicals

De Boer, D., and others. "More Data about the New Psychoactive Drug 2C-B." *Journal of Analytical Toxicology* (May-June, 1999): pp. 227-228.

"The Death of the Party." *FDA Consumer* (March, 2000): p. 14.

Kintz, P. "Interpreting the Results of Medico-Legal Analyses in Cases of Substance Abuse." *Journal of Toxicology: Clinical Toxicology* (March, 2000): p. 197.

Kowalski, Kathiann M. "What Hallucinogens Can Do to Your Brain." *Current Health* (April, 2000): p. 6.

Mackenzie, Dana. "Secrets of an Acid Head (Research on Hallucinogenic Drugs)." *New Scientist* (June 23, 2001): p. 26.

Romero, Dennis. "Sasha Shulgin, Psychedelic Chemist." *Los Angeles Times* (September 5, 1995).

Web Sites

"2C-B." *Fact Index Home Page.* http://www.fact-index.com/ (accessed June 16, 2005).

Buynovsky, Sarah. "New Drug Popping Up in the State." *News 10 Now (New York): 24-Hour Local News,* October 28, 2004. http://news10 now.com/content/top_stories/ (accessed June 30, 2005).

"Drugs and Chemicals of Concern: 4-Bromo-2,5-dimethoxyphenethyl-amine." *U.S. Department of Justice, Drug Enforcement Administration.* http://www.deadiversion.usdoj.gov/drugs_concern/ (accessed June 16, 2005).

Lallanilla, Marc. "New Rave Drugs Have Experts Concerned." *ABC News,* December 30, 2004. http://abcnews.go.com/Health/story?id=366370&page=1 (accessed June 30, 2005).

Monitoring the Future. http://www.monitoringthefuture.org/ and http://www.nida.nih.gov/Newsroom/04/2004MTFDrug.pdf (both accessed June 30, 2005).

National Institute on Drug Abuse. http://www.nida.nih.gov/ and http://www.drugabuse.gov (both accessed June 30, 2005).

"An Overview of Club Drugs: Drug Intelligence Brief, February 2000." *U.S. Department of Justice, Drug Enforcement Administration, Intelligence Division.* http://www.usdoj.gov/dea/pubs/intel/20005intell-brief.pdf (accessed June 16, 2005).

See also: Ecstasy (MDMA); Ephedra; GHB; Ketamine; LSD (lysergic acid diethylamide); Mescaline; Methamphetamine

Adderall

Official Drug Name: Adderall (ADD–ur–all), Adderall XR; a mixed amphetamine sulfate (am–FETT–uh–meen SUL–fate)
Also Known As: Speed, uppers
Drug Classifications: Schedule II, stimulant

attention-deficit/hyperactivity disorder (ADHD): a disorder characterized by impulsive behavior, difficulty concentrating, and hyperactivity that interferes with social and academic functioning

narcolepsy: a rare sleep disorder characterized by daytime tiredness and sudden attacks of sleep

impulsive behavior: (sometimes called impulsivity) acting quickly, often without thinking about the consequences of one's actions

What Kind of Drug Is It?

Adderall and Adderall XR are amphetamines (pronounced am-FETT-uh-meens), which are drugs that increase mental alertness. Adderall is manufactured by Shire Pharmaceuticals Group, a drug company headquartered in the United Kingdom with offices throughout the UK, the United States, Canada, and parts of Europe. Amphetamines are stimulants, or substances that increase the activity of a living organism or one of its parts.

In the 2003 edition of their book *Drugs 101: An Overview for Teens,* Margaret O. Hyde and John F. Setaro defined stimulants as "drugs used to increase alertness, relieve fatigue, [and make users] feel stronger and more decisive."

Adderall tablets are blue or orange, depending on the dosage, and are imprinted with the letters "AD." Adderall extended–release capsules are also blue or orange, depending on the dosage, and are imprinted with the name "Adderall XR." One side of each capsule is transparent. Both the tablets and the capsules are marked with a number (for instance, 5, 10, or 20) to identify the strength of the medication in milligrams.

Overview

The active ingredients in Adderall are used to treat symptoms of ATTENTION-DEFICIT/HYPERACTIVITY DISORDER (ADHD), NARCOLEPSY, and sometimes obesity. In the 1960s, the drug was marketed under the name Obetrol. The U.S. Food and Drug Administration (FDA) approved a new formulation of the drug, known as Adderall, for the treatment of ADHD in early 1996.

ADHD is a disorder that begins during childhood. However, in many cases, it is not diagnosed until adulthood. It is very difficult for people with ADHD to focus their attention and control their behavior. Children with ADHD are easily distracted and have difficulty concentrating, especially on schoolwork. They may also talk excessively, interrupt conversations, and have trouble waiting their turn. In many cases, people with ADHD display IMPULSIVE BEHAVIOR, which frequently continues into adulthood.

More About ADHD

The terms *hyper* and *hyperactive* are often used negatively when referring to people with ADHD. Such terms are stereotypes—labels, often negative, used to describe all people within a certain group regardless of whether they are true about everyone or not. It is important to note, however, that not everyone who talks a lot has ADHD. Not everyone who fidgets or gets antsy has ADHD. Not everyone who taps a pencil when taking a test has ADHD.

The truth is that ADHD affects people in completely different ways. Some of the symptoms are described in a booklet on the disorder published by the National Institute of Mental Health (NIMH). The authors note that some children with ADHD may "appear to be daydreaming, 'spacey,' easily confused, [or] slow moving" rather than overly active. Either way, the authors explain, it is important to realize that "many normal children may have these symptoms, but at a low level, or the symptoms may be caused by another disorder." The NIMH stressed the need for children with symptoms of "hyperactivity-impulsivity" or "inattention" to "receive a thorough examination and appropriate diagnosis by a well–qualified professional."

Adderall helps manage the symptoms of ADHD by increasing the release of DOPAMINE. Dopamine is a NEUROTRANSMITTER. It acts on the part of the brain responsible for filtering incoming information, making choices, judging behavior, and deciding when and how to act.

Speed

Amphetamines are drugs that give people more energy. This allows users to do more and stay awake longer without getting tired. This effect of "speeding up" people's actions explains how amphetamines came to be known by the street names "speed" and "uppers."

What Is It Made Of?

Amphetamines like Adderall do not occur naturally; they cannot be grown in a garden or dug up from the ground. Rather, amphetamines are synthetic, or manufactured, substances that consist of the elements carbon, hydrogen, and nitrogen.

The composition of amphetamine pills or capsules is actually a combination of various types of crystalline compounds called amphetamine *salts*. Adderall is a chemical compound that contains equal parts of four different amphetamine and dextroamphetamine salts. For this reason, it is referred to as a *mixed amphetamine*. (The only difference between amphetamine and dextroamphetamine is a few molecules of dextrose, which is a type of sugar.) (Entries on amphetamines and dextroamphetamine are also available in this encyclopedia.)

dopamine: pronounced DOPE–uh–meen; a combination of carbon, hydrogen, nitrogen, and oxygen that acts as a neurotransmitter in the brain

neurotransmitter: a substance that helps spread nerve impulses from one nerve cell to another

Many children with attention-deficit/hyperactivity disorder (ADHD) are given Adderall, Ritalin, or other drugs to control their behavior. Symptoms of ADHD include: acting impulsively, acting hyper or out of control, or having difficulty concentrating or focusing on something. *Photo by Steve Liss/ Time Life Pictures/Getty Images.*

How Is It Taken?

Adderall comes in both tablet and capsule form and is taken by mouth. Adderall tablets can be prescribed for patients as young as three years old. Adderall XR is the name given to the "extended release" form of the drug. It is recommended for use only in patients age six and older.

People who take Adderall tablets by prescription need to take two or three pills each day, one at a time, approximately four to six hours apart. Adderall XR is a once-a-day treatment for ADHD. The key to this extended relief formula lies in the two different types of tiny ball-shaped granules packaged in each capsule. These granules are known as amphetamine beads. Half of the beads in Adderall XR begin working immediately after their release from the capsule. The other half takes several hours to dissolve. This bead mixture "extends" the effect of the drug throughout the day, relieving the symptoms of ADHD for a full twelve hours. It is very important that the full contents of the capsule are taken at the same time to ensure the proper timing of the drug's release.

The starting dose of Adderall for new patients is 5 to 10 milligrams daily. The maximum dose is 30 milligrams per day. It takes about 30 to 60 minutes for a prescription-strength dose of Adderall to begin working on the symptoms of ADHD.

What's the Difference between ADD and ADHD?

According to the Attention Deficit Disorder Association's Fact Sheet on ADHD, "the difference is mainly one of terminology, which can be confusing at times. . . . Many people use the term ADD as a generic term for all types of ADHD. . . . Whether we call it ADD or ADHD, however, we are all basically referring to the same thing."

Are There Any Medical Reasons for Taking This Substance?

The FDA has approved the use of mixed amphetamine salts to treat ADHD and the sleep disorder narcolepsy. As of 2005, the main medical use for Adderall was as a treatment for ADHD. In *Internal Medicine Alert,* William T. Elliott and James Chan stated that mixed amphetamine salts like Adderall are as effective as Ritalin and other methylphenidates in the treatment of ADHD in children, adolescents, and adults. (An entry on Ritalin and other methylphenidates is also available in this encyclopedia.)

Amphetamines are successful in the treatment of ADHD because they help improve the user's ability to concentrate. Drugs like Adderall and Adderall XR have been shown to increase performance accuracy, improve short-term memory, speed up reaction time, aid in solving mathematical problems, and even increase problem-solving abilities in games. In November of 2004, the Washington Neuropsychological Institute released the results of a series of tests involving simulated driving experiences in nineteen- to twenty-five-year-old ADHD patients. *Asia Africa Intelligence Wire* reported that Adderall XR was shown to improve driver safety for up to twelve hours in the young adults who took it before participating in the driving experiment.

In 2003, Jessi Castro, a high school student in Miami, wrote a letter to *Time* magazine about her experience with ADHD and Adderall. She credited her straight-A success in school to Adderall. "I may be naturally smart," she wrote, "but I never could have applied myself as much without it [Adderall]."

The pressure to do well on college entrance exams, such as the SAT, has prompted some students to use prescription drugs like Adderall illegally. Such students claim the drug helps them focus and concentrate better.

Photo by John Nordell/The Christian Science Monitor via Getty Images.

Adderall and Narcolepsy

Adderall has also relieved the symptoms of narcolepsy, an unusual condition that causes people to fall asleep quickly and unexpectedly. A narcoleptic's sleep is often brief but quite deep and usually unplanned. The possibility of falling into an uncontrollable sleep at any time makes everyday life very difficult. Thus, ordinary activities such as driving can be very dangerous for people with narcolepsy.

Like all amphetamines, Adderall speeds up bodily functions. In fact, one of the most common side effects reported among Adderall users is an inability to sleep. Although this side effect can be troublesome for patients taking Adderall to treat the symptoms of ADHD, it produces a much-desired feeling of alertness in people with narcolepsy. By decreasing the frequency and severity of narcoleptic sleeping episodes, Adderall allows people with this condition more freedom to engage in the activities of normal daily life.

Adderall and Weight Loss

Adderall was originally manufactured and prescribed as a weight loss drug called Obetrol. Amphetamines tend to decrease feelings of hunger in people who take them, making them an often-abused drug among dieters. Amphetamine use for weight loss can be very dangerous. Most doctors agree that the best way to regulate weight is through moderate exercise and a healthy diet. Drugs like Adderall are only available with a doctor's prescription and are rarely used legally for weight control.

ADHD: Not Just Kids' Stuff

According to a 2004 *Pharma Business Week* article, "Up to 65 percent of children with ADHD may still exhibit symptoms into adulthood and an estimated 4.4 percent of the U.S. adult population is affected by ADHD." Based on U.S. Census Bureau information released on January 7, 2005, 4.4 percent of the adult population adds up to more than 8.8 million people over the age of eighteen.

In September of 2004, Adderall XR was approved for use by adults with ADHD. Results of a U.S. survey cited by *Pharma Business Week* revealed that "adults with ADHD are twice as likely to be divorced or separated and have had almost twice as many jobs ... compared to adults without ADHD. Importantly, 43 percent of adults with ADHD report that they lost or left one or more jobs due in some part to their ADHD symptoms." In addition, survey takers found that adults with ADHD run a greater risk of depression, antisocial behavior, and low educational achievement.

Usage Trends

The use of Adderall among overstressed high school and college students became a problem in the early 2000s. "In the past,

"What's It Like to Have ADD?"

Author and physician Edward M. Hallowell has ADD himself. In the article "What's It Like to Have ADD?," available on the *Attention Deficit Disorder Association* Web site, he describes his experiences:

It's like driving in the rain with bad windshield wipers. Everything is smudged and blurred and you're speeding along, and it's really frustrating not being able to see very well. Or, it's like listening to a radio station with a lot of static and you have to strain to hear what's going on. Or, it's like trying to build a house of cards in a dust storm. You have to build a structure to protect yourself from the wind before you can even start on the cards.

In other ways it's like being super-charged all the time. You get one idea and you have to act on it, and then, what do you know, but you've got another idea before you've finished up with the first one, and so you go for that one, but of course a third idea intercepts the second, and you just have to follow that one, and pretty soon people are calling you disorganized and impulsive and all sorts of impolite words that miss the point completely. Because you're trying really hard. . . .

Plus which, you're spilling over all the time. You're drumming your fingers, tapping your feet, humming a song, whistling, looking here, looking there, scratching, stretching, doodling, and people think you're not paying attention or that you're not interested, but all you're doing is spilling over so that you can pay attention. I can pay a lot better attention when I'm taking a walk or listening to music or even when I'm in a crowded, noisy room than when I'm still and surrounded by silence. . . .

The adult syndrome of ADD, so long unrecognized, is now at last bursting upon the scene. Thankfully, millions of adults who have had to think of themselves as defective or unable to get their acts together, will instead be able to make the most of their considerable abilities. It is a hopeful time indeed.

pick-me-ups like coffee, Diet Coke, or over-the-counter caffeine pills have been popular choices among students to get an extra buzz for studying," wrote Jillian Foley in *America's Intelligence Wire* in December 2004. "But in recent years, some . . . students have started turning to Adderall . . . to help them study, take tests, and write papers." But why would so many students without ADHD want to take a medicine for a disorder they do not have? Nicholas Zamiska offered an explanation in the November 8, 2004 issue of the *Wall Street Journal.* He explained that "studies conducted by the National Institutes of Health in the late 1970s found that low-dose stimulants increase concentration and alertness in everyone, not just people with attention disorders."

"The effects that make [Adderall] appealing to many students include decreased drowsiness and increased attentiveness for hours," wrote Omid Fatemi in *America's Intelligence Wire* in 2004. "[B]ut Adderall is a prescription drug for a reason." Many of the students

Prescription drugs like Adderall and Ritalin are taken illegally by some students. They claim that the drugs help them get better grades. Other students believe that taking such drugs is cheating. They note that hard work and study is the path to follow for better grades. © *Jose Luis Pelaez, Inc./Corbis.*

who use the drug know very little about the way it works, how it interacts with other drugs, and how easy it is to overdose. Side effects, Fatemi stated, range "from stomach pain to insomnia to an irregular heartbeat, and it can even cause brain damage." More and more media reports describe how Adderall is being used for academic success in increasingly competitive school environments. Many members of the educational community predict that the issue will need to be addressed head on in the coming years.

Effects on the Body

Technically, Adderall is a PSYCHOSTIMULANT. As Dr. Robert Hart explained in an article for *Drug Topics* by pharmacist Katie Rodgers, "Psychostimulants, in a sense, put your foot on the brake and help with the stopping." This is what makes them so effective in the

psychostimulant: pronounced SY–koh STIM–yew–lent; a stimulant that acts on the brain

treatment of ADHD. Patients who take Adderall are better able to ignore distractions and focus solely on the task at hand, whatever that task may be.

The most frequently observed side effect of Adderall is difficulty sleeping. Adderall can also cause nervousness, dizziness, restlessness, rapid heart rate, headache, stomachache, nausea, decreased appetite, weight loss, dry mouth, and skin rashes. A study cited in the *Journal of the American Academy of Child and Adolescent Psychiatry* (2001) showed that younger patients are more likely to experience a loss of appetite when taking Adderall than older ones. In addition, as noted in *Psychopharmacology Update* in 2005, Adderall and other psycho-stimulants used in the treatment of ADHD may cause users to develop jitters, motor tics (repeated blinking or tapping of feet or fingers, for example), and/or vocal tics (such as frequent throat clearing).

A two-year study showed reductions in both the average height and the average weight of preteens taking Adderall for their ADHD, according to Sherry Boschert in *Pediatric News.* Results of the study indicate that higher dosages of Adderall affected the growth rate more than lower doses did. Overall, however, the children's growth was slowed by about one-half inch per year. Adderall tends to decrease the appetite, so some scientists believe that the children who take it are not eating as well as they should. This could play a role in their slower gains in height and weight. "No one knows whether these children might catch up in growth during adolescence or if stopping the medication would lead to catch-up growth," noted Boschert. "And no one knows if the growth lag could be modified by good nutrition."

Dangers

"Taking Adderall for ADHD when you do not have ADHD can have serious consequences," noted Jillian Foley in *America's Intelligence Wire.* The human body needs sleep in order to function properly. Sleep deprivation is just one of the many dangers associated with amphetamine use. Frequent use can result in a PSYCHOLOGICAL ADDICTION, which can develop quickly, especially in people who already show signs of depression. Overdose of amphetamines can result in fever, convulsions, HALLUCINATIONS, and even death.

A *Psychopharmacology Update* article published in January 2005 warned that Adderall can increase the severity of "behavior disturbances and thought disorder in psychotic patients." Psychotic patients suffer from one or more forms of PSYCHOSIS, which disrupts

psychological addiction: the belief that a person needs to take a certain substance in order to function

hallucinations: visions or other perceptions of things that are not really present

psychosis: pronounced sy–KOH–sis; a severe mental disorder that often causes hallucinations and makes it difficult for people to distinguish what is real from what is imagined

Is It Cheating?

By the early 2000s, Adderall abuse among high school and college students had become a significant problem. "Overall, prescriptions for stimulants have risen to 2.6 million a month in 2004, from 1.6 million in 2000," according to a *Wall Street Journal* article. About 850,000 of those prescriptions are for Adderall. Students without ADHD reportedly find it fairly easy to get the drug from fellow students who have a prescription for it.

High school students of the early twenty-first century seemed to face increasing pressure to perform well on standardized tests. Many students feel like their "entire future may be riding on the results," explained Frances Mejia in an article for *CNNfyi.com*. The results of these tests weigh heavily in the college admissions process. Higher scores on standardized tests like the SAT and the ACT improve students' chances of being able to attend the schools of their choice. "[P]art of a [high school guidance] counselor's role these days is not only to prepare a student for the test academically, but also emotionally."

Some high school students admit taking Adderall in the hopes of improving their performance. They reported a jump of up to 200 points in their overall SAT scores. One twelfth grader interviewed in the *Wall Street Journal* claimed that Adderall helped her get her highest-ever SAT score in March of 2004. "It's a crazy kind of feeling, looking at a problem and saying I can do this in five seconds," she recalled.

Reports like this raise questions about drug use, academic fairness, and the law. Are students who deliberately use drugs like Adderall to improve their school performance guilty of cheating? Can they get into legal trouble for their actions? What about the students who do not take any performance-enhancing drugs? Will the Adderall-taking students gain an academic edge over their drug-free peers? High schools usually suspend students caught using other drugs on school grounds. However, a guidance counselor from Bethesda, Maryland's Chevy Chase High School sees a different trend with Adderall use to boost standardized test scores. He told the *Wall Street Journal* that as of 2004, the school had "never suspended or otherwise punished a student for using a prescription drug to help on an SAT."

the way the mind functions. As a result, people suffering from a psychotic episode can become completely withdrawn from reality.

Reactions with Other Drugs or Substances

Children taking a doctor-prescribed dosage of Adderall or Adderall XR for ADHD should be given their dose early in the day and should avoid high-fat breakfasts. In the early 2000s, medical researchers were investigating the possibility that high-fat foods might delay how quickly the drug is absorbed throughout the body. It has also been noted in several medical journals, including

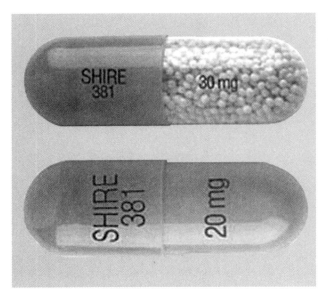

Adderall 20 mg and 30 mg capsules. *Copyright © 2005 Thomson Micromedex. All rights reserved. Information is for End User's use only and may not be sold, redistributed or otherwise used for commercial purposes.*

Psychopharmacology Update, that some fruit juices may interfere with the release of Adderall into the system.

Adderall should not be used by people with depression or suicidal tendencies or by people taking medicine to control their high blood pressure. In late 2004 the FDA called for changes in how boxes of Adderall XR were labeled. New labels warn that "misuse of amphetamine may cause sudden death and serious cardiovascular adverse events." This means that people who take Adderall XR without a doctor's prescription run the risk of suffering serious heart damage and could even die.

Treatment for Habitual Users

In the question-and-answer section of a fact sheet titled "Evidence–based Medication Management for Children and Adolescents with ADHD," researchers reported significant findings. The authors note: "Multiple studies that have followed children with ADHD for 10 years or more support the conclusion that the clinical use of stimulant medications does not increase the risk of later substance abuse." In fact, when children with ADHD receive the appropriate drug treatment, their risk of later drug or alcohol problems is the same as that of any other non-ADHD individual. The researchers further stated that "although there is potential for abuse when misused, psychostimulant medications do not cause addictions to develop in those being treated appropriately."

Regular users who stop taking Adderall should be taken off the drug slowly and are advised to do so under the care of a physician. Long periods of sleep, increased irritability, and severe depression can result if users discontinue Adderall suddenly rather than gradually.

Consequences

Abuse of Adderall can lead to TOLERANCE and psychological dependence. This means that, over time, the frequent user will begin to feel that he or she needs more and more of the drug to function effectively. "For now," wrote Sheena Smith in *America's*

tolerance: a condition in which higher and higher doses of a drug are needed to produce the original effect or high experienced

Intelligence Wire in late December of 2004, "there is little regulation concerning the illegal use of Adderall."

The Law

Adderall is a controlled substance. Its use is regulated by certain federal laws. The Controlled Substances Act (CSA) of 1970 called for the assignment of all controlled drug substances into one of five categories called schedules. These schedules are based on a substance's medicinal value, harmfulness, and potential for abuse and addiction. Schedule I is reserved for the most dangerous drugs that have no recognized medical use.

Amphetamines like Adderall fall under Schedule II, dangerous drugs with genuine medical uses that also have a high potential for abuse and addiction.

Possessing amphetamines without a medical doctor's prescription is against the law and can result in imprisonment and stiff fines. People convicted of distributing amphetamines—selling or giving away prescribed drugs—face lengthy prison terms and fines of up to $2 million.

For More Information

Books

Bayer, Linda. *Amphetamines and Other Uppers.* Broomall, PA: Chelsea House Publishers, 2000.

Hyde, Margaret O., and John F. Setaro. *Drugs 101: An Overview for Teens.* Brookfield, CT: Twenty-first Century Books, 2003.

Kuhn, Cynthia, Scott Swartzwelder, Wilkie Wilson, and others. *Buzzed: The Straight Facts about the Most Used and Abused Drugs from Alcohol to Ecstasy,* 2nd ed. New York: W.W. Norton, 2003.

Pellowski, Michael J. *Amphetamine Drug Dangers.* Berkeley Heights, NJ: Enslow Publishers, Inc., 2001.

Schull, Patricia Dwyer. *Nursing Spectrum Drug Handbook.* King of Prussia, PA: Nursing Spectrum, 2005.

Westcott, Patsy. *Why Do People Take Drugs?* New York: Raintree Steck-Vaughn Publishers, 2001.

Periodicals

"Adderall." *Psychopharmacology Update* (January, 2005).

"Adderall XR Effective in Adolescents with ADHD, Study Results Show." *Drug Week* (November 19, 2004): p. 68.

Boschert, Sherry. "Growth Delay Seen with Long-Term Adderall Use." *Pediatric News* (February, 2002): p. 29.

"Breakfast Choice May Affect Reliability of ADHD Medication." *Health & Medicine Week* (August 5, 2002): p. 13.

Castro, Jessi. "I Am a Different Person." *Time* (November 3, 2003): p. 58.

Elliott, William T., and James Chan. "Adderall XR—A New Long-Acting Drug for ADHD." *Internal Medicine Alert* (July 29, 2002): p. 110.

Fatemi, Omid. "Adderall: A Prescription Drug for a Reason." *America's Intelligence Wire* (October 29, 2004).

"FDA Approves Adderall XR to Treat ADHD in Adults." *Pharma Business Week* (September 6, 2004): p. 15.

Findling, Robert L., and others. "Developmental Aspects of Psychostimulant Treatment in Children and Adolescents with Attention-Deficit/Hyperactivity Disorder." *Journal of the American Academy of Child and Adolescent Psychiatry* (December, 2001): p. 1441.

Foley, Jillian. "Academic Aspirations Lead to Adderall Abuse." *America's Intelligence Wire* (December 16, 2004).

"Medicating Young Minds." *Time* (November 3, 2003): pp. 48–53, 55–56, 58.

"Preliminary Data Suggest Adderall XR ... Improved Simulated Driving Performance in Young Adults with ADHD." *Asia Africa Intelligence Wire* (November 19, 2004).

Rodgers, Katie. "ADHD Med Reformulated: An Old Drug Reenters the Market." *Drug Topics* (March 18, 1996): p. 31.

Smith, Sheena. "Adderall Craze Hits Campuses." *America's Intelligence Wire* (December 30, 2004).

"Warnings Added to Labeling for Adderall XR." *Brown University Child and Adolescent Psychopharmacology Update* (November, 2004): p. 5.

Zamiska, Nicholas. "Pressed to Do Well on Admissions Tests, Students Take Drugs; Stimulants Prescribed for Attention Disorders Find New Unapproved Use." *Wall Street Journal* (November 8, 2004): p. A1.

Web Sites

"18 and Older Population Estimates." *U.S. Census Bureau, Population Division, Information and Research Services.* http://www.census.gov/popest/estimates.php (accessed June 16, 2005).

"Adderall." *Hardin Library for the Health Sciences.* http://www.lib.uiowa.edu/hardin/md/adderall.html (accessed June 16, 2005).

"Attention-Deficit/Hyperactivity Disorder." *National Institute of Mental Health.* http://www.nimh.nih.gov/publicat/adhd.cfm (accessed June 16, 2005).

"Evidence-based Medication Management for Children and Adolescents with ADHD." *Children and Adults with Attention-Deficit/*

Hyperactivity Disorder (CHADD). http://www.chadd.org/fs/fs3.htm (accessed June 16, 2005).

"Fact Sheet on ADHD/ADD." *Attention Deficit Disorder Association (ADDA).* http://www.add.org/articles/factsheet.html (accessed June 16, 2005).

Hallowell, Edward M. "What's It Like to Have ADD?" *Attention Deficit Disorder Association (ADDA).* http://www.add.org/articles/whats_it_like.html (accessed June 16, 2005).

Mejia, Frances. "Under Pressure: Students Fret Over Powerful SAT College Entrance Exam." *CNNfyi.com: Student Bureau,* March 28, 2000. http://cnnstudentnews.cnn.com/2000/fyi/sb/03/22/sat.prep/ (accessed June 16, 2005).

"New Research in Animals Reveals Possible Long-Term Effects of Stimulants on Brain and Behavior" (press release). *National Institutes of Health (NIH) News.* http://www.nih.gov/news/pr/dec2003/nida-08.htm (accessed June 16, 2005).

See also: Amphetamines; Dextroamphetamine; Ritalin and Other Methylphenidates

Alcohol

Official Drug Name: Ethyl alcohol, ethanol, grain alcohol
Also Known As: Booze, hooch, moonshine, sauce, spirits (for alcohol in general); brew, suds (for beer); vino (for wine)
Drug Classifications: Not classified, depressant

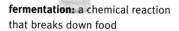

fermentation: a chemical reaction that breaks down food

inhibitions: inner thoughts that keep people from engaging in certain activities

sedative: a drug used to treat anxiety and calm people down

What Kind of Drug Is It?

Alcohol is an ancient drug. Beer and wine jugs well over 5,000 years old have been excavated from archaeological sites in southwest Asia and northern Africa. Prehistoric peoples are thought to have produced the first alcoholic beverages by accident. This occurred when mixtures of water, a bit of fungus, and wild berries left alone in the sun turned into alcohol through a process known as FERMENTATION.

Alcohol acts as a depressant. A depressant is a substance that slows down the activity of an organism or one of its parts. At the same time, drinking alcohol also lowers one's INHIBITIONS. When this happens, someone might act more recklessly than he or she would normally.

Overview

Through the ages, alcohol has been used as an all-purpose drug: a painkiller, an antiseptic, a disinfectant, a teething aid for babies, a SEDATIVE, a battlefield medicine, and a drowner of sorrows. It is also associated with celebrations: offering a toast to a newly married couple is a common tradition.

During the Middle Ages (c. 500–c. 1500), alcohol became something of a status symbol among Europe's upper classes. Wine production became very important to the economies of Italy and France throughout the Renaissance period, which spanned the fourteenth through the early seventeenth centuries. Meanwhile, in the New World, the first distillery opened in 1640 in what would later become the state of New York. In the 1700s, home brewing processes were replaced largely by the commercial manufacture of beer and wine in Europe.

Laws banning the sale of alcoholic beverages date back to the fourteenth century, when Germany banned the sale of alcohol on Sundays and other religious holidays. Even earlier, Switzerland instituted laws requiring drinking establishments to close at certain times to combat public drunkenness. The United States has seen historical increases and decreases in alcohol use as well. High periods of alcohol consumption coincided with periods of war: during the American Civil War (1861–1865), World War I (1914–1918), and

During the Prohibition era in the United States, people found various ways to conceal and transport alcohol. The image on the left shows how a woman of the era might dress to go out in public. The image on the right shows that she is actually hiding two tins of alcohol strapped to her legs under her overcoat. © *Underwood & Underwood/Corbis.*

World War II (1939–1945), drinking increased among Americans. These peaks in alcohol usage were interrupted by so-called "dry" periods in U.S. history—times when the consumption of alcohol dropped to very low levels throughout the nation.

The Era of Prohibition in the United States

The longest span of dry years in the United States occurred during PROHIBITION, which lasted from 1920 to 1933. At that time,

Prohibition: a ban on the manufacture and sale of alcoholic beverages

Nearly 80 percent of high school students have consumed alcohol illegally. The legal drinking age is twenty-one throughout the United States. *Photo by Lezlie Light.*

many Americans viewed alcohol as a destructive force in society. Crime, poverty, gambling, prostitution, and declining family values were blamed on alcohol consumption. A ban on the manufacture and sale of all alcoholic beverages in the United States began on January 16, 1920, with the passage of the Eighteenth Amendment to the Constitution. However, Prohibition did not stop all drinking in the United States. Some people produced alcohol in illegal stills, especial in rural areas. The brew created in these stills was often referred to as Moonshine. The liquor was then sold on the BLACK MARKET. Other people brewed alcoholic beverages at home, hoping to not get caught.

During Prohibition, some people even went to other countries, such as Canada, to buy alcohol and smuggle it back into the United States. Smugglers used all sorts of methods to hide the illegal drink. They hid it under false floors in trucks, under their clothing, and even in vials placed within walking sticks or canes. Prohibition proved to be highly unpopular. Thirteen years after it

black market: the illegal sale or trade of goods; drug dealers are said to carry out their business on the "black market"

had begun, Prohibition ended and alcohol was once again deemed a legal substance in the United States.

Alcohol consumption rose considerably in the early and middle 1980s, when many states lowered the drinking age to eighteen. Because of the increase in the number of teen deaths tied to drinking and driving, the legal drinking age was raised to twenty-one throughout the nation in 1987. The rate of alcohol consumption dipped in the 1990s, but alcohol remains the most commonly used legal drug. Consumption of alcohol by young people is very high.

Much could be written on the topic of alcohol as an addictive substance. The following entry attempts to provide as much relevant information as possible for the scope and intended audience of this encyclopedia.

> ## No Nutritional Value
>
> Alcohol contains what are called "empty calories." Beer, wine, wine coolers, and liquor have no nutritional value, but they still cause weight gain. Drinking alcohol is bad for the skin as well as the waistline. It increases the number and severity of acne breakouts. It is also known for causing bad breath among users.

What Is It Made Of?

The chemical composition for ETHANOL or ethyl alcohol, otherwise known as alcohol, is C_2H_5OH. That means it is composed of two atoms of carbon, one atom of oxygen, and six atoms of hydrogen. Ethanol is a colorless liquid that is highly flammable. Aside from being an ingredient in alcoholic beverages, it is used in fuels, solvents, disinfectants, and preservatives.

Pure alcohol is too strong to drink by itself. It must be diluted with water and other substances to create alcoholic beverages. Ethyl alcohol is the only alcohol considered safe to drink. Other alcohols such as methanol (also called wood alcohol) and isopropyl alcohol (pronounced EYE-so-PROPE-uhl; also called rubbing alcohol) are not used in beverages. They are highly toxic (poisonous) to the body. Methanol, in particular, can cause blindness and even death if swallowed.

Types of Alcoholic Beverages

Wines and beers are produced by fermenting fruits, vegetables, and grains. Fermentation occurs when sugar in berries or grains is combined with yeast, which is a fungus. A fungus is a sort of recycler that dissolves nutrients and changes them. A chemical reaction takes place as yeast cells eat up the sugars in food. Those sugars are changed into carbon dioxide and alcohol. Wine is formed when

ethanol: the colorless flammable liquid in alcoholic drinks; ethanol is the substance that gets people drunk

Hard Liquors

The difference between hard liquors lies in the grains or vegetables that are used to make them. Rye, corn, and barley are used to make whiskey. Vodka is distilled from potatoes, rye, or wheat. Scotch is derived from malted barley. Gin is a combination of distilled spirits (alcohol) flavored with juniper berries. Rum is made from molasses.

Adding carbonated drinks to hard liquor—mixing rum with cola or whiskey with ginger ale, for instance—produces a drink that seems stronger than liquor mixed with plain water. Carbonation speeds up the absorption of alcohol into the bloodstream.

the combination of sugar, yeast, and berries reaches an alcohol concentration point between 9 and 15 percent. Similarly, when sugar, yeast, and grains such as barley are combined and reach an alcohol concentration of 3 to 6 percent, beer is made and fermentation stops.

Hard liquor is produced by a process called DISTILLATION, which adds an extra step to the fermentation process. In distillation, liquids that have already been fermented are boiled to remove the alcohol. At the boiling point, the alcohol separates from the fermented liquid to create a vapor. The vapor is captured and then held separately in a cooling tube until it turns back into a liquid. The resulting alcohol, now removed from the original fermented liquid, becomes hard liquor when mixed with water.

Alcohol makes up 50 percent of distilled liquors such as whiskey, rum, vodka, scotch, and gin. The percentage of alcohol in hard liquor is used to determine the "PROOF" number printed on every bottle. Proof is determined by doubling the percentage of pure alcohol in a liquor and then dropping the percentage sign. For instance, whiskey that is 50 percent alcohol is said to be 100 proof.

Liqueurs (pronounced lick-OARZ) are distilled from grain and mixed with fruit, herbs, spices, and sugary syrups. They are extremely sweet and very high in alcohol content. They are intended to be drunk in very small quantities, usually as an "after dinner" drink. Popular liqueurs include Cointreau (pronounced KWANN-troh), Tia Maria, and Drambuie (pronounced dram-BOO-ee).

Sweet and powerful drinks like brandy and port are made from distilled wine, which increases the alcohol content of 12 percent to two to three times that amount. "The original idea of distillers," wrote Andrew Weil and Winifred Rosen in *From Chocolate to Morphine,* "was to concentrate wine to a smaller volume to make it easier to ship it in barrels overseas. At the end of the voyage the brandy was to be diluted with water back to an alcohol content of 12 percent. What happened . . . was that when people got their hands on what was in the barrels, no one waited to add water. Suddenly a new and powerful form of alcohol flooded the world."

distillation: the separation of liquids by a process of evaporation

proof: the measure of the strength of an alcoholic beverage

How Is It Taken?

Alcohol is swallowed, usually in a liquid form. It is also swallowed in gel form in semi-solid "Jell-O shots." These Jell-O shots are medicine-cup-sized mixtures of gelatin and hard liquor, such as vodka, which are chilled before serving. The high sugar content in the gelatin hides the taste of the alcohol, making Jell-O shots particularly dangerous. Fruit punch spiked with hard liquor can have the same powerful effect. Users could accidentally consume far more alcohol than they intended in a short period of time.

According to Ron Weathermon and David W. Crabb in *Alcohol Research & Health,* a standard drink is defined as one 12-ounce can of beer or bottle of wine cooler, one 5-ounce glass of wine, or 1.5 ounces of distilled liquor. Each of these drinks contains the equivalent of 1 ounce of pure alcohol.

Are There Any Medical Reasons for Taking This Substance?

"Alcohol actually blocks some of the messages trying to get to the brain," according to the *TeensHealth* Web site. That is the primary reason it has been used for thousands of years to suppress pain, treat injuries and infections, and prepare people for surgery. In the past, alcohol has been used as an ANESTHETIC, a sedative, and even a treatment for a lung disease called typhus.

Research in the 1990s showed that moderate amounts of alcohol could help reduce the risk of heart attacks. Abuse of alcohol, however, has been connected to heart disease. "Between the extremes of heavy and light drinking lies a 'gray area' that is not completely understood," explained Cynthia Kuhn and her coauthors in their book *Buzzed: The Straight Facts about the Most Used and Abused Drugs from Alcohol to Ecstasy.* "Moreover, this gray area appears to be rather small. That is, while an average of one-half to one drink per day may be healthy for your heart, it is perfectly clear that an average of two drinks per day significantly increases your risk of dying from heart disease or cancer." As of 2005, there were no known therapeutic uses for alcohol.

The facts about youth & alcohol

Alcohol use is widespread among today's teenagers
- Nearly 70% of 8th graders perceive alcoholic beverages as "fairly easy" or "very easy" to get.
- By the time they complete high school nearly 80% of teenagers have consumed alcohol, 30% report having been drunk in the past month, and 29% report having 5 or more drinks in a row in the past two weeks.

Alcohol use increases substantially from middle to high school
- Approximately 20% of 8th graders report having recently (within the past 30 days) consumed alcohol compared to 35% of 10th graders and almost 50% of 12th graders.
- A little over 20% of 8th graders report having been drunk at least once in their life compared to almost 45% of 10th graders and 60% of 12th graders.

The consequences of underage drinking
- A person who begins drinking as a young teen is four times more likely to develop alcohol dependence than someone who waits until adulthood to use alcohol.
- During adolescence significant changes occur in the body, including the formation of new networks in the brain. Alcohol use during this time may affect brain development.
- Motor vehicle crashes are the leading cause of death among youth ages 15 to 20, and the rate of fatal crashes among alcohol-involved drivers between 16 and 20 years old is more than twice the rate for alcohol-involved drivers 21 and older. Alcohol use also is linked with youthful deaths by drowning, suicide, and homicide.
- Alcohol use is associated with many adolescent risk behaviors, including other drug use and delinquency, weapon carrying and fighting, and perpetrating or being the victim of date rape.

SOURCE: "The Facts About Youth & Alcohol," National Institute on Alcohol Abuse and Alcoholism, National Institutes of Health, U.S. Department of Health and Human Services, Bethesda, MD [Online] http://www.niaaa.nih.gov/publications/PSA/factsheet.pdf#search='the%20facts%20about%20youth%20&%20alcohol' [accessed May 24, 2005]

anesthetic: a substance used to deaden pain

Usage Trends

"Next to tobacco and caffeine, alcohol is the world's most popular drug," wrote Paul M. Gahlinger in *Illegal Drugs: A Complete Guide to Their History, Chemistry, Use, and Abuse.* Peer pressure, depression, and a need to fit in are all factors leading to alcohol use by teens.

Alcoholism Defined

There is a difference between alcohol abuse and ALCOHOLISM. In 1956, the American Medical Association defined alcoholism as a disease. Alcoholism is described as a loss of control over drinking—a preoccupation with drinking despite negative consequences to one's physical, mental, and emotional makeup as well as one's work and family life. Problem drinkers might start out by abusing alcohol occasionally without being addicted to it. However, Kuhn pointed out that "continued exposure to alcohol changes the brain in ways that produce dependence." Therefore, anyone who drinks heavily over a long period of time "will become physically dependent on the drug."

According to the National Council on Alcoholism and Drug Dependence (NCADD), about 18 million Americans have alcohol problems. Excessive drinkers are generally defined as: 1) men who consume more than two drinks per day, every day, or more than three drinks at a time; and 2) women who consume more than one drink per day, every day, or more than three drinks at a time. Women used to make up one-third of the problem drinking population, but they are quickly catching up to men in terms of abuse. In general, if a woman and a man consume the same amount of alcohol, the woman will become more intoxicated in a shorter period of time. And because of their physical makeup, women are more likely than men to damage their hearts, livers, and brains due to drinking. An increased risk of breast cancer has also been linked to drinking.

Problem drinkers can be rich or poor, young or old, male or female. They come from all racial and ethnic backgrounds. Although anyone can become an alcoholic, a child with an alcoholic parent runs a greater risk of developing the disease of alcoholism than a child of non-alcoholic parents.

Young People and Alcohol

alcoholism: a disease that results in habitual, uncontrolled alcohol abuse; alcoholism can shorten a person's life by damaging the brain, liver, and heart

New York Times contributor Howard Markel wrote, "Because the brains of teenagers are still developing, many experts believe they are at greater risk for becoming addicted." According to the National Institutes of Health (NIH), young people who begin drinking before the age of thirteen are four times more likely to develop an addiction to alcohol than people who begin drinking at age twenty-one.

Before she can enter the prom, a student is given a breathalyzer test by the school's principal in Grant, Nebraska. All students, faculty, and chaperones had to pass the test before they were allowed into the dance. *AP/Wide World Photos.*

The results of the 2004 Monitoring the Future (MTF) study were released to the public on December 21, 2004. Conducted by the University of Michigan (U of M), the MTF was sponsored by research grants from the National Institute on Drug Abuse (NIDA). Since 1991, U of M has tracked patterns of alcohol and drug use, as well as attitudes toward alcohol and drugs, among students in the eighth, tenth, and twelfth grades. (Prior to that, from 1975 to 1990, the MTF survey was limited to twelfth graders.)

The 2004 MTF survey results indicate that alcohol use among students in the eighth and tenth grades has fallen each year since 2001. Researchers noted, however, that "drinking and drunkenness did not continue to decline" among twelfth graders in 2004. According to MTF charts for 2003 to 2004, about three in every ten high school seniors reported "being drunk in the past 30 days." The ease with which seniors said they would be able to get the drug held

Alcohol and the Entertainment Industry

Nels Ericson, a writer for the U.S. Office of Juvenile Justice and Delinquency Prevention, pointed out that alcohol is a standard prop in more than 90 percent of America's most popular movie rentals. Television is another media source that bombards youth with pro-drinking messages. The National Council on Alcoholism and Drug Dependence (NCADD) reported that "the typical American young person will see 100,000 beer commercials before he or she turns 18."

The New York Times reported in 2002 that a link may exist between movie-viewing habits and alcohol usage among teens. A Dartmouth College survey based on information from more than 4,500 fifth through eighth graders in the eastern United States revealed that "teenagers whose parents place no restrictions on their viewing R-rated movies appear much more likely to use tobacco or alcohol." Most of the students interviewed were fourteen years old or younger. By law, moviegoers are supposed to be seventeen or older to view an R-rated film at a theater. Nearly half of the students who saw R-rated films on a regular basis admitted they had tried alcohol, versus only 4 percent of the students who were not allowed to view R-rated films.

steady, with more than 94 percent of the twelfth graders surveyed saying it would be "fairly easy" or "very easy" to obtain alcohol. Only 26 percent of twelfth graders disapproved of kids their age "trying one or two drinks of an alcoholic beverage." Beer and fruit-flavored alcoholic beverages, such as wine coolers, seemed to be a favorite among middle school and high school drinkers.

The 2004 Monitoring the Future survey also showed that:

- 44 percent of eighth-grade students, 64 percent of tenth-grade students, and 77 percent of twelfth-grade students admit to having tried alcohol.
- 20 percent of eighth-grade students, 42 percent of tenth-grade students, and 60 percent of twelfth-grade students report having been drunk from alcohol use at least once.

Binge Drinking

In the late 1990s, "BINGE DRINKING" became an accepted term for a night of heavy drinking or simply for heavy alcohol consumption at one sitting. The NCADD claimed that in 1999 "44 percent of college students reported binge drinking (five or more drinks in a row for males or four or more drinks in a row for females)" at some point in their college years. This does not make them *frequent* binge drinkers; it means that they have engaged in binge drinking at least once. As of 2002, about one in four students could be classified as a *frequent* binge drinker. To make matters worse, "59 percent of frequent binge drinkers report driving after drinking," noted Dr. Henry Wechsler, director of the Harvard School of Public Health's College Alcohol Study, in his book *Dying to Drink: Confronting Binge Drinking on College Campuses,* written with Bernice Wuethrich.

Research conducted by the National Institute on Alcohol Abuse and Alcoholism (NIAAA) indicates that some 1,400 college students die each school year in alcohol-related incidents. Another 100,000 became victims of sexual assault after drinking too much.

binge drinking: consuming a lot of alcohol at one time

Paying the Price

In addition to the high one gets when drinking alcohol, the substance produces a variety of other potentially embarrassing, not to mention uncomfortable, effects. Read on to learn more.

- The human body has all sorts of natural protective mechanisms. Vomiting is one of them. Nausea and stomach cramps are two ways that the brain alerts the body to the presence of poisons—like alcohol—in the system. The stomach rids itself of the poison by vomiting. People who have too much alcohol in their systems often end up clutching a toilet bowl and heaving up every bit of food and drink in their stomachs. And those are the lucky ones. Vomiting in a toilet is preferable to vomiting somewhere else, and sometimes people under the influence of alcohol just cannot reach a toilet in time. Accidental urination can occur under the influence of alcohol as well, compounding the embarrassment.

- Alcohol makes the blood vessels inside the brain expand. Drinking to the point of intoxication (drunkenness) often results in an uncomfortable set of physical effects known as a "hangover." Contrary to popular belief, drinking coffee, eating high-sugar foods, or taking a cold shower will not relieve hangover symptoms. The pounding headache, upset stomach, and trembling feelings that often follow a night of heavy drinking will not subside until the brain's blood vessels return to their normal size. In short, nothing but time will get rid of a hangover.

Effects on the Body

Even though alcohol is considered "one of the most widely accepted recreational drugs," noted Gahlinger, its overall impact on public health "is far worse than all illegal drugs combined." Prolonged use of alcohol can have serious negative effects on the body. Long-term alcohol use can result in memory loss. Alcohol can suppress the immune system, making people more susceptible to infections. Heavy drinking can increase the user's risk of nutritional deficiencies, ULCERS, high blood pressure, heart disease, STROKE, certain cancers, and liver disease.

The NIAAA reported that "alcohol-induced liver disease is a major cause of illness and death in the United States." The liver is the organ that breaks down alcohol in the body. It removes alcohol from the blood, leaving water, carbon dioxide gas, and energy as by-products. The carbon dioxide gas leaves the body through the lungs, and the water is eliminated in urine. Depending on the size, gender, and general health of the drinker, it can take the liver between one and two hours to process a glass of wine, a single beer, a shot of hard liquor, or one mixed drink.

ulcers: the breakdown of mucus membranes, usually in the stomach

stroke: a loss of feeling, consciousness, or movement caused by the breaking or blocking of a blood vessel in the brain

A young alcoholic man is shown lying against a building on a busy street in California. He cries as he begs for money to feed his addiction. His drinking habit has caused cirrhosis of the liver. *AP/Wide World Photos.*

If large quantities of alcohol are present in the body, the liver has to work overtime to break it down and eliminate it from the body. Until the liver has a chance to filter all of the toxins, or highly poisonous substances, out of a drinker's blood, the remaining alcohol will simply stay in the bloodstream and recirculate. "There are limits on the number and amounts of toxic substances a liver can handle without harm to it," explained Laurence Pringle in *Drinking: A Risky Business.* Heavy drinking can lead to CIRRHOSIS of the liver, a deadly disease common among alcoholics. "In cirrhosis," continued Pringle, "cells of the liver are actually being killed by alcohol. . . . Continued heavy drinking may cause the liver to fail entirely."

cirrhosis: pronounced sir-OH-sis; destruction of the liver, possibly leading to death

Down the Hatch, and Then What?

After alcohol is swallowed, it passes first into the stomach and then into the small intestine. Most of the alcohol is absorbed into the

If police suspect someone is driving drunk, they give the driver a sobriety test. Here, a youth is instructed to walk a straight line. If he cannot do so without stumbling, chances are that he is intoxicated. © *Richard Hutchings/Corbis.*

bloodstream through the small intestine and carried to the brain through the blood. Alcohol has profound effects on the brain's ability to function effectively. Even though alcohol is a depressant, low doses of it can cause the release of certain brain chemicals that produce a sense of euphoria. This "HIGH" is misleading because it makes alcohol seem like a stimulant.

First and foremost, alcohol causes a loss of inhibition in those who drink it. "Judgment is the first function of the brain to be affected," wrote Gail Gleason Milgram of the Rutgers University Center of Alcohol Studies in an online article. "The ability to think and make decisions becomes impaired." People with lowered inhibitions tend to take more chances and engage in riskier behavior than they would if they had not been drinking. A self-conscious individual who has had a drink or two may become more confident. A shy person may become more talkative. People who have had too much to drink often engage in unsafe sex and are at a much greater risk for contracting sexually transmitted diseases, including HIV (the human immunodeficiency virus), which can lead to AIDS (acquired immunodeficiency syndrome).

The most obvious physical effects of alcohol consumption are slowed reflexes, a lack of coordination, difficulty walking "a straight line," and slurred speech. As more alcohol is consumed, drinkers

high: drug-induced feelings ranging from excitement and joy to extreme grogginess

Blood alcohol concentration (BAC) levels and effects

Blood alcohol concentration	Changes in feelings and personality	Impaired activities (continuum)
0.01–0.05	Relaxation Sense of well being Loss of inhibition	Alertness Judgment
0.06–0.10	Pleasure Numbness of feelings Nausea, sleepiness Emotional arousal	Coordination (especially fine motor skills) Visual tracking
0.11–0.20	Mood swings Anger Sadness Mania	Reasoning and depth perception Inappropriate social behavior (e.g., obnoxiousness)
0.21–0.30	Aggression Reduced sensations Depression Stupor	Slurred speech Lack of balance Loss of temperature regulation
0.31–0.40	Unconsciousness Death possible Coma	Loss of bladder control Difficulty breathing
0.41 and greater	Death	Slowed heart rate

SOURCE: Adapted from "Table 4," in *Understanding Alcohol*, Biological Sciences Curriculum Study, for the National Institute on Alcohol Abuse and Alcoholism, National Institutes of Health, Bethesda, MD [Online] http://science.education.nih.gov/supplements/nih3/alcohol/guide/info-alcohol.htm [accessed May 24, 2005].

experience dizziness, nausea, dehydration, and an inability to reason. Having a large number of drinks in rapid succession puts many drinkers to sleep. Those who remain awake and continue drinking increase their likelihood of passing out, which can be very dangerous. Intoxicated people who throw up while unconscious risk choking on their vomit. This can be—and often is—fatal, because vomit easily blocks the drinker's airway, making breathing impossible.

"Chronic, repeated drinking damages and sometimes kills the cells in specific brain areas," noted Kuhn. "And it turns out that it might not take a very long history of heavy drinking to kill cells in certain areas of the brain" involved in memory formation and problem solving.

Effects May Vary

The physical effects of alcohol on the body depend on several different factors. Both the amount of food present in the stomach when drinking and the amount of time that elapses between drinks influence a person's physical response to alcohol. "Peak blood alcohol concentration [BAC] could be as much as three times greater in someone with an empty stomach than in someone who has just eaten," wrote Kuhn. Five drinks consumed in one hour will have drastically different effects on the drinker than five drinks consumed with food over five hours.

The gender, size, and mental outlook of the drinker also affect the body's response to alcohol. "Alcohol does not dissolve in fat tissues," explained Weathermon and Crabb. Because women have a larger proportion of body fat than men, they tend to feel the effects of alcohol after drinking smaller doses than men do. A smaller person will become intoxicated sooner than a larger person because the larger person has more blood and body fluids mixing with the alcohol he or she consumes. A person's reaction to alcohol also varies according to the circumstances under which it is consumed. "The same amount of wine that makes someone pleasantly high at a party may make a depressed person in a lonely room even more depressed," commented Weil.

Drinking and Driving

"Alcohol abuse kills some 75,000 Americans each year and shortens the lives of these people by an average of thirty years," noted *MSNBC.com* in the fall of 2004. The statistics, which were provided by the Centers for Disease Control and Prevention (CDC), indicate that about 35,000 of these people died from diseases connected with heavy drinking. The other 40,000 were killed in alcohol-related car crashes and other accidents, including falls, fires, and drownings. Young people under twenty-one years of age accounted for about 4,500 of alcohol-related deaths.

The rate of fatal motor-vehicle crashes in alcohol-involved drivers age sixteen to twenty is more than twice the rate for alcohol-involved drivers over the age of twenty-one. The probable reason for this statistic, according to an NIAAA "Alcohol Alert" from 2003, is that younger drivers have less experience behind the wheel. Adding alcohol to the mix is a recipe for disaster. In addition, *Newsweek* reported in 2005 that, according to the NIH, "the area of the brain that inhibits risky behavior isn't fully developed" in humans until they reach the age of twenty-five.

Alcohol and Pregnancy

Alcohol and pregnancy do not mix. Alcohol use can interfere with a woman's ability to become pregnant. It can also lower a man's sperm count and reduce his sexual drive.

There is no safe level of alcohol consumption for a woman at any time during a pregnancy. Every bottle of alcohol bears a warning label that reads: "According to the Surgeon General, women should

A Vermont state trooper examines a wrecked car that held four teens who died in a crash after a night of drinking in Canada. Some American teens go to Canada to drink because the legal drinking age is lower there. *AP/Wide World Photos.*

fetal alcohol syndrome (FAS): a pattern of birth defects, learning deficits, and behavioral problems affecting the children of mothers who drank heavily while pregnant

fetal alcohol effects (FAE): the presence of some—but not all—of the symptoms of fetal alcohol syndrome (FAS)

not drink alcoholic beverages during pregnancy because of the risk of birth defects." If a pregnant woman drinks alcohol, so does her baby. If she becomes drunk, so does her baby.

Drinking alcohol during pregnancy can cause miscarriages, stillbirths, and serious birth defects. Alcohol "disrupts [the] formation of nerve cells in a baby's brain," wrote Margaret O. Hyde and John F. Setaro in *Drugs 101: An Overview for Teens.* FETAL ALCOHOL SYNDROME (FAS) can occur when a woman drinks while she is pregnant. It is one of the leading causes of birth defects in children and the most preventable cause of mental retardation. FAS babies have low birth weights, small heads, slowed mental and physical growth rates, and certain facial and skeletal abnormalities. It is a hard condition to diagnose because its symptoms can mimic those of other disorders. Babies born with FETAL ALCOHOL EFFECTS (FAE) are less severely impaired than FAS babies. FAE babies do not have distinctive facial and skeletal abnormalities, nor do they suffer the same level of brain damage as FAS babies, but they can have physical and behavioral problems such as poor coordination, learning disabilities, and attention deficit disorders.

Reactions with Other Drugs or Substances

Alcohol should not be consumed with any over-the-counter or prescription medications because harmful interactions can occur. Sometimes, the effect of a medicine is increased by alcohol. In other cases, a medication may not be able to break down properly in the presence of alcohol. Drinking alcohol with antihistamines, for instance, will increase the drowsiness that can occur with cold-type medicines. Alcohol can cause liver damage when taken in combination with acetaminophen (best known by the brand name Tylenol).

Alcohol has additional negative effects when taken with other drugs. For example, when taken with aspirin, alcohol can irritate the stomach lining and cause gastrointestinal bleeding. Alcohol combined with antidepressants affects the user's coordination and reaction time, making the operation of motor vehicles and other machinery extremely risky. Alcohol taken with BARBITURATES ("downers" such as Nembutal, Seconal, Amytal, and Tuinal) can increase depression.

Mixing alcohol with TRANQUILIZERS, muscle relaxants, sleeping aids, and other medicines can cause serious side effects, especially in elderly people. Alcohol consumed with illegal drugs such as marijuana, cocaine, heroin, or amphetamines can be deadly.

Treatment for Habitual Users

There is no cure for alcoholism, but the advancement of the disease can be stopped if the user quits drinking. The Hazelden Foundation's "Alcohol Screening" Web page states that "for one in thirteen American adults, alcohol abuse or alcohol dependence (alcoholism) causes substantial harm to their health and disruption in their lives." In "Substance Abuse: The Nation's Number One Health Problem," Nels Ericson noted that "only a quarter of individuals who

---

Alcohol-Related Vehicle Crashes

According to the U.S. Department of Transportation's National Highway Traffic Safety Administration (www.nhtsa.dot.gov):

- 17,013 people in the United States died in alcohol-related motor-vehicle crashes in 2003
- Alcohol-related crashes on America's roads injure someone every two minutes
- Alcohol-related crashes in the United States cost roughly 51 billion dollars each year.

---

barbiturates: pronounced bar-BIH-chuh-rits; drugs that act as depressants and are used as sedatives or sleeping pills; also referred to as "downers"

tranquilizers: drugs such as Valium and Librium that treat anxiety; also called benzodiazepines (pronounced ben-zoh-die-AZ-uh-peens)

abuse alcohol and illicit drugs get treatment. . . . Treatment for alcoholism is successful for 40 to 70 percent of patients."

There are several types of treatment options available for alcoholics. Most incorporate at least some of the principles that make up the twelve-step program used by Alcoholics Anonymous (AA). AA offers a popular and effective approach to rehabilitation. It helps the user gain an understanding of alcoholism as a disease. The first AA group was formed in Akron, Ohio, in 1935, by Bill Wilson and Dr. Bob Smith. According to the *AA* Web site, there were more than 100,000 groups and over 2 million members in 150 countries as of 2005.

Inpatient programs, which are often found in hospital settings, usually begin with a period of DETOXIFICATION, followed by extensive counseling and, if necessary, a drug program to discourage the drinker from relapsing. (Certain medications are designed to make an alcoholic feel very sick when combined with alcohol.) Detoxification, or detox, addresses the physical aspect of "drying out" the drinker. Withdrawal symptoms can be intense and frightening to the recovering alcoholic. At their worst, symptoms can include HALLUCINATIONS, tremors (uncontrollable shaking), and seizures.

Detox is usually followed up with individual and/or family counseling and involvement in a twelve-step program such as the one offered by AA. Psychiatric hospitals address both the problem of alcohol abuse and the emotional issues that accompany it. Treatment includes individual, group, and/or family counseling, drugs to treat psychiatric illnesses, and the additional support of a twelve-step program.

Another type of inpatient program is the 28-day rehabilitation facility. This type of treatment program offers detoxification from alcohol as well as: 1) support from substance abuse counselors; 2) education on the disease concept of alcoholism; and 3) individual, group, and family therapy. In addition, it uses support group meetings both on and offsite. Residential programs are yet another alternative. In residential programs, patients stay at a home for recovering alcoholics. At these "sober houses," as they are called, several alcoholics work together to stay alcohol-free. They receive counseling, job assistance, and group support.

detoxification: often abbreviated as detox; a difficult process by which substance abusers stop taking those substances and rid their bodies of the toxins that accumulated during the time they consumed such substances

hallucinations: visions or other perceptions of things that are not really present

sober: not drunk

Consequences

People have been known to do things under the influence of alcohol that they would never consider doing when SOBER. Drinking too much can leave users with little or no recollection of what they did or said while drunk. NCADD statistics show that alcohol is

Groups like the Students Against Destructive Decisions (SADD) formed to warn teens and others about the dangers of driving drunk. Members of the group are seen here at the U.S. Capitol in Washington, D.C., promoting their cause. *AP/Wide World Photos.*

involved in one out of every four emergency room admissions, one out of every three suicides, and one out of every two homicides and incidents of domestic violence. "A report from the British Medical Association," stated Emma Haughton in *Drug Abuse?* (1997), estimated that up to 70 percent of all murders in the United Kingdom were somehow "associated with alcohol abuse."

People who drink heavily develop a tolerance to alcohol. As the disease of alcoholism progresses, an alcoholic will need to drink more and more to get the desired result that lower doses of alcohol had once produced. Tolerance actually changes the alcoholic's brain impulses and the chemical makeup of cell membranes.

Alcoholics typically go through several stages, changing their patterns of use to patterns of abuse. They may begin using alcohol as an occasional stress reliever. They promise themselves and others that their drinking is just a "temporary thing." But over several years it becomes a habit. Their families struggle to hide the drinkers' growing problems with alcohol. As the disease progresses, drinkers usually experience mood changes, problems with friends and family, and trouble on the job. In the final stage, alcoholics begin to suffer physical decline as a result of drinking and may develop illnesses like liver disease or heart failure.

The personal consequences of alcoholism reach far beyond the alcoholic. An alcoholic's drinking affects many people, especially the members of his or her family. Children of alcoholics sometimes continue the cycle of alcoholic behavior when they reach adulthood. Alateen is an international organization for teens who are relatives or friends of a problem drinker. Support groups like Alateen help young people break the cycle of addiction and lead healthy lives.

The Law

It is against the law to consume alcohol in the United States until the age of twenty-one, but, according to the *TeensHealth* Web site, nearly 80 percent of teens have done it. Underage drinking can lead to arrest. In the United Kingdom, it is illegal for anyone under the age of eighteen to buy alcohol, whether in a supermarket or a pub. It is also illegal to supply someone under the age of eighteen with alcohol.

For years, the legal blood alcohol concentration for adult drivers ranged from 0.08 percent to 0.1 percent throughout the United States. A stricter national standard of 0.08 was adopted by most states in the first few years of the twenty-first century. The BAC limit for drivers under twenty-one was set at 0.02 in every state. Penalties for driving while intoxicated vary from state to state and can include fines, jail sentences, probation, driver's license suspension, mandatory community service, or participation in an alcohol education program.

The National Center for Injury Prevention and Control (NCIPC), a division of the Centers for Disease Control and Prevention, released a summary of impaired-driving statistics in December of 2004. The latest information available for that report came from the records of the National Highway Traffic Safety Administration (NHTSA) for 2002 and 2003. According to the data, about 1.5 million people were arrested for driving under the influence (DUI) in 2002. More than 100 million other drunk drivers were on the roads but were not caught. Alcohol consumption was a factor in two out of every five traffic-related deaths in 2003. In addition, about 25 percent of all drivers under the age of twenty who were killed in motor vehicle crashes that year had a blood-alcohol level of 0.08 or higher.

Drunk on Mouthwash

Listerine mouthwash is 26.9 percent alcohol. In January of 2005, a Michigan woman was arrested for drunk driving after drinking three glasses of Listerine. Her blood alcohol concentration (BAC) was more than three times Michigan's legal limit of 0.08 percent.

Alcoholic beverage control laws (ABC laws) were developed in the United States to prevent the illegal sale of alcohol. ABC laws are enforced by federal, state, and local law enforcement agencies. Each state regulates where alcohol can be sold and where it can be consumed. Restaurants, convenience stores, grocery stores, and bars selling alcohol must have special licensing. A person must be twenty-one years old to purchase and consume alcohol. Buying alcohol for an underage drinker is illegal, even if the buyer is over twenty-one. Warning labels are required on all alcoholic beverages sold in the United States. These labels alert consumers to the possible dangers of alcohol use when pregnant, driving an automobile, or operating machinery.

For More Information

Books

Gahlinger, Paul M. *Illegal Drugs: A Complete Guide to Their History, Chemistry, Use, and Abuse.* Las Vegas, NV: Sagebrush Press, 2001.

Haughton, Emma. *Drug Abuse?* London: Franklin Watts, 1997.

Hyde, Margaret O., and John F. Setaro. *Drugs 101: An Overview for Teens.* Brookfield, CT: Twenty-first Century Books, 2003.

Kuhn, Cynthia, Scott Swartzwelder, Wilkie Wilson, and others. *Buzzed: The Straight Facts about the Most Used and Abused Drugs from Alcohol to Ecstasy,* 2nd ed. New York: W.W. Norton, 2003.

Milam, James R., and Katherine Ketcham. *Under the Influence.* New York: Bantam Books, 1984.

Nagle, Jeanne. *Polysubstance Abuse.* New York: Rosen Publishing Group, Inc., 2000.

Pringle, Laurence. *Drinking: A Risky Business.* New York: Morrow Junior Books, 1997.

Alcohol

Schull, Patricia Dwyer. *Nursing Spectrum Drug Handbook.* King of Prussia, PA: Nursing Spectrum, 2005.

Wechsler, Henry, and Bernice Wuethrich. *Dying to Drink: Confronting Binge Drinking on College Campuses.* New York: Rodale, 2002.

Weil, Andrew, and Winifred Rosen. *From Chocolate to Morphine.* New York: Houghton Mifflin, 1993, rev. 2004.

Periodicals

Black, Susan. "Dying for a Drink." *American School Board Journal* (August, 2003).

Brink, Susan. "Your Brain on Alcohol." *U.S. News & World Report* (May 7, 2001): pp. 50-57.

Croal, N'Gai. "Kids, Don't Talk and Drive." *Newsweek* (February 14, 2005): p. 12.

Ehrenfeld, Temma. "New Hope for Addicts? An Epilepsy Drug May Help Alcoholics Stop Drinking." *Newsweek* (June 13, 2005): p. 68.

Gegax, T. Trent. "An End to 'Power Hour': A Tragic Alcohol Fatality Spurs a Crackdown on the Time-Honored Custom of Bingeing Up North." *Newsweek* (June 6, 2005): p. 28.

Hingson, R., and others. "Magnitude of Alcohol-Related Mortality and Morbidity among U.S. College Students Ages 18-24." *Journal of Studies on Alcohol* (April 12, 2002): pp. 136-144.

Markel, Howard. "Tailoring Treatments for Teenage Drug Users." *New York Times* (January 7, 2003).

Nagourney, Eric. "Behavior: When 'R' Stands for Risky." *New York Times* (February 26, 2002).

Nagourney, Eric. "A Sobering Effect on Teenage Drivers." *New York Times* (May 8, 2001).

"Sex, Drugs, and Rock 'n' Roll." *Independent* (January 28, 1996): p. 8.

Weathermon, Ron, and David W. Crabb. "Alcohol and Medication Interactions." *Alcohol Research & Health,* vol. 23, no. 1 (1999): pp. 40-54.

Windell, James. "Teen Binge Drinking Is a Serious Health Problem." *Oakland Press* (December 16, 2004).

Web Sites

"A to Z of Drugs: Alcohol." *The BBC's Crime Web Site.* http://www.bbc.co.uk/crime/drugs/alcohol.shtml (accessed June 16, 2005).

Alateen. http://www.al-anon.alateen.org/alateen.html (accessed June 16, 2005).

"Alcohol." *TeensHealth.* http://kidshealth.org/ (accessed June 16, 2005).

"Alcohol Linked to 75,000 U.S. Deaths a Year." *MSNBC.com,* June 25, 2005. http://www.msnbc.msn.com/id/6089353/ (accessed June 30, 2005).

"Alcohol Screening." *Hazelden Foundation.* www.hazelden.org/ (accessed June 16, 2005).

"Alcoholism and Drug Dependence Are America's Number One Health Problem." *National Council on Alcoholism and Drug Dependence.* http://ncadd.org/ (accessed June 16, 2005).

"The Big Book Online Fourth Edition." *Alcoholics Anonymous.* http://www.aa.org/ (accessed June 16, 2005).

"The Cool Spot: The Young Teen's Place for Info on Alcohol and Resisting Peer Pressure." *National Institute on Alcohol Abuse and Alcoholism.* http://www.thecoolspot.gov/ (accessed June 16, 2005).

"Drinking: It Can Spin Your World Around: Facts for Teens." *American Academy of Family Physicians Family Doctor.org.* http://familydoctor.org/ (accessed June 16, 2005).

Ericson, Nels. "Substance Abuse: The Nation's Number One Health Problem: An Office of Juvenile Justice and Delinquency Prevention Fact Sheet." *National Criminal Justice Reference Service.* http://fulltextpubs.ncjrs.org/content/FullTextPubs.html (accessed June 16, 2005).

"Impaired Driving Facts." *Centers for Disease Control and Prevention, National Center for Injury Prevention and Control.* http://www.cdc.gov/ncipc/factsheets/drving.htm (accessed June 16, 2005).

Milgram, Gail Gleason. "Online Facts: The Effects of Alcohol." *Rutgers University Center of Alcohol Studies.* http://alcoholstudies.rutgers.edu/onlinefacts/effects.html (accessed June 16, 2005).

Monitoring the Future. http://www.monitoringthefuture.org/ and http://www.nida.nih.gov/Newsroom/04/2004MTFDrug.pdf (both accessed June 16, 2005).

National Institute on Drug Abuse. http://www.nida.nih.gov/ and http://www.drugabuse.gov (both accessed June 30, 2005).

The Robert Wood Johnson Foundation. http://www.rwjf.org (accessed June 16, 2005).

"Teens Targeted in Drugged Driving Campaign." *MSNBC.com,* December 3, 2004. http://www.msnbc.msn.com/id/6639590/ (accessed June 16, 2005).

"Traffic Safety Facts: 2003." *U.S. Department of Transportation, National Highway Traffic Safety Administration.* http://www-nrd.nhtsa.dot.gov/ (accessed June 16, 2005).

"Underage Drinking: A Major Public Health Challenge: Alcohol Alert No. 59." *National Institute on Alcohol Abuse and Alcoholism.* http://www.niaaa.nih.gov/publications/aa59.htm (accessed June 16, 2005).

Amphetamines

Official Drug Name: Amphetamine
(am-FETT-uh-meen); Benzedrine (BENZ-
uh-dreen)
Also Known As: Amp, bennies, pep pills,
speed, and uppers
Drug Classifications: Schedule II,
stimulant

What Kind of Drug Is It?

Amphetamines are stimulant drugs that improve concentration, reduce appetite, and help keep users awake. Stimulants heighten the activity of a living being. In the 2003 edition of their book *Drugs 101: An Overview for Teens,* Margaret O. Hyde and John F. Setaro defined stimulants as "drugs used to increase alertness, relieve fatigue, [and make users] feel stronger and more decisive." Caffeine, nicotine, cocaine, ecstasy (MDMA), and steroids are all stimulants. (An entry for each of these substances is available in this encyclopedia.) However, amphetamines have a great potential for abuse. The "HIGH" created by stimulants makes people feel good, but only temporarily. "They may elevate mood," wrote John B. Murray in the *Journal of Psychology,* but "their effects are short-lived."

Overview

Although they were discovered late in the nineteenth century, amphetamines did not receive much attention in the medical community until 1927, when a University of California researcher named Gordon Alles began studying their effects. Alles found that the drugs gave people a lot of energy, allowing them to do more and stay awake longer without getting tired. This effect of "speeding up" people's actions explains how amphetamines eventually came to be known by the street names "speed" and "uppers."

There are several different types of amphetamines. (For more information, see individual entries on Adderall, dextroamphetamine, and methamphetamine in this encyclopedia.) Generally, all amphetamines act the same way: as stimulants.

Early Amphetamines Treat Breathing Problems

The first amphetamine was made in a laboratory by a German chemist in the late 1880s. The drug was not used for medical purposes, however, until more than forty years later. By that time, scientists were looking to create a drug that would mimic the effects of ephedra, a natural Chinese remedy for ASTHMA. When boiled in

high: drug-induced feelings ranging from excitement and joy to extreme grogginess

asthma: pronounced AZ-muh; a lung disorder that interferes with normal breathing

water, stems from the ephedra bush produce a tea that helps dilate, or open up, the small sacs of the lungs. The active ingredient in this tea apparently eases breathing in asthmatics who drink it. (An entry on ephedra is also available in this encyclopedia.)

Research on asthma medications led to the manufacture of Benzedrine, the earliest and most basic form of amphetamine. In 1931, the pharmaceutical company Smith, Kline, and French introduced the Benzedrine inhaler to relieve the discomfort of nasal congestion due to colds, allergies, and asthma. As Murray pointed out, these first Benzedrine users reported trouble sleeping when they were on the drug. This sparked yet another branch of research on the effects of amphetamines. By 1935, drug companies were marketing amphetamines for the treatment of a daytime sleeping disorder known as NARCOLEPSY. Researchers did not yet realize that amphetamine use could be dangerous.

The ADHD Connection

As far back as 1937, doctors were looking for ways to help children who had problems concentrating. At the time, the condition that is now referred to as ATTENTION-DEFICIT/HYPERACTIVITY DISORDER (ADHD) was called "minimal brain dysfunction." Little was known about the disorder, and it was believed to affect only children. Since then, the misleading name "minimal brain dysfunction" has been dropped, and medical researchers have learned more about ADHD and its effects.

ADHD is a disorder that begins during childhood, although in many cases it goes undiagnosed until adulthood. It is very difficult for people with ADHD to focus their attention and control their behavior. Children with ADHD are easily distracted and have difficulty concentrating, especially on schoolwork. They may also talk excessively, interrupt conversations, and have trouble waiting their turn. In many cases, people diagnosed with ADHD display IMPULSIVE BEHAVIOR, which frequently persists into adulthood.

According to the Schaffer Library of Drug Policy's 1972 entry on amphetamines, early use of amphetamines in young patients with ADHD produced surprising results. "Instead of making them even more jittery, as might be expected, the amphetamines calm many of these children and noticeably improve their concentration and performance," commented the authors of the article. The use of amphetamines for ADHD in children and adults continues into the twenty-first century.

narcolepsy: a rare sleep disorder characterized by daytime tiredness and sudden attacks of sleep

attention-deficit/hyperactivity disorder (ADHD): a disorder characterized by impulsive behavior, difficulty concentrating, and hyperactivity that interferes with social and academic functioning

impulsive behavior: (sometimes called impulsivity) acting quickly, often without thinking about the consequences of one's actions

Usage Spikes after World War II

During World War II (1939–1945), soldiers used amphetamines to maintain alertness during combat. In the years following the war, many service personnel had trouble functioning without the drug. One major instance of widespread amphetamine abuse occurred in Japan after the war. Much of the country was devastated by bombs dropped during World War II, and the Japanese had to work long hours to rebuild their country. Japanese men who had been soldiers recalled how amphetamines had helped them face one battle after another when the war was in full swing. Demand for the drug increased, and amphetamines were released for sale in Japan without a prescription. This led to a decade of abuse throughout the nation. In the mid-1950s, though, the Japanese government restricted access to amphetamines and passed stricter laws against illegal amphetamine use.

Around the same time, Americans were becoming hooked on amphetamines, too. Users found they could lose weight quickly and effortlessly. Amphetamines quickly earned a reputation as a "wonder drug" that allowed users to work harder without feeling tired. "Pharmaceutical companies encouraged doctors to prescribe amphetamines to depressed housewives in the 1960s," wrote Andrew Weil and Winifred Rosen in *From Chocolate to Morphine.* The drugs were even given to racehorses, since it was thought the drug would make them run faster. Throughout the decade, public health authorities noted a new and disturbing trend in amphetamine use among drug users in San Francisco, California. Individuals, soon to be known as "speed freaks," were injecting liquefied amphetamines into their veins.

Amphetamine use also went up dramatically in the United Kingdom in the 1960s. According to Hilary Klee in the *Journal of Drug Issues,* "the 'Swinging Sixties' was a period of revolutionary social change and experimentation with psychoactive drugs.... 'Pop idols' became major ... influences on British youth. The role models in the United Kingdom were ... young and working class, like many of their fans. Amphetamine was popular among them because it provided the energy to perform all night and survive periods on tour."

The massive increase in drug use in the 1960s prompted countries throughout the world to pass new anti-drug laws and regulations. In the United States, Congress passed the Controlled Substances Act (CSA) of 1970, which cut down considerably on the production, importation, and prescription of amphetamines. Many forms of amphetamine, particularly diet pills, were removed from the over-the-counter market. But this crackdown on amphetamines led to the development of illegal labs in many countries. By the 1990s, ILLICIT amphetamine production had emerged worldwide, with large numbers of illegal labs being reported especially in the western United States, the United Kingdom,

illicit: unlawful

"Speed Kills"

The people who made the phrase "Speed Kills" popular were not talking about driving responsibly. The saying was used in the psychedelic era of the 1960s and early 1970s. It was coined by people who saw many of their peers fall victim to intravenous (IV) drug abuse.

Shooting amphetamines directly into the bloodstream is the most dangerous of all methods of use. This is because of the "speed" with which the drug flows throughout the body. The high is almost immediate, the shock to the system is intense, and the results can be deadly. Long-term speed use increases the risk of a drug-related fatality. Users build up a tolerance for the drug, meaning that they need more and more speed to get the same high. Taking higher and higher doses of the drug can lead to overdose and even death.

An anti-drug button from the 1960s warns of the dangers of taking speed. *Photo by Herbert Orth/Time Life Pictures/Getty Images.*

The phrase "Speed Kills" was not just used by anti-drug activists. It was also popular among drug users who knew firsthand the dangers of amphetamine abuse. The slogan appeared on various mementos of the psychedelic era. The anti-amphetamine message adorned buttons, posters, and even stickers that schoolchildren put on their notebooks.

and eastern Europe. The problem persisted into the early twenty-first century, especially among unemployed youth.

What Is It Made Of?

Amphetamines do not occur naturally; they cannot be grown in a garden or dug up from the ground. Rather, amphetamines are synthetic, or manufactured, substances that consist of the elements carbon, hydrogen, and nitrogen.

The chemical structure of amphetamines is related to two natural substances known to boost energy within the human body. Those substances are EPHEDRINE and ADRENALINE. Ephedrine is a

ephedrine: pronounced ih-FEH-drinn; a chemical substance that eases breathing problems

adrenaline: pronounced uh-DREN-uh-linn; a natural stimulant produced by the human body; also known as epinephrine (epp-ih-NEFF-run)

Some speed abusers use a razor blade to chop amphetamine tablets into a fine powder to snort the drug. *Science Photo Library.*

natural stimulant found in the ephedra bush. It is the active ingredient in a Chinese herbal drug that relieves the symptoms of asthma. Adrenaline is a natural stimulant that the human body produces all by itself. It sets off the body's "fight or flight" reaction in times of emergency. When adrenaline is released, heart rate and blood pressure increase, the muscles that control breathing relax, and the pupils of the eyes dilate.

How Is It Taken?

Amphetamines come in both tablets and capsules and are usually swallowed. However, drug abusers sometimes crack open the capsule to get to the flecks of the drug inside it, or they grind the tablets into a fine powder. Amphetamine powder obtained from either method is then inhaled or "snorted." Users also mix it with tobacco or marijuana and then smoke it.

Beginning in the 1960s, some hardcore drug abusers started mixing the amphetamine powder into a liquid and then injecting it. This is called INTRAVENOUS, OR IV, DRUG ABUSE. When injected, the amphetamine high occurs almost immediately, increasing the

intravenous, or IV, drug abuse: injection of a liquid form of a drug directly into the bloodstream

danger of addiction. Weil and Rosen described the physical and mental effects of a few weeks of continued intravenous use. Addicts "became EMACIATED and generally unhealthy," the authors reported. "They stayed up for days on end, then 'crashed' into stupors. They became jumpy, paranoid, and even psychotic."

Many high-dose amphetamine abusers become psychotic, or mentally deranged, after a week or so of continuous use. A disruption occurs in the way their minds function, making it difficult for people suffering from a psychotic episode to distinguish between what is real and what is imagined. Users who increase "their dose rapidly to enormous levels ... swallowing whole handfuls of amphetamine tablets" can develop an "amphetamine PSYCHOSIS." According to the Schaffer Library of Drug Policy, this condition makes them feel as if "ants, insects, or snakes [are] crawling over or under the skin."

Are There Any Medical Reasons for Taking This Substance?

Historically, amphetamines have been prescribed by doctors as an appetite suppressant and as a treatment for both ADHD and an unusual sleep disorder called narcolepsy.

Amphetamines tend to decrease feelings of hunger in people who take them, making them an often-abused drug among dieters. Although the use of amphetamines for weight control was popular in the 1950s and again in the 1980s and part of the 1990s, this practice is no longer common. Amphetamine use for weight loss can be very dangerous. Most doctors agree that the best way to regulate weight is through moderate exercise and a healthy diet.

As of 2005, amphetamines were most commonly prescribed to treat ADHD and narcolepsy. Amphetamines are successful in the treatment of ADHD because they help improve the user's ability to concentrate. In prescription form, amphetamines also have been found to be helpful in treating narcolepsy, a fairly rare condition that causes people to fall asleep quickly and unexpectedly. Amphetamines speed up bodily functions, producing a much-desired feeling of alertness in people with narcolepsy.

Usage Trends

Amphetamine abuse is very widespread and often unintended. Cynthia Kuhn and her coauthors summarized the dangers of amphetamines in their book *Buzzed: The Straight Facts about the Most Used and Abused Drugs from Alcohol to Ecstasy.* In a word, the buzz from

emaciated: pronounced ee-MASE-ee-ate-ed; very thin and sickly looking

psychosis: pronounced sy-KOH-sis; a severe mental disorder that often causes hallucinations and makes it difficult for people to distinguish what is real from what is imagined

In the 1930s, Benzedrine inhalers were introduced to treat asthma. But some users reported that the amphetamine-based drug made sleeping difficult. Today's inhalers (shown above) no longer contain Benzedrine.
Photograph by Leitha Etheridge-Sims.

amphetamines is "pleasurable." Overuse typically stems from the drug's effects. Amphetamines make most users feel good, at least in the short term. Experimentation with amphetamines can get out of hand quite easily, though. Even legal users—those individuals taking the drug with a doctor's prescription—can get hooked.

Not Just a Nasal Spray

Generations ago, over-the-counter nasal inhalers contained amphetamines. The reasoning behind amphetamine treatment for nasal congestions was quite simple: stimulants are known to constrict blood vessels. Constricting the blood vessels in the nose and sinuses cuts down on congestion because it shrinks the nasal tissues, allowing air to flow more freely through the nose. This effect is only temporary, though, and when it wears off, a "rebound effect" occurs. The nasal passages actually end up more severely blocked than they were before the amphetamine was inhaled.

The first users of any new drug are a bit like human guinea pigs. "Because of the incredible complexity of the brain," explained Kuhn, "most drugs that affect it have actions in addition to those for which they were developed." Aside from the problems with the rebound effect, some users of early nasal inhalers "experienced general stimulation from them" as well, wrote Weil and Rosen. "Some got high, and some became dependent." Because of their side effects and the potential for abuse, amphetamines are no longer dispensed in over-the-counter decongestants.

Who's Using Amphetamines?

The results of the 2004 Monitoring the Future (MTF) study were released to the public on December 21, 2004. Conducted by the University of Michigan (U of M), it was sponsored by research grants from the National Institute on Drug Abuse (NIDA). Since 1991, U of M has tracked patterns of drug use and attitudes toward drugs among students in the eighth, tenth, and twelfth grades. (Prior to that, from 1975 to 1990, the MTF survey was limited to twelfth graders.)

The 2004 MTF survey results indicate that nonprescription amphetamine use among students in the eighth and tenth grades had fallen. Researchers noted "a steady decline among eighth graders since 1996; in fact, their annual . . . use has fallen by almost half since then," from 9.1 to 4.9 percent. Amphetamine use was also down among tenth graders, "but not among twelfth graders, who . . . remain near their recent peak levels of use." According to MTF charts for 2003 to 2004, about one in every ten high school seniors reported using amphetamines "in the last twelve months." The ease with which seniors said they would be able to get the drug held steady. More than half of the twelfth graders surveyed said it would be "fairly easy" or "very easy" to obtain amphetamines.

The MTF survey does not track drug use among people after their high school years. However, amphetamine use in the general population can be determined by other data. Experts in the field of drug research periodically gather together all of the information available on certain drugs to create a profile, or description, of a typical user. Based on these studies, the typical amphetamine user of the 1960s, 1970s, 1980s, and part of the 1990s was young, white, male, single, and often unemployed. More recent findings cited in the *Journal of Psychology* in 1998 indicate that the population of amphetamine users is becoming broader and now includes:

- more women
- more married, divorced, and widowed people
- fewer whites
- people of all age groups, from middle school students to retirees.

In mid-2003, *Alcoholism & Drug Abuse Weekly* reported the results of the Quest Diagnostics 2002 Drug Testing Index, a measure of drug use among American workers. Based on 7 million urine tests performed by the lab throughout 2002, the overall use of drugs in the workplace apparently decreased. The incidence of amphetamine usage, however, went up significantly. According to Quest, positive test results among U.S. workers "increased 70 percent over the past five years" from 1998 through 2002.

The use and abuse of amphetamine-like stimulants is a growing global problem that poses "a serious threat to the health, social and economic fabric of families, communities and nations," according to the *World Health Organization* Web site. The United Nations estimated that in the year 2000, 29 million people around the world had abused various types of amphetamine stimulants in the previous decade.

Effects on the Body

Amphetamines are PSYCHOSTIMULANTS. As a prescription drug for the treatment of ADHD, amphetamines have been shown to increase performance accuracy, improve short-term memory, improve reaction time, aid in solving mathematical problems, increase problem-solving abilities in games, and help individuals concentrate.

"If stimulants simply increased energy and alertness," commented Kuhn, "they indeed would be [a] miracle medicine.... However, these drugs also cause an unmistakable euphoria and sense of well-being that is the basis of addiction." The effect of amphetamines is similar to the effect of cocaine, another widely abused psychostimulant. However, amphetamine highs are generally longer lasting.

Amphetamine users often feel that the drug puts them in a better mood and increases their level of confidence. "It gives me a lot of energy," remarked one user in an interview with Klee. "I can get out and do things, meet people, things like that. And you don't let anything get to you. You're on top of the world."

Amphetamines are often abused by people who want to boost their energy and enhance their physical performance. Athletes on amphetamines may find that they can play longer, harder, and better. Students on speed can endure longer studying sessions and remain focused on their homework for hours, sometimes without even taking a break to eat. Truck drivers who take amphetamines are able to cover more miles without falling asleep at the wheel. But the high generated by amphetamines eventually wears off.

psychostimulants: pronounced SY-koh-STIM-yew-lents; stimulants that act on the brain

In 2001, track star Justin Gatlin received a two-year suspension from competing after testing positive for amphetamines. He successfully fought the suspension, however, showing that the drug was prescribed to him to treat ADHD. Gatlin stopped taking the medication and later won a gold medal at the 2004 Olympic Games. *AP/Wide World Photos.*

After the Buzz

"A single oral dose of amphetamine usually stimulates the body for at least four hours," wrote Weil and Rosen. After that, more of the drug is needed to maintain the high. Once the buzz of uppers has worn off, users who felt awake, energized, and full find themselves very tired, grumpy, and extremely hungry. A person coming down from an amphetamine high may sleep an entire day away before the drug leaves his or her system entirely.

"Irritability and/or aggression is common when 'coming down' off the drug, when using [it] heavily, and when [it is] combined with alcohol," reported Klee. "You get to the point where you're shouting at people and causing trouble and the amphetamine gives you the energy to do it . . . which is a problem," noted one of the users Klee quoted. Such behavior can ruin long-standing relationships and, in some cases, result in social rejection for users.

Addiction and Other Dangers

Long-term amphetamine use can result in a PSYCHOLOGICAL ADDICTION OR PSYCHOLOGICAL DEPENDENCE. Psychological dependence can develop quickly, especially in people who already show signs of depression. As Kuhn put it, "We know that the drive to use cocaine or amphetamine is considerably stronger than that for any of the other addictive drugs."

The use of amphetamines can cause an upset stomach, diarrhea, headache, dizziness, nervousness, weight loss, and insomnia. The drug can also lead users to perform bizarre, repetitive actions. "Assembling and disassembling radios, cars, and gadgets is common among . . . users. [They] are aware that their activity is meaningless but report not being able to stop," noted Murray. Higher doses result in fever, an unusually fast heartbeat, chest pain, blurred vision, tics, tremors, and antisocial behavior.

Amphetamines can kill. Prolonged abuse of amphetamines can lead to TOLERANCE. Taking greater quantities of amphetamines increases the chance of an overdose. Signs of an overdose include convulsions, followed by coma, and then possibly death. The cause of death may be from the bursting of blood vessels in the brain, a heart attack, or an extremely high fever.

Lab Studies

The National Academy of Sciences revealed in 2003 that exposure to amphetamines can reduce "the ability of certain brain cells to change in response to life experiences." With funding provided by the National Institute on Drug Abuse (NIDA), drug researchers from the University of Lethbridge in Canada and U of M-Ann Arbor worked together, conducting experiments with amphetamines on lab rats.

Amphetamine-treated rats seemed confused by changes that were introduced to their surroundings during the course of the testing. Rats that were not given amphetamines, however, had no problems maneuvering around ramps, bridges, tunnels, and toys that had been relocated in their cages. Even after three and a half months, the amphetamine-treated rats were unable to adjust to changes in their environment. Analysis of the brains of both treated and untreated rats showed definite differences in their physical appearance.

These findings correspond with drug experiments conducted by three researchers on human volunteers in 1969. Those experiments, according to Murray, indicated that high doses of amphetamines affect the brain. The volunteers, who were hospitalized for the six-week-long study, experienced wide mood swings that began with euphoria, or a feeling of great happiness, and ended with deep

psychological addiction or psychological dependence: the belief that a person needs to take a certain substance in order to function

tolerance: a condition in which higher and higher doses of a drug are needed to produce the original effect or high experienced

depression. They also went for days without eating or sleeping well, talked nonstop for hours at a time, and showed signs of PARANOIA before the experiment was concluded.

Reactions with Other Drugs or Substances

Amphetamines are dangerous drugs. The dangers increase when they are taken with other addictive substances. Amphetamines are frequently combined with other drugs to prolong or add to the high they produce alone. Caffeine is one substance that is known to add to the effects of amphetamines. When combined with alcohol, "amphetamines have the potential to produce unprovoked, random, and often senseless violence," noted Murray. Amphetamines raise blood pressure, so they should not be taken by people who are on medication to reduce their blood pressure. In addition, the drug should not be taken with over-the-counter cold medications or with certain antidepressant medications.

Treatment for Habitual Users

Tolerance to amphetamines occurs quickly. In an attempt to sustain the high that results from amphetamine use, users often begin taking more of the drug than they should. They then find themselves unable to stop on their own. The WITHDRAWAL process can last days or weeks. Besides feeling intense cravings for the drug, long-time users who attempt to kick their habit experience other unpleasant effects. These include extreme anxiety, abdominal pain, shortness of breath, vivid or unpleasant dreams, fever, decreased energy, and depression. Even "long after the withdrawal period, past users may experience urgings and cravings," added Murray. Addiction experts consider behavioral therapy and emotional support essential for the successful treatment and rehabilitation of amphetamine abusers.

Consequences

Amphetamines can be extremely toxic. When uppers are "used without medical supervision, they are potentially dangerous, even for first-time users," warned Murray. People who are high on amphetamines are more likely to take chances and engage in riskier behavior than they would if they were not high. This increases the danger of becoming infected with HIV (the human immunodeficiency virus), which can lead to AIDS (acquired immunodeficiency syndrome), either through unsafe sex or by sharing needles.

Drug abuse among young people is associated with early sexual activity, increased involvement in criminal activities, and higher

paranoia: abnormal feelings of suspicion and fear

withdrawal: the process of gradually cutting back on the amount of a drug being taken until it is discontinued entirely; also the accompanying physiological effects of terminating use of an addictive drug

Many countries destroy illegal drugs seized in police raids. Here, Thailand officials load packs of amphetamines onto a cart to be burned in an incinerator in December 2004. The amphetamines were among 3.5 tons of drugs taken to the incinerator. *Pornchai Kittiwongsakul/AFP/Getty Images.*

school dropout rates. Amphetamine users often take other drugs along with uppers. This can increase the likelihood of becoming involved in accidents. It can also contribute to the development of physical, mental, and emotional problems, including high rates of infection, PHOBIAS, depression, and suicidal tendencies.

Infants born to mothers dependent on amphetamines have an increased risk of premature delivery and low birth weight. The infants may actually experience symptoms of drug withdrawal. Mothers taking the drug should not breast-feed their babies, since amphetamine is excreted in human milk. A number of studies using rodents as test animals indicate that women should not take amphetamines at all when pregnant.

phobias: extreme and often unexplainable fears of certain objects or situations

The Law

Amphetamines are controlled substances: their use is regulated by certain federal laws. The Controlled Substances Act (CSA) of 1970 called for the assignment of all controlled drug substances into one of five categories called schedules. These schedules are based on a substance's medicinal value, harmfulness, and potential for abuse and addiction. Schedule I is reserved for the most dangerous drugs that have no recognized medical use. Amphetamines fall under Schedule II: dangerous drugs with genuine medical uses that also have a high potential for abuse and addiction.

Possessing amphetamines without a medical doctor's prescription is against the law and can result in imprisonment and stiff fines. The length of the jail sentence and the amount of the fine are increased when a person is convicted of a second or third offense of amphetamine possession. People convicted of distributing amphetamines—selling or giving away prescribed drugs—face lengthy prison terms and fines of up to $2 million.

For More Information

Books

Bayer, Linda. *Amphetamines and Other Uppers.* Broomall, PA: Chelsea House Publishers, 2000.

Clayton, Lawrence. *Amphetamines and Other Stimulants.* New York: Rosen Publishing Group, 1994.

Gahlinger, Paul M. *Illegal Drugs: A Complete Guide to Their History, Chemistry, Use, and Abuse.* Las Vegas, NV: Sagebrush Press, 2001.

Hyde, Margaret O., and John F. Setaro. *Drugs 101: An Overview for Teens.* Brookfield, CT: Twenty-first Century Books, 2003.

Kuhn, Cynthia, Scott Swartzwelder, Wilkie Wilson, and others. *Buzzed: The Straight Facts about the Most Used and Abused Drugs from Alcohol to Ecstasy,* 2nd ed. New York: W.W. Norton, 2003.

Pellowski, Michael J. *Amphetamine Drug Dangers.* Berkeley Heights, NJ: Enslow Publishers, Inc., 2001.

Schull, Patricia Dwyer. *Nursing Spectrum Drug Handbook.* King of Prussia, PA: Nursing Spectrum, 2005.

Weil, Andrew, and Winifred Rosen. *From Chocolate to Morphine.* New York: Houghton Mifflin, 1993, rev. 2004.

Westcott, Patsy. *Why Do People Take Drugs?* Austin, TX, and New York: Raintree Steck-Vaughn Publishers, 2001.

Periodicals

Klee, Hilary. "The Love of Speed." *Journal of Drug Issues* (Winter, 1998): pp. 33-55.

Murray, John B. "Psychophysiological Aspects of Amphetamine-Methamphetamine Abuse." *Journal of Psychology* (March, 1998): pp. 227-237.

"Workplace Drug Use Declines, Amphetamine Use Increases." *Alcoholism & Drug Abuse Weekly* (June 16, 2003): p. 8.

Web Sites

"The Amphetamines." *Schaffer Library of Drug Policy.* http://www.druglibrary.org/schaffer/ (accessed June 16, 2005).

"Amphetamine-Type Stimulants." *World Health Organization.* http://www.who.int/substance_abuse/facts/ATS/en/ (accessed June 16, 2005).

"Mind over Matter: Stimulants." *NIDA for Teens: The Science behind Drug Abuse.* http://teens.drugabuse.gov/mom/mom_stim2.asp (accessed June 16, 2005).

Monitoring the Future. http://www.monitoringthefuture.org/ and http://www.nida.nih.gov/Newsroom/04/2004MTFDrug.pdf (both accessed June 16, 2005).

Proceedings of the National Academy of Sciences of the United States of America. http://www.pnas.org/ (accessed June 16, 2005).

See also: Adderall; Cocaine; Dextroamphetamine; Diet pills; Ephedra; Methamphetamine

Amyl Nitrite

What Kind of Drug Is It?

Amyl nitrite is a clear, yellowish, flammable (burns easily) liquid with a strong fruity odor. Some sources describe it as having a sweet smell similar to a ripe banana; others compare it to the slightly sickening sweetness of a rotten apple. Old amyl nitrite takes on a vinegary smell similar to dirty, sweaty socks.

Amyl nitrite is a stimulant, meaning that it increases the rate at which chemical reactions occur in the body. Stimulants are substances that increase the activity of a living organism or one of its parts. Amyl nitrite EVAPORATES into the air at room temperature and is not intended to be swallowed. Instead, the fumes from liquid amyl nitrite are inhaled by the user, usually through the nose. For this reason, amyl nitrite is called an INHALANT. It is available legally in the United States only with a prescription.

Overview

Amyl nitrite was discovered in the United Kingdom in the mid-1800s and used to treat severe chest pain. People with heart disease (also called coronary artery disease) often experience shortness of breath and feelings of intense pain and pressure in their chests. This pain, called ANGINA PECTORIS, is felt when the blood supply to the heart is restricted. Blood carries oxygen to all parts of the body. Without oxygen, the body's cells die. Chest pain is the brain's way of telling a person with coronary artery disease that the heart needs more oxygen. In order to get that oxygen, the flow of blood to the heart must increase.

Amyl nitrite helps relax the muscles around the blood vessels of the heart, making it easier for blood to flow through them. The blood vessels that carry oxygen to the heart are called arteries. Amyl nitrite acts on those arteries by dilating or opening them up. As a result, the pumping action of the heart improves, and blood circulates more freely throughout the body. When oxygen-rich blood reaches the heart, the chest pain goes away. Amyl nitrite acts very quickly, relieving the pain of angina in heart patients within a few minutes.

Official Drug Name: Amyl nitrite (AM-ull NITE-rite), Aspirols, Vaporole; sometimes referred to as amyl nitrate; this substance is closely related to butyl nitrite, isobutyl nitrite, and other nitrites, including nitroglycerin.
Also Known As: Amys (pronounced like the girl's name Amy), pearls, poppers, and snappers. Note that butyl nitrite and isobutyl nitrite have their own street names, including liquid gold, locker room, rush, and thrust. The most frequently used nickname for nitrites in general is *poppers*.
Drug Classifications: Not scheduled, inhalant

evaporate: to change from a liquid into a vapor

inhalant: a chemical that gives off fumes or vapors that are sniffed

angina pectoris: pronounced an-JINE-uh peck-TOR-ess; a feeling of suffocation and pain around the heart that occurs when the blood supply to the heart is not adequate

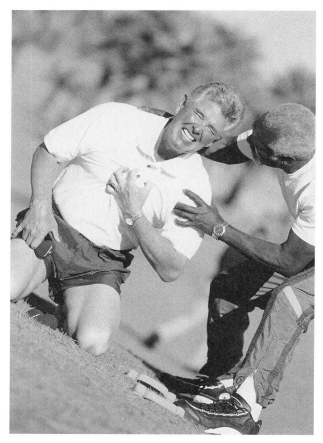

Amyl nitrite was originally manufactured and prescribed to treat angina pectoris, a heart condition marked by severe chest pain and shortness of breath. More effective treatments exist today. © *Royalty-Free/Corbis.*

People who use amyl nitrite as a RECREATIONAL DRUG find its side effects appealing. Sniffing amyl nitrite brings on a short but dizzying burst of euphoria, making it a prime target for abuse. Its use as a recreational drug began growing in popularity in the 1950s. Because of the way in which amyl nitrite is taken, however, "it is very difficult to control the dose," explained Ruth Stalnikowicz in a *Journal of Toxicology* article. This can pose serious health threats to users. Throughout the 1960s, though, amyl nitrite was actually available to the public as an over-the-counter drug. According to Andrew Weil and Winifred Rosen in *From Chocolate to Morphine,* abuse of the substance skyrocketed during that time, and by 1969, the U.S. Food and Drug Administration (FDA) declared that amyl nitrite could only be obtained with a doctor's prescription.

Over time, amyl nitrite was used less and less to treat angina, but it became fashionable on the club scene following rumors that it intensified sexual pleasure. It found particular acceptance among gay men in cities across the United States and the United Kingdom. Usage later spread to straight dance clubs, where both men and women sniffed it to achieve a quick HIGH that supposedly added to the wild dance club experience.

recreational drug: a drug used solely to achieve a high, not to treat a medical condition

high: drug-induced feelings ranging from excitement and joy to extreme grogginess

nitrite: a negatively charged molecule of nitrogen and oxygen

What Is It Made Of?

A NITRITE is a chemical compound that contains one nitrogen atom joined to two oxygen atoms. The chemical symbol for a nitrite is NO_2. In medical applications, nitrites are used to enlarge blood vessels. In the food industry, nitrites are often used as preservatives.

How Is It Taken?

Amyl nitrite vapor is usually inhaled through the nose and more rarely inhaled through the mouth. Small doses—0.3 millilitres each—of the prescription drug come in very fragile, airtight glass vials or containers called ampules. These ampules are covered with a layer of cotton material and topped off with an outer mesh wrapping. The containers are easily crushed between the thumb and fingers. That's how vials of amyl nitrite became known as *poppers*—because of the "popping" sound they make when crushed. In fact, the term *poppers* is so closely associated with amyl nitrite that it has been listed as a slang name for the drug in the last three editions of *Merriam-Webster's Collegiate Dictionary*. (The definition, according to *Webster's 11th Edition*, is "a vial of amyl nitrite or butyl nitrite used [illegally] as an inhalational APHRODISIAC.")

After the ampules are broken, the layer of cotton surrounding the popper becomes soaked with the drug. When the vapors from the liquid are inhaled, the amyl nitrite triggers an almost immediate jump in heart rate and a drop in blood pressure. Heart patients experiencing severe chest pain are instructed to wave the broken ampule under their noses and inhale the amyl nitrite vapors up to six times (while seated because dizziness may occur). Amyl nitrite begins working very quickly—within fifteen to thirty seconds—and its pain-relieving effects are dramatic.

Because a prescription is required to obtain amyl nitrite in the United States, two variants of the drug, butyl nitrite and isobutyl nitrite, became popular in the 1970s. These and other nitrites are now generally sold in small, dark-colored glass bottles and sniffed in concentrated form. Nitrite-based inhalants produce an almost instant high that is felt for two to five minutes.

Are There Any Medical Reasons for Taking This Substance?

Amyl nitrite was originally manufactured and prescribed to treat angina pectoris, a heart condition marked by severe chest pain and shortness of breath. More effective treatments for angina now exist, and it is rarely prescribed for this purpose in the twenty-first century.

The most important medical use for amyl nitrite since the late 1980s has been as an ANTIDOTE for CYANIDE poisoning. By the turn of the twenty-first century, the possibility of chemical weapons use in times of war had become increasingly real. The most extreme use of cyanide is as a chemical weapon, since high doses can kill large groups of people at one time. The terrorist attacks of September 11, 2001, against the United States sparked considerable concern about the need for antidotes to poisons such as cyanide. According

aphrodisiac: pronounced aff-roh-DEE-zee-ack; a drug or other substance that excites or increases sexual desire

antidote: a remedy to reverse the effects of a poison

cyanide: a poisonous chemical compound that shuts down the respiratory system, quickly killing people who have been exposed to it

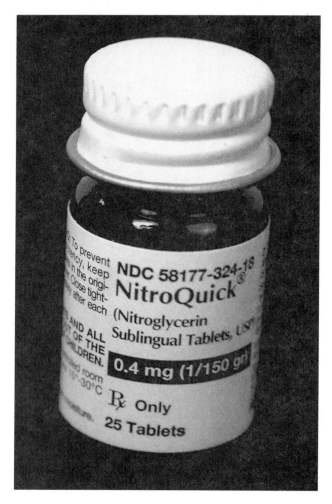

Nitroglycerin, when used in very small doctor-prescribed amounts, relieves the pain of angina pectoris in heart patients. *Scott Camazine/Photo Researchers, Inc.*

to the *Seattle Post-Intelligencer,* the U.S. Centers for Disease Control and Prevention hoped to have stocks of antidotes called "chem-packs" distributed to every state by 2006. Amyl nitrite is one of the drugs included in these chem-packs.

Usage Trends

The use of amyl nitrite as a prescription drug for angina pectoris has dropped considerably since the 1960s. Doctors now use other drugs more commonly to control chest pain in heart patients. One of those drugs is nitroglycerin—a heavy, oily, highly explosive liquid. When used in very small doctor-prescribed amounts, it relieves the pain of angina pectoris. It is easier to administer than amyl nitrite, causes fewer side effects, and is considered a more reliable form of treatment for angina pectoris.

Since the growth in popularity of butyl nitrite and isobutyl nitrite in the 1970s, other nitrites have been produced and continue to be sold through Web sites and catalogs as an industrial chemical, specifically as a room deodorizer or liquid incense. These substances are widely known, however, for the high they give users who sniff them in concentrated form.

Clifford Sherry cited statistics from the National Institute on Drug Abuse (NIDA) in his 1994 book *Inhalants.* According to Sherry, more than 5 million Americans were abusing nitrites at least once a week in the early 1990s. At that time, the primary abusers of amyl nitrite were adults around twenty-five years of age—not students in middle school or high school. There are several reasons for this, and the main one is accessibility. Amyl nitrite is a prescription drug, which makes it harder for teens to obtain. Different inhalants, such as glue, paint, nail polish, hair spray, and other aerosol propellants, were—and still are—far easier to get and can produce a quick high of their own. (An entry on inhalants is available in this encyclopedia.)

Raves are often associated with illegal drug use, including nitrites, 2C-B, ecstasy (MDMA), GHB, and ketamine. Such drug use is not common at all raves, however. Some groups sponsor drug-free raves where people can go just to enjoy the dancing and music. *AP/Wide World Photos.*

Another reason for the historic popularity of amyl nitrite among people twenty-five and older had to do with the muscle-relaxing effects of the drug. Sherry points out that "nitrite abusers tend to be looking for different effects from the other inhalant abusers." The heart isn't the only muscle that amyl nitrite relaxes; other muscles throughout the body are affected by it as well. As a result, amyl nitrite has gained a reputation as a sexual aid, especially among gay men. In fact, the drug has a long history of use by members of the gay community. Medical experts have linked amyl nitrite abuse with unsafe sexual activity, prompting fears that users have a higher risk of developing AIDS (acquired immunodeficiency syndrome) and other sexually transmitted diseases.

Frequent Abusers

As of 2005, nitrite abuse could be found across all ethnic groups, age levels, and genders. However, the most frequent users fell into one of two groups: 1) older, white, usually male adolescents from families with low to average incomes, and 2) teenagers and young adults who attend all-night dance parties, known as RAVES, on a regular basis.

raves: wild overnight dance parties that typically involve huge crowds of people, loud techno music, and illegal drug use

Nitrites are often used in combination with other so-called rave or club drugs, such as 2C-B, ecstasy (MDMA), GHB, and ketamine.

Few studies focus specifically on amyl nitrite abuse; the drug is usually lumped into the general category of inhalants. However, researchers and other members of the scientific community generally believe the amyl nitrite problem is not as severe as that posed by other, more readily available, inhalants.

Monitoring the Future Study

Data from national and state surveys show that, generally speaking, inhalant abuse is most common among middle school and high school students. The results of the 2004 Monitoring the Future (MTF) study, conducted by the University of Michigan (U of M) and sponsored by research grants from NIDA, were released to the public on December 21, 2004. Since 1991, U of M has tracked patterns of drug use and attitudes toward drugs among students in the eighth, tenth, and twelfth grades. (Prior to that, from 1975 to 1990, the MTF survey was limited to twelfth graders.)

Results of the 2004 MTF survey indicate that, overall, the abuse of inhalants among eighth graders increased between 2003 and 2004. (Note that this information refers to inhalants in general, not specifically to nitrites.) MTF study authors called the increase in inhalant use "among younger students ... one of the more troublesome findings this year." Researchers were unsure what caused the increase.

Information on nitrite usage, particularly among eighth-grade and tenth-grade students, was not available, but nitrite abuse appears to have trickled down to adolescents. About 4 out of every 300 twelfth graders surveyed admitted using a nitrite of some kind at some point in their lives. The perceived availability of amyl and butyl nitrites (the ease with which seniors said they would be able to get the drugs) was high: 20 percent of those surveyed said it would be "fairly easy" or "very easy" to obtain.

Trends in the United Kingdom

A similar trend has occurred in the United Kingdom. Neville Hodgkinson, writing in the London *Sunday Times* in 1994, revealed the results of a study of amyl nitrite use among fourteen and fifteen year olds in Manchester, United Kingdom. Fourteen percent of the students in the study admitted that they had sniffed poppers in the past. "It has become increasingly popular as a 'rave' drug [but now it's] even for playground use," concluded Hodgkinson.

In a 2003 *Guardian* article, Alan Travis reported: "Illegal drug use in England and Wales remains among the highest in Europe with around 4 million people—12% of the population between 16 and 59—having used some kind of illicit substance in the last year.... But the new figures from the British Crime Survey," added Travis, "show ... that the legal prescription drug amyl nitrite or poppers is now more widely used by 16 to 24-year-olds."

Do You Know What Nitrites Do?

The effects of amyl nitrite go far beyond bad breath, a headache, and a case of the giggles. Remember what it does to some muscles? It relaxes them. Two of the muscles it works on are those associated with bowel and bladder control. Put plainly, nitrites can cause users to have accidents before they can reach a toilet.

Effects on the Body

British writer Georgie Dales admits to having manufactured illegal drugs with her classmates many years ago when they were young chemistry students. She described poppers in the London *Independent Sunday* as "a heady brew which when sniffed makes the heart race and the head spin as it kills a couple of million brain cells." She and her cohorts had plans to manufacture more illicit drugs, but, as she put it, "Luckily, we got busted first."

Amyl nitrite is absorbed into the bloodstream rapidly and reaches the brain quickly, with effects usually beginning ten to fifteen seconds after inhaling. The initial effects include an almost immediate sense of happiness and pleasure called a "head rush," or simply a "rush." The RUSH is caused by a temporary cut in the amount of oxygen to the brain and the faster pumping of the heart. These feelings last just two to five minutes and are usually followed by a headache.

Amyl nitrite and other poppers tend to impair the judgment of the user, increasing the likelihood that he or she will make bad decisions—especially when it comes to sexual behavior. Virtually every available reference source on nitrites states that these drugs cause a decrease in the user's INHIBITIONS, providing a sense of well-being, intensified emotions, and enhanced sexual desire. People with lowered inhibitions tend to take more chances and engage in riskier behavior than they would if they were not high.

Poppers cause confusion, dizziness, giddiness, drowsiness, facial flushing, skin irritations around the mouth and nose, and a slowed perception of time, not to mention bad breath. They also cause certain muscles in the body to relax involuntarily. Despite these side effects, users claim that nitrites heighten their sense of sexual arousal.

rush: a feeling of euphoria or extreme happiness and well-being

inhibitions: inner thoughts that keep people from engaging in certain activities

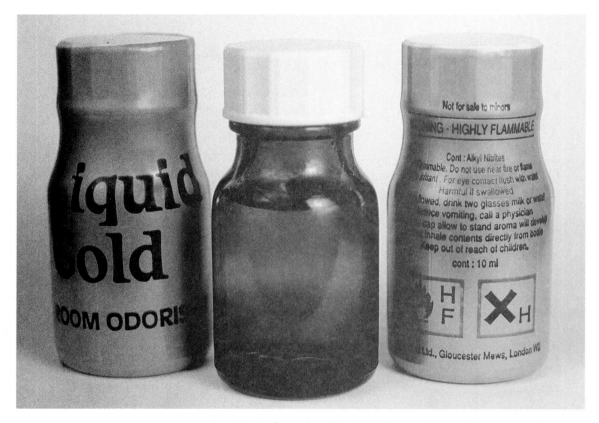

Amyl nitrite (center) and Liquid Gold are nicknamed "poppers." They are stimulant drugs that are often abused at all-night dance parties called raves. *Science Photo Library.*

Dangers

Sniffing amyl nitrite can be dangerous to anyone because nitrites reduce blood pressure. The inhalation of nitrites by pregnant women or by people with the blood condition ANEMIA, the eye disease glaucoma, high blood pressure, heart disease, respiratory (or breathing) problems, or a recent injury to the head sets the stage for extremely severe health risks, and possibly death, according to the NIDA. Poppers can also trigger a short-term deficiency of oxygen reaching the tissues of the body, a condition called HYPOXIA.

Overdose symptoms include nausea, vomiting, dangerously low blood pressure, difficulty breathing, cold skin, blue lips or fingernails, a rapid heartbeat, an unbearable headache and/or a strong feeling of pressure in the head, and eventual unconsciousness. The

anemia: a blood condition that results in the decreased ability of the blood to transport enough oxygen throughout the body

hypoxia: a dangerous condition brought on by an inadequate amount of oxygen circulating throughout the body

inhalation of nitrites can damage red blood cells and affect the blood's ability to carry oxygen from the lungs to the rest of the body. Swallowing nitrites can be fatal.

Other long-term effects of popper use are unclear. Mood swings and personality changes have been reported but have not been studied. Tolerance to nitrites develops with repeated use.

Recent data from the NIDA indicate that the inhalation of nitrites can damage the cells of the immune system and make it more difficult for users to fight off certain infections. Among HIV-positive individuals (people who test positive for the human immunodeficiency virus, which can lead to AIDS), amyl nitrite usage can increase the rate at which the virus multiplies. The higher the number of viral cells in a person's body, the greater the risk for developing AIDS. In a 2004 article for *AIDS Treatment News,* John S. James reported on a United States-based study of infections among men who have sex with men. Nearly half the men in the study used poppers, "suggesting a potentially large impact on the spread of HIV." James also noted that animals exposed to poppers have shown an increased risk of "cancer growth and bacterial growth, probably by suppressing the animals' natural immunity."

> ## "A Feeling ... of Bursting of the Head"
>
> According to the *Medsafe* Web site of New Zealand, "inhaled doses of 5 to 10 drops of amyl nitrite may cause violent flushing of the face, accompanied by a feeling of imminent bursting of the head and very excessive heart action. The inhalation of larger amounts may produce a feeling of suffocation and muscular weakness."

Reactions with Other Drugs or Substances

Sniffing amyl nitrite is dangerous. Combining amyl nitrite use with other drugs or alcohol can be deadly. The effects of nitrites are intensified by substances such as aspirin, high blood pressure medication, and alcohol. Drug users frequently use nitrites to enhance the high brought on by the other illicit drugs they take—marijuana, cocaine, methamphetamines, and hallucinogens, among others. Doing so increases the risk of harmful reactions. According to various British sources, a majority of young people at dance clubs and raves in the early 2000s regularly used more than one drug at a time, with amyl nitrite often part of the mix.

Amyl nitrite is particularly dangerous when combined with the prescription drug Viagra, used to help men who have problems with their sexual performance. Tobias Jones reported in the London *Independent Sunday* that "Viagra can have a lethal effect if mixed with amyl nitrite 'poppers.'" Since both act to dilate

Jail Time or Anti-Drug Treatment?

In 2000, California voters approved Proposition 36, also known as the Substance Abuse and Crime Prevention Act. Proposition 36, which took effect on July 1, 2001, allows state courts to sentence first- and second-time drug-use offenders to probation and drug abuse treatment programs rather than jail time. Treatment can include outpatient care, inpatient treatment at a halfway house, psychotherapy, and drug education and prevention classes. This law applies to persons convicted of possession of amyl nitrite without a prescription. Its goal is to reduce repeat drug use.

A follow-up study on the success of Proposition 36 was conducted by the University of California at Los Angeles. According to a press release dated September 23, 2004, "California's groundbreaking 'drug treatment instead of incarceration'" program produced "excellent results in its first two years of implementation." More than 66,000 people entered the program, saving the state hundreds of millions of dollars in incarceration costs. Proposition 36 could become a model for other states to follow in the ongoing fight against drug abuse.

blood vessels, a mixture of the two can cause blood pressure to drop to dangerously low levels. This can lead to a heart attack, STROKE, coma, or death.

Treatment for Habitual Users

"We really don't know exactly why the nitrites have the mental effects that make them attractive for people to use," explained Cynthia Kuhn and her coauthors in the 2003 edition of *Buzzed: The Straight Facts about the Most Used and Abused Drugs from Alcohol to Ecstasy*. Nitrites, in fact, are not considered addictive substances. The biggest problem for amyl nitrite abusers stems from their tendency to combine it with other drugs. Habitual nitrite sniffers are likely to benefit from drug dependency treatment programs, including counseling.

Education and knowledge regarding the dangers of inhaling nitrites is a key to preventing their use. Studies show that most youths who try drugs do so because of peer pressure. Therefore, it is important that young people not only resist the pressure, but try to persuade friends who are using amyl nitrite—or abusing any drug—to get help.

Consequences

Studies and surveys in the United States and the United Kingdom show that people who use poppers generally tend to underperform academically and are less likely to graduate from high school. Historical trends show that dropouts are more likely to end up with low-paying jobs or to become part of the welfare system. In addition, a number of studies show that people who abuse drugs are much more prone to illness, particularly viruses and other infections. Unlike other inhalants, amyl nitrite is abused primarily because it is believed to enhance sexual pleasure and performance through loss of inhibition. Users often engage in unsafe sex and are at a much greater risk for contracting sexually transmitted diseases, including HIV.

stroke: a loss of feeling, consciousness, or movement caused by the breaking or blocking of a blood vessel in the brain

The Law

Laws governing the possession, use, or sale of nitrites can seem very confusing. Not all nitrites are considered drugs. In fact, of all the nitrites used as inhalants, only amyl nitrite is classified as a drug. In the United States, the only legal way to get amyl nitrite is by prescription. The other nitrites fall into a different category. These substances are not considered foods or drugs, and this is where the legal complexities begin.

The FDA made the possession, use, or sale of amyl nitrite without a prescription illegal in the United States in 1969. In 1988, the U.S. Consumer Products Safety Commission banned the sale of butyl nitrite, and the law was amended, or changed, in 1990 to include a broader range of nitrites. The laws regarding the possession, use, or sale of poppers in the United States vary from state to state but usually involve prison terms and stiff fines.

Still, some dishonest manufacturers have found ways to dodge the laws covering amyl and butyl nitrites. They simply make slight alterations to the chemical compounds that bind to the nitrites. One example of an altered popper is a substance called cyclohexyl nitrite, commonly sold in drug paraphernalia or "head" shops and adult bookstores as a head cleaner for VCRs. Researchers point out that regardless of the legal status, the dangers of using any type of nitrite remain the same.

In the United Kingdom, the laws concerning nitrites are somewhat different. The Medicines Act (1968) states that it is illegal to sell amyl nitrite without a prescription. However, possession or use of amyl nitrite without a prescription is not a crime. Most other nitrites sold as poppers are not covered by the Medicines Act, since distributors market them as room deodorizers and liquid incense, not medicines. Therefore, the sale, possession, and use of butyl and isobutyl nitrites are not restricted in any way under British law.

For More Information

Books

Gahlinger, Paul M. *Illegal Drugs: A Complete Guide to Their History, Chemistry, Use, and Abuse.* Las Vegas, NV: Sagebrush Press, 2001.

Kuhn, Cynthia, Scott Swartzwelder, Wilkie Wilson, et al. *Buzzed: The Straight Facts about the Most Used and Abused Drugs from Alcohol to Ecstasy,* 2nd ed. New York: W. W. Norton, 2003.

Merriam-Webster's Collegiate Dictionary. 11th edition. Springfield, MA: Merriam-Webster, Inc., 2003.

Monroe, Judy. *Inhalant Drug Dangers.* Berkeley Heights, NJ: Enslow Publishers, Inc., 2002.

Schull, Patricia Dwyer. *Nursing Spectrum Drug Handbook.* King of Prussia, PA: Nursing Spectrum, 2005.

Sherry, Clifford. *Inhalants.* New York: Rosen Publishing Group, 1994.

Weil, Andrew, and Winifred Rosen. *From Chocolate to Morphine.* New York: Houghton Mifflin, 1993, rev. 2004.

Periodicals

"Antidotes to Chemical Weapons Distributed." *Seattle Post-Intelligencer* (July 14, 2004): p. A3.

Dales, Georgie. "Life Stories: What I Learned in Chemistry." *Independent Sunday* (April 20, 2003): p. 3.

Elliott, Stuart. "The Media Business: Advertising—Why Poppers Can Be Found in the Freezer Aisle, and Does New York Have an Official Uniform?" *New York Times* (May 26, 1998).

Hodgkinson, Neville. "'Poppers' Face New Legal Curb." *Sunday Times* (June 12, 1994): p. 5.

Jones, Tobias. "Real People: Uppers and Downers . . . Some Clubbers Will Try Just about Anything." *Independent Sunday* (January 31, 1999): p. 2.

Lyttle, John. "Try and Ban Them If You Like, But You Won't Change the Undeniable Fact: Poppers Rule." *Independent* (January 17, 1997): p. 4.

McGarvey, E. L., and others. "Adolescent Inhalant Abuse: Environments of Use." *American Journal of Drug and Alcohol Abuse* (November, 1999): pp. 731-741.

"Men Combining Viagra, Illicit Drugs." *Alcoholism & Drug Abuse Weekly* (September 3, 2001): p. 8.

Meyerhoff, Michael K. "Facts about Inhalant Abuse." *Pediatrics for Parents* (July, 2001): p. 9.

O'Neal, Shelby. "Inhalant Abuse: The Neglected Problem—Inhalants Are Seen by Children and Adolescents as an Easy Way to Achieve Up to a Two-Hour High." *Alcoholism & Addiction Magazine* (November, 1989): p. 39.

Scheller, Melanie. "Inhalants—Don't Let Them Take Your Breath Away." *Current Health 2: A Weekly Reader Publication* (September, 2000): p. 16.

Schwartz, Richard H. "When to Suspect Inhalant Abuse." *Patient Care* (May 30, 1989): p. 39.

"Sex, Drugs, and Rock 'n' Roll." *Independent* (January 28, 1996): p. 8.

Stalnikowicz, Ruth, and others. "Aphrodisiac Drug-Induced Hemolysis." *Journal of Toxicology: Clinical Toxicology* (April 2004): p. 313.

Stapleton, Stephanie. "'Household High' Found to Be Growing Threat to Teen Health." *American Medical News* (April 10, 2000): p. 32.

Travis, Alan. "Dance Drug Ecstasy Falls Out of Favor as Young Clubbers Find New Highs." *Guardian* (December 5, 2003): p. 3.

Web Sites

"Amyl Nitrite." *WholeHealthMD*. http://www.wholehealthmd.com/ (accessed June 16, 2005).

California Proposition 36: The Official Home Page of the Substance Abuse and Crime Prevention Act of 2000. http://prop36.org/ (accessed June 16, 2005).

"Information for Health Professionals Data Sheet: Amyl Nitrite." *Medsafe: New Zealand Medicines and Medical Devices Safety Authority.* http://www.medsafe.govt.nz/ (accessed June 16, 2005).

James, John S. "Poppers, Some Other Drugs, May Increase HIV Infection Risk." *AIDS Treatment News Archive.* http://www.aids.org/ (accessed June 16, 2005).

Johnston, Lloyd. "Overall Teen Drug Use Continues Gradual Decline, but Use of Inhalants Rises." *Monitoring the Future* (press release). http://www.monitoringthefuture.org/ (accessed June 16, 2005).

National Institute on Drug Abuse. http://www.nida.nih.gov/ and http://www.drugabuse.gov (both accessed June 16, 2005).

See also: Inhalants

Antidepressants

Official Drug Name: Amitriptyline (amm-uh-TRIP-tuh-leen; Elavil), bupropion (byoo-PROH-pee-on; Wellbutrin), citalo-pram (sye-TAL-oh-pram; Celexa), clomi-pramine (kloh-MIPP-ruh-meen; Anafranil), escitalopram (EE-sye-TAL-oh-pram; Lexapro), fluoxetine (flu-AKS-uh-teen; Prozac), imipramine (ih-MIPP-ruh-meen; Tofranil), mirtazapine (murr-TAZ-uh-peen; Remeron), paroxetine (purr-OKS-uh-teen; Paxil), phenelzine (FENN-uhl-zeen; Nardil), sertraline (SURR-truh-leen; Zoloft), venlafaxine (venn-luh-FAKS-een; Effexor). The twelve drugs listed here are a sampling of the various types of antidepressants in use as of 2005.
Also Known As: Happy pills
Drug Classifications: Not scheduled, psychotherapeutic drugs with "black box" warnings

What Kind of Drug Is It?

Antidepressant drugs are used to relieve the symptoms of depression and anxiety. Depression is a mood disorder that causes people to have feelings of overwhelming and lasting hopelessness, sadness, despair, and self-blame. The condition can also bring on changes in sleeping and eating habits, a loss of pleasure, feelings of apathy, and even suicidal thoughts. Anxiety is a disorder that causes feelings of being extremely overwhelmed, restless, fearful, and worried. Symptoms of anxiety include loss of sleep, dizziness, sweating, and shaking, among others.

Antidepressants play an important role in the treatment of depression and anxiety. They help to rebalance brain chemistry so the symptoms of depression and anxiety are alleviated. A large number of people take antidepressants. Richard Jerome, writing in *People,* reported that "133 million prescriptions for antidepressants were written in 2002" in the United States alone.

Overview

Depression is a condition that affects the way people feel, think, and act. "Ten to 20 percent of adults in the United States experience depression at some point in their lifetime," noted Adrienne Z. Ables and Otis L. Baughman III in an article for the journal *American Family Physician.*

Sometimes depressive episodes are sparked by an especially upsetting event in life such as the death of a loved one, the breakup of a relationship, a change in jobs, separation from friends or family, or a severe illness. Because depression seems to run in families, scientists are investigating possible biological causes for the condition. The authors of "Depression: Help Is at Hand," a publication of the Royal College of Psychiatrists (RCP), stated that people who have a parent who has become severely depressed "are about eight times more likely to become depressed" themselves. This may be due to an abnormality in the brain involving chemical messengers called NEUROTRANSMITTERS.

neurotransmitters: substances that help spread nerve impulses from one nerve cell to another

76

Depressed people often have a hard time tracing their sadness to a particular cause. Certain medicines and even some physical illnesses such as the flu can bring on depression, so it is extremely important for people to educate themselves about its signs, symptoms, and treatments.

Symptoms of depression include:

- A long-lasting sad mood
- A change in sleep patterns—either sleeping all the time or having difficulty getting enough sleep
- A change in eating habits—some people eat more when they get depressed, others stop eating altogether and begin losing significant amounts of weight
- A loss of interest in activities or hobbies that used to bring pleasure
- Self-destructive thoughts or actions
- Difficulty making decisions
- A loss of confidence
- Increased irritability
- Problems with school or work
- Problems with friends or family members
- A feeling of hopelessness, as if things will never be any better.

Depression occurs in people of all ages, from small children to the elderly. "In contrast to the normal emotional experiences of sadness, loss, or passing mood states, depression is extreme and persistent and can interfere significantly with an individual's ability to function," stated the authors of the "Depression Research" page of the *National Institute of Mental Health* (NIMH) Web site.

A study sponsored by the World Health Organization and the World Bank is cited in "Depression Research." The study noted that major depression was found "to be the leading cause of disability in the United States and worldwide." Regardless of what triggers their depression, those who suffer from it require medical assistance. This assistance might include PSYCHOTHERAPY, medication, or a combination of both. Many depressed people from all age groups have responded well to treatment.

Depression is common among people who have experienced a life-threatening event, such as these teenagers who grieved following the shootings at Columbine High School in 1999. Counselors are often brought in to help students deal with the loss of friends when a tragedy occurs. *AP/Wide World Photos.*

psychotherapy: the treatment of emotional problems by a trained therapist using a variety of techniques to improve a patient's outlook on life

Depression Statistics

Doctors and research scientists continuously seek to learn more about depression. They have learned that:

- Nearly 10 percent of the adult population in the United States suffers from a depressive illness. That is about 19 million Americans over the age of eighteen.
- One in five children and adolescents in the United States suffers from some kind of emotional problem that affects his or her daily life.
- As of 2004, doctors were writing about 11 million prescriptions for antidepressants to teenagers and children each year.
- More women than men have been diagnosed with depression, but that does not necessarily mean that more women are depressed than men. Researchers suggest that women are just more likely to seek help than men.

Anxiety, which is often associated with depression, can also be helped by medication. Severe anxiety can result in PANIC ATTACKS. These attacks can make a person feel like he or she is dying. They cause rapid heartbeat, tightness in the chest, shaking, shortness of breath, and dizziness. Antidepressants can help a person focus on dealing with his or her fears before an attack occurs, and the drugs can alleviate the physical symptoms of an attack.

An Accidental Find

Chemists seem to have stumbled upon drugs with antidepressive effects while working on treatments for other medical problems. The very first antidepressants, iproniazid (sold under the brand name Marsilid) and imipramine (sold under the brand name Tofranil), were developed in the 1950s. Since then, great strides have been made in understanding how the human brain works. These strides contributed to the creation of the four main types of antidepressant drugs known as of 2005: 1) tricyclics, 2) monoamine oxidase inhibitors (MAOIs), 3) selective serotonin reuptake inhibitors (SSRIs), and 4) "others," including serotonin and norepinephrine reuptake inhibitors (SNRIs). All of these drugs get their names from the way they act on chemicals called neurotransmitters located in the human brain.

Tricyclics and MAOIs were available years before the SSRIs came on the scene. Richard DeGrandpre, writing in *Nation,* stated that "SSRIs have not been clinically proven to be more effective" than the older tricyclics. The SSRIs gained a reputation for safety because they are generally less toxic, or harmful to the body, when taken in overdoses. In normal doses, however, both the new and the old classes of antidepressants have been shown to relieve the symptoms of depression in some patients. Because each patient will respond differently to the various antidepressants, physicians may try several different kinds—or even combine one with another—in the search for the most effective treatment for a particular patient.

panic attacks: unexpected episodes of severe anxiety that can cause physical symptoms such as shortness of breath, dizziness, sweating, and shaking

Main types of antidepressants			
Tricyclics (try-SICK-licks)	**MAOIs (monoamine oxidase inhibitors)**	**SSRIs (selective serotonin reuptake inhibitors)**	**Others, including SNRIs (serotonin and norepinephrine reuptake inhibitors)**
amitriptyline (amm-uh-TRIP-tuh-leen; Elavil)	mirtazapine (murr-TAZ-uh-peen; Remeron)	citalopram (sye-TAL-oh-pram; Celexa)	bupropion (byoo-PROH-pee-on; Wellbutrin)
clomipramine (kloh-MIPP-ruh-meen; Anafranil)	phenelzine (FENN-uhl-zeen; Nardil)	escitalopram (EE-sye-TAL-oh-pram; Lexapro)	venlafaxine (venn-luh-FAKS-een; Effexor)
imipramine (ih-MIPP-ruh-meen; Tofranil)		fluoxetine (flu-AKS-uh-teen; Prozac)	
		paroxetine (purr-OKS-uh-teen; Paxil)	
		sertraline (SURR-truh-leen; Zoloft)	

SOURCE: Prepared by Barbara C. Bigelow for Thomson Gale, 2005.

The Ultimate Problem Solver?

The most popular antidepressants are the SSRIs. Prozac was the first SSRI approved for use in the treatment of depression. It became available in 1987, received extensive coverage in the media, and within a few years became a household name. Some people were under the impression that Prozac was the ultimate problem solver—a sort of "happy pill" that gave everyone who took it a more positive outlook on life. It had no reported side effects and was even thought to help in weight loss. What most people failed to realize, however, is that antidepressants have no psychological effects on people who don't suffer from depression. They only help depressed patients reach a normal level of functioning.

Still, the market for antidepressants grew wildly in the 1990s and early 2000s. According to *The Pill Book,* seven of the top fifty prescriptions written by U.S. doctors in 2003 were for antidepressants. Associated Press reporter Bruce Smith, as recorded on the *ABC News* Web site, noted that 32.7 million prescriptions for Zoloft, another SSRI, were written that year. This made Zoloft the most widely prescribed antidepressant in the United States.

What Is It Made Of?

A variety of substances have antidepressant actions. The antidepressants available in the United States are classified in two main ways: 1) by their chemical structure, as in the case of tricyclics (three-ring structure), or 2) by their actions on neurotransmitters, as in the case of MAOIs, SSRIs, and SNRIs. Tricyclics work to increase the levels of the neurotransmitters NOREPINEPHRINE and SEROTONIN in the

norepinephrine: pronounced nor-epp-ih-NEFF-run; a natural stimulant produced by the human body

serotonin: a combination of carbon, hydrogen, nitrogen, and oxygen; it is found in the brain, blood, and stomach lining and acts as a neurotransmitter and blood vessel regulator

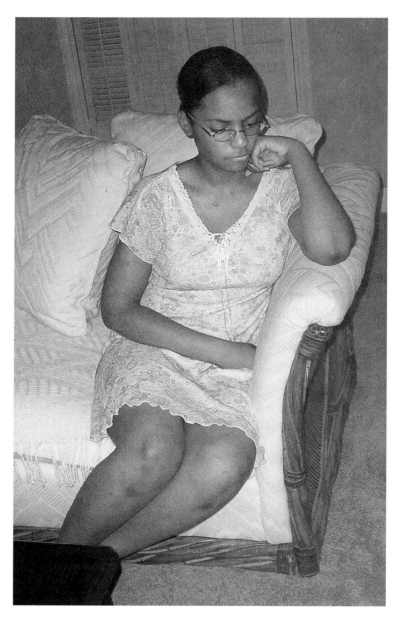

Many people experience depression at some time in their lives. Depression is a mood disorder that causes people to have feelings of overwhelming and lasting hopelessness, sadness, despair, and self-blame. *Photograph by Leitha Etheridge-Sims.*

brain. These neurotransmitters are usually at low levels in people who suffer from depression. The problem with tricyclics is that they can affect other neurotransmitters as well, causing a number of side effects. MAOIs stop the protein in the brain known as monoamine oxidase from breaking down serotonin, norepinephrine, and another neurotransmitter called dopamine after they deliver their messages to the brain. This leaves high levels of these chemicals in the brain and subsequently keeps depression at bay.

However, MAOIs also keep monoamine oxidase from destroying tyramine (found in various foods), which can cause fatal increases in blood pressure. SSRIs were specifically designed by scientists to stop the "reuptake," or reabsorption, of only serotonin in the brain, allowing levels of serotonin to build and remain high while not affecting the levels of other chemicals. They are the most prescribed forms of antidepressants because they usually have fewer side effects and interactions with other drugs. SNRIs focus on stopping the reuptake of serotonin and norepinephrine so that they both build and remain at a high level.

How Is It Taken?

Prescription antidepressants are taken orally, usually once a day, and usually in capsules or tablets. Some are available in liquid form for swallowing. It is very important that patients on antidepressants take their medications exactly as prescribed, even if the drugs do not seem to be working at first. In some cases, three to four weeks of antidepressant use may be needed before the effects of the drug can be observed.

The usual daily dose prescribed of an antidepressant can differ. For the SSRI Prozac, a patient is typically prescribed 20 to 40 milligrams per day. In higher doses, it has been used to treat OBSESSIVE-COMPULSIVE DISORDER (OCD) and the eating disorder BULIMIA. In 2002, Prozac became available in a once-a-week capsule-form that contains 90 milligrams of fluoxetine granules that are released over time. The effect of one of these capsules is equivalent to seven daily doses of 20 milligrams of Prozac.

Dosages of Zoloft, another SSRI, typically begin at 50 milligrams per day for adults and may be raised to 100 or 200 milligrams per day. When the SSRI Paxil is prescribed for depression, the initial dose is usually 20 milligrams per day. This dose may be increased to about 40 milligrams per day. Citalopram (Celexa) and escitalopram (Lexapro) are SSRIs that are gaining popularity for two reasons. First, their side effects are said to be minimal. Second, the risk of harmful interactions with other drugs is low. As of 2005, drug

obsessive-compulsive disorder (OCD): an anxiety disorder that causes people to dwell on unwanted thoughts, act on unusual urges, and perform repetitive rituals such as frequent hand washing

bulimia: pronounced bull-EEM-eeh-yuh; an eating disorder that involves long periods of bingeing on food, followed by self-induced vomiting and abuse of laxatives

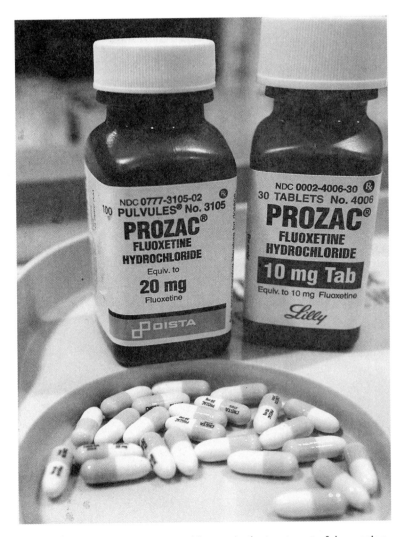

Prozac was the first SSRI approved for use in the treatment of depression.

Photo by Stephen Chernin/Getty Images.

researchers noted a definite increase in the number of prescriptions being written for these two particular antidepressants.

Are There Any Medical Reasons for Taking This Substance?

Antidepressants are used mainly to relieve the symptoms of depression, which include feelings of sadness, helplessness, and hopelessness. They may also be used to treat severe anxiety, panic attacks, POST-TRAUMATIC STRESS DISORDER (PTSD), obsessive-compulsive disorders, eating disorders, chronic pain, severe PREMENSTRUAL SYNDROME, and postpartum depression. Affecting more than one in ten new mothers, postpartum depression causes sadness, anxiety, irritability, tiredness, interrupted sleep, a loss of enjoyment or desire to do anything, and guilt over not being able to care properly for the baby.

Sometimes severely ill individuals become depressed. The symptoms of depression can have very negative effects on their recovery. STROKE patients are especially vulnerable to depression. After-stroke, or post-stroke, effects can include a loss of voluntary movement (usually on one side of the body), a loss of sensation (especially in affected limbs), weakness, and difficulty speaking. The long process of rehabilitation for stroke patients is often hampered by depression. Antidepressants have proven very effective in post-stroke patients. A positive attitude is crucial to recovery and helps patients stick to their intensive and often exhausting physical therapy schedules. Treating post-stroke depression improves the chances of the stroke patient regaining both physical strength and mental sharpness.

Usage Trends

"I think the categorical belief is that depression is something you get over rather than something you take medication for," stated Dr. Zachary N. Stowe in an interview with Laurie Tarkan for the *New York Times.* Indeed, some "four out of five people with depression will get completely better without any help," noted the authors of "Depression: Help Is at Hand." Episodes of depression frequently last for eight months to a year before going away. For some depressed people, however, the symptoms hang on even longer.

Of the one in five people with depression that does *not* go away on its own, treatment is recommended. Without help, those people are twice as likely to fall into a pattern of repeated depressive episodes. A 2003 *Time* magazine article pointed to the potential seriousness of the condition. "Untreated depression has a lifetime suicide rate of 15 percent—with still more deaths caused by related behaviors like self-medicating with alcohol and drugs."

September 11, 2001

Doctors reported that requests for antidepressants increased dramatically after the terrorist attacks of September 11, 2001, on American soil. Fear, depression, and anxiety were common among Americans after terrorists hijacked planes and flew them into the World Trade Center in New York City and the Pentagon in Washington, D.C.

post-traumatic stress disorder (PTSD): an illness that can occur after experiencing or witnessing life-threatening events, such as serious accidents, violent assaults, or terrorist attacks; symptoms include reliving the experience through nightmares and flashbacks, having problems sleeping, and feeling detached from reality

premenstrual syndrome: symptoms that occur in some women about a week before the start of their monthly period and may include irritability, fatigue, depression, and abdominal bloating

stroke: a loss of feeling, consciousness, or movement caused by the breaking or blocking of a blood vessel in the brain

Defining Depression

Depression is hard to define, and not all doctors agree on whether it is a mood disorder or the more serious definition: a disease. In his 2005 book, *Against Depression,* Peter Kramer notes that his work presents "an insistent argument that depression is a disease." In fact, he calls depression one of the worst diseases to afflict humankind.

Dr. Peter R. Breggin sees the situation differently. In his 2001 work, *The Antidepressant Fact Book,* he states that "it is a mistake to view depressed feelings or even severely depressed feelings as a 'disease.'" He continues: "Depression . . . is an emotional response to life. It is a feeling of unhappiness—a particular kind of unhappiness that involves helpless self-blame and guilt, a sense of not deserving happiness, and a loss of interest in life. . . . A human emotion or psychological state—basically, a feeling—should not be considered a 'disease' simply because it becomes extreme."

The Debate over SSRI Safety and Suicide Risks in Children and Teens

As more and more children and teens are diagnosed with depression, the effects of the drugs used to treat it must be evaluated in young people. Some experts worry that antidepressants may act differently in people under the age of eighteen because their brains are not yet fully mature. "Our knowledge of antidepressant treatments in youth, though growing substantially, remains limited when compared with what we know about treatment of depression in adults," stated the authors of the NIMH article "Antidepressant Medications for Children and Adolescents: Information for Parents and Caregivers."

According to *Christian Science Monitor* correspondent Patrik Jonsson, two separate congressional hearings revealed that the U.S. Food and Drug Administration (FDA) had "known about problems with [antidepressant] drugs since 1996, but failed to take decisive action." These "problems" included higher rates of aggression and an increase in suicidal thinking among young patients being treated with antidepressants. By 2000, even more studies had emerged "showing a possible link between hallucinations and aggression in children and teens taking Zoloft, Paxil, and Prozac," reported "FindLaw" columnist Elaine Cassel on *CNN.com.* Despite these findings, in January of 2003 the FDA approved the use of Prozac in depressed children as young as seven years old. As of 2005, only Prozac has been approved to treat depression and OCD in children. Zoloft, Luvox, and Anafranil are only approved for children for OCD. As of 2005, no other antidepressant is approved for use in children.

Treatment for Adolescents with Depression Study (TADS): To gain more information on the effects of antidepressants in young people, the NIMH spent $17 million on the Treatment for Adolescents with Depression Study (TADS), which was conducted between 2000 and 2003. More than 400 depressed adolescents were divided into groups that received varying forms of treatment. One group was treated with Prozac alone. Another group received a combination of Prozac and COGNITIVE BEHAVIORAL THERAPY (CBT), a type of psychotherapy that stresses positive thinking. A third group received CBT without the Prozac. A fourth group received only a PLACEBO.

cognitive behavioral therapy (CBT): a type of therapy that helps people recognize and change negative patterns of thinking and behavior

placebo: pronounced pluh-SEE-boh; a "sugar pill" or "dummy pill" that contains no medicine

Some antidepressants have been linked to increased suicides in users. Here, the mother (left) of a deceased teen waits to testify at a public hearing before the FDA. Her son, Jacob, committed suicide at age 14 while taking antidepressant drugs. *AP/Wide World Photos.*

The results of the study were released to the press by the NIMH in August of 2004. The participants were monitored for improvement in their depression and for trends in their suicidal thinking. The combination of medication and therapy proved the most effective in relieving the symptoms of depression. The data concerning suicidal thinking were more difficult to interpret.

The results of TADS revealed that 7 percent of adolescents receiving Prozac either attempted suicide or threatened to do so. Only 4 percent of participants in the placebo group had a suicide-related event. Still, the NIMH concluded that "it is extremely difficult to determine whether SSRI medications do or do not increase the risk of . . . suicide, especially since depression itself increases the risk for suicide." Experts believe that a larger study is needed to resolve unanswered questions.

Results Lead to "Black Box" Warnings

In 2004, the FDA examined information from more than twenty studies, including TADS, on antidepressants and adolescents. Together, the studies involved about 4,300 patients under the age of eighteen. Overall, the results mirrored the TADS findings. The rate of suicidal thinking or behavior was twice as high among

Testing New Drugs

The word *placebo* is Latin for "I shall please." Placebos, often called "sugar pills" or "dummy pills," are used in experiments that test the effectiveness of new drugs. Doctors give one group of patients regular doses of a placebo and one group of patients regular doses of the real drug that is being tested for a particular condition. Patients are not told what they have been taking until the testing period is over. After a few months, both groups are compared. A higher rate of improvement among patients in the test-drug group is good news for drug researchers. It indicates that the new drug is truly effective in treating the condition it was designed to treat.

Patients' conditions may improve for a time if they *believe* they are taking a medication that will relieve their symptoms. In the treatment of depression, an average of 35 percent of placebo-treated individuals will improve, compared with about 60 percent of SSRI-treated individuals.

adolescents taking SSRIs as it was in adolescents who were not. This prompted the FDA to announce in late 2004 that "black box" labeling of antidepressants would become mandatory. In "Antidepressant Medications for Children and Adolescents," the authors noted: "A black-box warning is the most serious type of warning in prescription drug labeling." Black box warnings for antidepressants state that the drugs may be linked with an increased risk of suicidal thinking or behavior. On its Web site, the FDA specifies the language to be used on the black box warnings. Part of the standard warning follows:

> Antidepressants increased the risk of suicidal thinking and behavior (suicidality) in short-term studies in children and adolescents with Major Depressive Disorder (MDD) and other psychiatric disorders. Anyone considering the use of [drug name] or any other antidepressant in a child or adolescent must balance this risk with the clinical need. Patients who are started on therapy should be observed closely for clinical worsening, suicidality, or unusual changes in behavior. Families and caregivers should be advised of the need for close observation and communication with the prescriber.

According to *MSNBC.com*, antidepressant use among children and teens has declined by about 10 percent since the information on suicide risks was released.

Effects on the Body

Neurotransmitters, such as serotonin and norepinephrine, are chemical substances that transmit information from one nerve to another. By the middle of the twentieth century, researchers had found that depressed people seemed to have lower concentrations of neurotransmitters coating the nerve endings in their brains. Antidepressants help stop the reuptake of these chemical substances in the brain, creating a kind of bath of neurotransmitters like serotonin for the nerve endings to soak in. Raising the concentration of neurotransmitters in the brains of depressed individuals works to reduce the symptoms of their depression.

The actions of antidepressants on the brain are not fully understood, but scientists are learning more about them every day. Studies show little difference in the effectiveness of the various antidepressants, but some individual patients appear to do better on one drug than another. In the search for the most effective drug for a particular patient, a physician may prescribe various antidepressant drugs or even try some in combination.

General side effects of antidepressants can include stomach upset, agitation, anxiety, dizziness, INSOMNIA, and a dry mouth (which usually increases a user's thirst). Since SSRIs were discovered, the older MAOIs are prescribed less often for the treatment of depression. Side effects of MAOIs can be severe and include a sudden elevation of blood pressure. Tricyclics may cause dryness of the mouth and eyes. A dry mouth can lead to the formation of dental cavities, and dry eyes can result in blurred vision. Use of tricyclics may also result in reduced urine output, constipation, and weight gain. Older patients are cautioned against tricyclic use because the drugs can disrupt the normal rhythm of the heartbeat. SNRIs should not be used by people with heart problems.

News from Around the Globe

Depression and anxiety are common problems throughout the world. Were you aware that:

- The National Institute on Mental Health in England (NIMHE) reported that about 1 in every 100 deaths in the United Kingdom is a suicide.
- Canada's labeling of SSRIs carries an additional warning of a potential increase in hostility, aggression, and "harm to others." A reference to harming others does not appear on the black box warnings of SSRIs in the United States, however.

The Question of Addiction

Until the early 2000s, antidepressants were not believed to cause addiction in users. A traditional feature of addictive substances is the "HIGH" or "buzz" they cause in users. "Antidepressants will not make you high," stated Andrew Weil and Winifred Rosen in *From Chocolate to Morphine.*

Ables and Baughman mentioned in 2003 that some degree of WITHDRAWAL occurs with all antidepressants. This contradicts the belief that antidepressants are not addictive. The withdrawal symptoms, which are usually mild, begin about a week after the antidepressant medication is stopped. They include dizziness, nausea, headache, and flu-like symptoms, but agitation and even panic attacks may occur. Withdrawal symptoms usually end within three weeks for SSRIs. However, "withdrawal from paroxetine [SSRI Paxil]," explained Ables and Baughman, "was shown to cause more severe symptoms that may occur more quickly, even after the second missed dose."

insomnia: difficulty falling asleep or an inability to sleep

high: drug-induced feelings ranging from excitement and joy to extreme grogginess

withdrawal: the process of gradually cutting back on the amount of a drug being taken until it is discontinued entirely; also the accompanying physiological effects of terminating use of an addictive drug

Zoloft on Trial

Christopher Pittman threatened suicide and was hospitalized after his parents' final breakup in 2001. Pittman's mother had first left home when Pittman was just two years old. His parents' repeated attempts to get back together failed. After hearing that their relationship was really over, Pittman, then twelve years old, became desperate and ran away from his Florida home. After he was found, he spent a couple of weeks in a psychiatric hospital and was diagnosed with depression and defiant behavior. Doctors put him on Paxil, an SSRI, briefly. Days later he was prescribed Zoloft, a different SSRI. Zoloft was the most widely used antidepressant for both adults and teens in the United States at that time.

Pittman went to live with his father's parents in South Carolina later in 2001. He was there for only a matter of weeks, and life seemed to be going well for him. Then, one day that November, Pittman and his

grandfather had a serious argument. They fought about some trouble that Pittman had caused on his school bus. Pittman was told that he might have to return to his father's home in Florida because of the incident. That night, the twelve-year-old boy shot his grandparents to death in their bed, set their home on fire, and drove away in their car with his dog. Pittman's lawyers argued that "the killings occurred for a reason beyond the boy's control—a reaction to the antidepressant Zoloft," noted Barry Meier in the *New York Times*. "Such defenses," Meier continued, have been used in the past but "have rarely succeeded."

Pittman's case did not go to trial until three years after the tragic incident. While in jail awaiting his trial, Pittman repeatedly claimed that he loved his grandparents. His own father even came to his defense, stating that the boy had always been especially

Researchers in the United Kingdom noted similar findings. According to the Royal College of Psychiatrists, "up to a third of people who stop SSRIs and SNRIs have withdrawal symptoms. These include: stomach upsets, flu-like symptoms, anxiety, dizziness, vivid dreams at night, and sensations in the body that feel like electric shocks." These symptoms are more often associated with paroxetine (sold under the brand name Paxil in the United States and Seroxat in the United Kingdom) and venlafaxine (sold under the brand name Effexor in the United States and Efexor in the United Kingdom) than any other SSRIs and SNRIs. Research continues on the still-baffling question of addiction and withdrawal issues among antidepressant users.

Reactions with Other Drugs or Substances

Anyone prescribed an antidepressant should consult with a physician before taking any other drug, including over-the-counter

Defense attorney Paul Waldner (left) tries to comfort his client, Christopher Pittman, who was on trial for murdering his grandparents. *AP/Wide World Photos.*

close to the couple. Pittman told police that on the night of the murders, he had heard voices urging him to kill his grandparents. Those voices in his head, claimed defense lawyers, were caused by the Zoloft, and possibly even the Paxil, he had been taking for depression.

The so-called "Zoloft defense" did not work for Christopher Pittman. On February 15, 2005, he was sentenced to thirty years in prison for the murders of his grandparents.

The Pittman case fueled the growing debate about the safety of antidepressants in children and teens. Between 2001 and 2004, the FDA stepped up its investigations into the effects of antidepressants on patients under the age of eighteen. In June of 2003, the FDA recommended against prescribing Paxil (the first medication prescribed by Pittman's doctors) for depression in children and adolescents.

medications. Patients taking MAOIs must avoid certain foods such as aged meats, cheeses, and pickles because they contain tyramine, which can cause harmful reactions when combined with MAOIs. These foods should not be consumed until well after a person stops taking the drug.

It is important to know that the effects of alcohol are greatly increased when combined with antidepressants. In addition, combining large amounts of caffeine with antidepressants may intensify the jitters and agitation that sometimes accompany depression.

The reactions of RECREATIONAL DRUGS with antidepressants are unpredictable and possibly very dangerous. The symptoms of depression are often intensified by ILLICIT drug use. To help avoid problems, it is important that patients taking antidepressants stick to their prescribed dosage and stay away from other drugs, unless prescribed by a physician. In addition, the effectiveness of a drug can only be measured when the prescription is followed accurately.

recreational drugs: drugs used solely to achieve a high, not to treat a medical condition

illicit: unlawful

Alternatives to Medicine

Antidepressants are believed to help relieve the symptoms of depression, but there are other things depressed people can do to feel better. Among these are:

- Talking with trusted friends, family members, and counselors
- Identifying and solving the problem that may have caused the depression in the first place
- Getting regular exercise
- Eating well
- Staying away from alcohol and other depressants
- Practicing relaxation techniques
- Setting time aside for enjoyable activities or hobbies

Treatment for Habitual Users

Antidepressants are not abused in the traditional sense. This means that they are not taken by users to get high. If antidepressant drug therapy is discontinued, it should be done under a doctor's care using the "step-down method" in order to reduce the risk of side effects. This method involves gradually lowering the dose of the drug until the patient is weaned off it entirely.

Consequences

Depression and anxiety can interfere with a person's happiness, success, and relationships. The symptoms of depression and anxiety should not be ignored. About 80 percent of people with depression respond very positively to treatment, but that leaves a significant number—the other 20 percent—without help. Thus, an important goal of NIMH research is to advance the development of more effective treatments for depression, especially those "hard-to-treat" forms that don't respond well to currently available medications and/or counseling.

Major depression can occur just once in a person's lifetime, but it is usually recurring. Depressive episodes will interfere with the ability to work, eat, sleep, concentrate, and take pleasure in formerly enjoyed activities. Treatment for depression is often a long-term process, but it can help those with the condition lead fuller and happier lives.

Taking antidepressants for depression and/or anxiety does have consequences. They all have side effects, some dangerous, that need to be monitored. A number of people believe that taking drugs for depression and/or anxiety is not necessary. In fact, they claim, it can even be harmful. In 2005, actor Tom Cruise spoke out against the use of antidepressants, citing vitamins and exercise as better alternatives. However, others state that their lives have greatly improved since they started taking antidepressants.

The Law

Antidepressants are only available by prescription. It is illegal for people to take drugs that have not been prescribed for them. It is also illegal for patients to share prescribed drugs with other people.

Since users of antidepressants do not achieve a high with these drugs (as may occur with the STIMULANT drugs AMPHETAMINES and other drugs of abuse), they are rarely abused. No market for the illegal sale of antidepressants has been reported.

stimulant: a substance that increases the activity of a living organism or one of its parts

amphetamines: stimulant drugs that increase mental alertness, reduce appetite, and help keep users awake

For More Information

Books

Appleton, William S. *Prozac and the New Antidepressants.* New York: Plume, 2000.

Breggin, Peter R. *The Antidepressant Fact Book.* Cambridge, MA: Perseus, 2001.

Katzung, Bertrum G. *Basic and Clinical Pharmacology.* New York: Lange Medical Books/McGraw-Hill, 2001.

Kramer, Peter. *Against Depression.* New York: Viking, 2005.

Morrison, Andrew L. *The Antidepressant Sourcebook.* New York: Broadway Books, 1999.

Schull, Patricia Dwyer. *Nursing Spectrum Drug Handbook.* King of Prussia, PA: Nursing Spectrum, 2005.

Silverman, Harold M. *The Pill Book,* 11th ed. New York: Bantam, 2004.

Weil, Andrew, and Winifred Rosen. *From Chocolate to Morphine.* New York: Houghton Mifflin, 1993, rev. 2004.

Periodicals

Ables, Adrienne Z., and Otis L. Baughman III. "Antidepressants: Update on New Agents and Indications." *American Family Physician* (February 1, 2003): pp. 547-554.

Cheakalos, Christina. "A Big Letdown?" *People* (May 12, 2003): pp. 191-192.

DeGrandpre, Richard. "Trouble in Prozac Nation." *Nation* (January 5, 2004): pp. 6-7.

Dewan, Shaila, and Barry Meier. "Boy Who Took Antidepressants Is Convicted in Killings." *New York Times* (February 16, 2005).

Harris, Gardiner. "FDA Panel Urges Stronger Warning on Antidepressants." *New York Times* (September 15, 2004).

Jerome, Richard. "The Prozac Kids." *People* (July 28, 2003): pp. 46-49.

Jonsson, Patrik. "'Zoloft Defense' Tests Whether Pills Are Guilty." *Christian Science Monitor* (February 11, 2005).

"Medicating Young Minds." *Time* (November 3, 2003): p. 48.

Meier, Barry. "A Drug on Trial." *New York Times* (August 23, 2004).

"Post-Stroke Depression Impedes Recovery." *New England Journal of Medicine Health News* (September, 2000).

"Prescription for Suicide?" *Time* (February 9, 2004): pp. 59-60.

Schuster, Mark A. "A National Survey of Stress Reactions after the September 11, 2001, Terrorist Attacks." *New England Journal of Medicine* (November 15, 2001).

Shute, Nancy. "Teens, Drugs, and Sadness." *U.S. News & World Report* (August 30, 2004): pp. 36, 38.

Tarkan, Laurie. "Dealing with Depression and the Perils of Pregnancy." *New York Times* (January 13, 2004).

Web Sites

"Antidepressant Eases Late-Life Anxiety Disorders." *Yahoo! News.* http:// news.yahoo.com (accessed January 5, 2005).

"Antidepressant Medications for Children and Adolescents: Information for Parents and Caregivers." *National Institute of Mental Health.* http://www.nimh.nih.gov/healthinformation/antidepressant_child.cfm (accessed June 30, 2005).

"Antidepressants." *Royal College of Psychiatrists.* http://www.rcpsych.ac.uk/ info/factsheets/pfacanti.asp (accessed June 30, 2005).

Cassel, Elaine. "Did Zoloft Make Him Do It?" *CNN.com,* February 7, 2005. http://www.cnn.com/2005/LAW/02/07/cassel.pittman/index.html (accessed June 30, 2005).

"Changing Minds." *Royal College of Psychiatrists.* http://www.rcpsych.ac.uk/ campaigns/cminds/depression.htm (accessed June 30, 2005).

"Class Suicidality Labeling Language for Antidepressants." *U.S. Food and Drug Administration, Center for Drug Evaluation and Research.* http:// www.fda.gov/cder/drug/antidepressants/PI_template.pdf (accessed June 26, 2005).

Collins, Jeffrey. "Dad Cites Boy's Antidepressants in Deaths." *ABC News,* December 5, 2004. http://abcnews.go.com/Health/wireStory?id= 303933&CMP=OTC-RSSFeeds0312 (accessed June 16, 2004).

"Combination Treatment Most Effective in Adolescents with Depression" (press release). *National Institute of Mental Health.* http:// www.nimh.nih.gov/press/prtads.cfm (accessed June 16, 2005).

"Depression." *National Institute of Mental Health.* http://www.nimh.nih.gov/ publicat/depression.cfm (accessed June 16, 2005).

"Depression: Help Is at Hand." *Royal College of Psychiatrists.* http:// www.rcpsych.ac.uk/info/help/dep/index.asp (accessed June 30, 2005).

"Depression Research." *National Institute of Mental Health.* http:// www.nimh.nih.gov/publicat/depresfact.cfm (accessed June 30, 2005).

"Fewer Kids Taking Antidepressants." *MSNBC.com,* February 1, 2005. http://www.msnbc.msn.com/id/6894036 (accessed June 16, 2005).

"NIMH Research on Treatment for Adolescents with Depression Study (TADS): Combination Treatment Most Effective in Adolescents with Depression." *National Institute of Mental Health.* http://www.nimh. nih.gov/healthinformation/tads.cfm (accessed June 16, 2005).

"ParentsMedGuide—The Use of Medication in Treating Childhood and Adolescent Depression: Information for Patients and Families." *Parents-MedGuide.org.* http://www.parentsmedguide.org/parentsmedguide.htm (accessed June 30, 2005).

Polk, Jim. "Doctor: Boy Not Responsible for Killing Grandparents." *CNN.com,* February 9, 2005. http://www.cnn.com/2005/LAW/02/08/zoloft.trial/index.html (accessed June 30, 2005).

Smith, Bruce. "Teen Gets 30 Years in Zoloft Murder Case." *ABC News,* February 15, 2005. http://abcnews.go.com/US/wireStory?id=502403 (accessed June 16, 2005).

See also: Herbal drugs

Barbiturates

Official Drug Name: Amobarbital (AMM-oh-BAR-bit-al; Amytal), aprobarbital (AH-pro-BAR-bit-al; Alurate), barbital (BAR-bit-al; Veronal), butabarbital (BYOOT-uh-BAR-bit-al; Butisol), butalbital (byoo-TAHL-bit-al; Fioricet and Fiorinal), mephobarbital (MEFF-oh-BAR-bit-al; Mebaral), pentobarbital (PENT-oh-BAR-bit-al; Nembutal), phenobarbital (FEEN-oh-BAR-bit-al; Luminal), secobarbital (SEK-oh-BAR-bit-al; Seconal), secobarbital with amobarbital (Tuinal), thiopental (THY-oh-PENN-tal; Pentothal).

Also Known As: Barbs, downers, and sleeping pills (general names). Certain barbiturates have their own street names, often based on the color of the pill: blues or blue dolls for Amytal; purple hearts for Luminal; rainbows for Tuinal; reds, red birds, or red devils for Seconal; yellows or yellow jackets for Nembutal.

Drug Classifications: Schedule II, III, IV; depressant

What Kind of Drug Is It?

Barbiturates (pronounced bar-BIH-chuh-rits) are drugs that act as DEPRESSANTS and are used as SEDATIVES or sleeping pills. Because they are depressants, they are often called "downers." According to Lawrence Clayton in *Barbiturates and Other Depressants*, "Any depressant will kill if taken in a large enough quantity." Accidental overdose can occur quite easily among barbiturate users.

The effects of barbiturates are very similar to those of alcohol and include increased feelings of relaxation, sleepiness, and a decrease in INHIBITIONS. Barbiturates are habit-forming drugs and should not be used on an everyday basis. They can cause depression in high doses and addiction when taken over a long period of time.

Overview

Barbiturates have an extremely high potential for abuse. Ever since their introduction in the early 1900s, barbiturates have been considered addictive drugs. Barbiturates slow down both the mind and the body. In his book *A Brief History of Drugs: From the Stone Age to the Stoned Age,* Antonio Escohotado pointed to their "high capacity to produce numbness" by putting the user in a state somewhere between drunkenness and sleep. Aside from those effects, he continued, is their "almost inevitable ability to kill in high doses: a detail that converted these drugs into the most common means of committing suicide" from the 1940s through the 1960s.

Discovered in the 1860s

The story of barbiturates began "when a chemist combined animal urine and acid from apples," explained Clayton. That chemist was German professor and future Nobel prizewinner Adolf von Baeyer (1835–1917). The substance he created became known as barbituric (bar-bih-CHUR-ik) acid. It received its name because Baeyer first produced it on St. Barbara's Day (a day of religious recognition observed each year on December 4) of 1863.

Following Baeyer's discovery, two German researchers, Dr. Joseph von Mering (1849–1908) and Nobel prizewinner Emil Hermann

depressants: substances that slow down the activity of an organism or one of its parts

sedatives: drugs used to treat anxiety and calm people down

inhibitions: inner thoughts that keep people from engaging in certain activities

Fischer (1852–1919), produced barbital, the first barbiturate. Barbiturates are compounds derived from barbituric acid. Doctors recognized barbital's sleep-enhancing effects as far back as 1882. More than twenty years later, in 1903, barbital was marketed as a sleeping pill under the brand name Veronal. The second barbiturate, phenobarbital, arrived on the scene in 1912 under the name Luminal. Since then, several thousand barbituric acid-type drugs have been SYNTHESIZED. At the beginning of the twenty-first century, only about twelve were still being used.

Barbiturates were found to reduce the activity of nerves that control emotions and bodily functions such as breathing. Because of the drugs' soothing effects, they were commonly prescribed as sedatives for nearly fifty years. Other uses include EPILEPSY treatment and anesthesia before surgery.

Nobel prizewinner Emil Hermann Fischer produced barbital, the first barbiturate. *Photo courtesy of the Library of Congress.*

Intoxicating Effects Lead to Abuse

During the 1930s, many Americans received barbiturate prescriptions to help them sleep or relax. Barbiturates quickly gained a reputation as an intoxicant, a substance that makes users seem drunk. People began taking barbiturates as recreational drugs. They also began the dangerous practice of combining the pills with alcohol to increase the intoxication.

The 1938 Food, Drug, and Cosmetic Act gave authority over drug production to the U.S. Food and Drug Administration (FDA). The federal agency used those powers to restrict access to drugs that had a potential for abuse or misuse. The use of barbiturates without a medical doctor's prescription became illegal in the United States. But that didn't keep the drugs from becoming more and more popular throughout the 1940s.

At that time, researchers in the United States and the United Kingdom began noticing a disturbing trend. Over the years, the production of barbiturates had grown from thousands to millions of doses per year. Higher rates of barbiturate production and consumption seemed to coincide with a growing number of deaths from barbiturate poisoning. As late as 1964, Joel Fort, author of "The Problem of Barbiturates in the United States of America," argued

synthesized: made in a laboratory

epilepsy: a disorder involving the misfiring of electrical impulses in the brain, sometimes resulting in seizures and loss of consciousness

Prescription Abuse

In 1948, the Supreme Court of the United States gave the Food and Drug Administration (FDA) permission to investigate pharmacies' records of barbiturate prescriptions. The results showed a shocking pattern of abuse. In one case a single prescription for barbiturates was refilled sixty-one times. The last three of those refills were approved *after* the patient had already died from a barbiturate overdose. In another incident, more than 180,000 barbiturates simply disappeared from a Tennessee drug store. Records indicated that drug manufacturers had sent the pills to the store, but the staff at the store was unable to explain where they went.

Soon after these discoveries were made public, pharmacies began complying with laws regarding the sale and refill of prescription barbiturates. Illegal transactions made by pharmacists, drug store owners, and drug store employees dropped dramatically. This led to the growth of a black market—a market in which barbiturates are supplied and sold illegally—beginning in the 1960s.

against the wide availability of barbiturates. "Despite conclusive evidence to the contrary," he wrote, "many physicians in the United States appear to think and act as though barbiturates are completely harmless drugs that can be prescribed in unlimited quantities." His report was prepared for the United Nations Office on Drugs and Crime.

Downers and Uppers

The pairing of barbiturates with AMPHETAMINES became a significant problem throughout the United States in the 1940s and 1950s. It all began when record numbers of people started taking barbiturates to help them sleep at night. To counteract the grogginess and lack of energy they suffered the next morning, users would take amphetamines to help them wake up. Amphetamines are STIMULANTS or "uppers." At night, users still "up" from an amphetamine HIGH would take "downers," or barbiturates, to rid themselves of their extra energy and get to sleep. The next day the drug-taking cycle would start again. The regular use of barbiturates with amphetamines was so widespread by the 1950s that the U.S. government classified them as the most abused drugs in the country.

New Generation, New Drugs

During the 1960s, a new generation of young people began experimenting with a wide variety of mind-altering substances. Barbiturates were among the drugs abused by these new users, mainly because the pills were widely available and frequently used by the generation that came before them—their parents. According to the 1972 *Consumers Union Report on Licit and Illicit Drugs,* 10 billion barbiturate doses were scheduled for production in 1969 alone. That figure represented an 800-percent increase in the amount produced twenty-seven years earlier in 1942.

Passage of the Controlled Substances Act (CSA) in 1970 restricted access to barbiturates in the United States. Another category of anti-anxiety drugs, the benzodiazepines (pronounced ben-zoh-die-AZ-uh-peenz), were promoted as a safer alternative to

amphetamines: pronounced am-FETT-uh-meens; stimulant drugs that increase mental alertness, reduce appetite, and help keep users awake

stimulants: substances that increase the activity of a living organism or one of its parts

high: drug-induced feelings ranging from excitement and joy to extreme grogginess

Drugs and Fame

"Until recently," wrote Paul M. Gahlinger in *Illegal Drugs: A Complete Guide to Their History, Chemistry, Use, and Abuse,* "about 3,000 people a year died from barbiturates, about half of them suicides." Film star and sex symbol Marilyn Monroe died of an overdose on August 5, 1962, after taking nearly fifty Nembutal tablets. The popular blonde had appeared in such films as *Some Like It Hot, How to Marry a Millionaire, Bus Stop,* and *Gentlemen Prefer Blondes.* Her death was controversial as it was deemed a suicide. But many of her fans insisted that she would never take her own life.

Other celebrity deaths can be attributed to barbiturate use as well. Electric guitarist Jimi Hendrix died of suffocation brought on by a barbiturate overdose on September 18, 1970. Hendrix thrilled audiences with his performance at Woodstock in 1969. Among his popular songs were "Purple Haze," "All Along the Watchtower," and an electrifying guitar rendition of "The Star Spangled Banner."

Barbiturates may have played a role in the death of Elvis Presley, the King of Rock 'n' Roll, as well. He died on August 16, 1977, of a drug overdose. A mixture of methaqualone, morphine, codeine, and several barbiturates were found in his system at the time of his death. (Entries on

Film star Marilyn Monroe's death, resulting from an overdose of barbiturates, shocked her fans around the world. *© Hulton-Deutsch Collection/Corbis.*

each of these drugs are available in this encyclopedia.) Remembered for his many movies, he recorded such hits as "Hound Dog," "Jailhouse Rock," "Love Me Tender," "Don't Be Cruel," and "Return to Sender." Each year, thousands of people visit his former home, Graceland, in Memphis, Tennessee.

barbiturates. Prescriptions for benzodiazepines rose because health providers considered them less addictive than barbiturates, with a lower risk of accidental overdose among users. As barbiturates became harder to obtain, drug abusers turned to other illegal substances during the 1970s and 1980s. U.S. Drug Enforcement Administration (DEA) reports indicate that the use of marijuana, heroin, and cocaine began to rise after 1970.

What Is It Made Of?

Barbiturates are compounds derived from barbituric acid, a substance made from carbon, hydrogen, nitrogen, and oxygen. The *uric acid* portion of the name is taken from the main ingredient in urine, which provides the basis for barbituric acid.

Barbiturate users often refer to the pills they take in terms of the color of the capsule. These street names include blues or blue dolls for Amytal; reds, red birds, or red devils for Seconal; yellows or yellow jackets for Nembutal; purple hearts for Luminal; and rainbows for Tuinal.

How Is It Taken?

In the United States, barbiturates are manufactured in various forms. Most barbiturates come in pills and capsules that patients swallow. Some are available as liquids that are swallowed. Others are produced in injectable forms. Some abusers have been known to mix up their own injectable liquid barbiturates by crushing pills and combining the powdered drug with water.

Drugs made from barbituric acid are classified in one of four categories: ultrashort-, short-, intermediate-, or long-acting. These categories are defined by the amount of time that it takes for the barbiturate to produce effects in the user and how long those effects last.

DEA reports indicate that drug abusers favor short- and intermediate-acting barbiturates. These types of barbiturates take effect within fifteen to forty minutes of being swallowed, and their depressant effects last from five to six hours. Drugs in this category include amobarbital, aprobarbital, butabarbital, pentobarbital, and secobarbital.

Are There Any Medical Reasons for Taking This Substance?

For many years, barbiturates were used as daytime sedatives. Since the discovery of another type of anti-anxiety drug called benzodiazepine, which is considered safer, barbiturates are not prescribed for this purpose as frequently as they once were.

When combined with an aspirin or nonaspirin pain reliever and caffeine, the barbiturate butalbital is effective in treating severe pain. It is sometimes prescribed to relieve the pain associated with migraine headaches.

The "Death with Dignity" Debate

The use of barbiturates in assisted suicides in Oregon has fueled a storm of controversy throughout the United States. In 1997 Oregon became the only state in the nation to permit assisted suicide. Oregon voters approved the Death with Dignity Act, allowing doctors to pre-scribe lethal doses of barbiturates, most often secobarbital, to terminally ill people.

The terms of the act defined terminally ill people as those individuals estimated to have fewer than six months to live. That diagnosis had to be verified by two physicians, who would also determine whether the terminally ill person was competent to make such a decision. "During the six years since the Oregon law took effect," wrote Jim Barnett in a 2004 article for the *Oregonian,* "171 Oregonians have died by doctor-assisted suicide."

The administration of President George W. Bush has fought against the Death with Dignity Act since 2001. Opponents of the assisted sui-cide law argue that the state of Oregon is breaking federal laws that govern the use of controlled substances. However, supporters of the Death with Dignity law believe that it repre-sents the will of the people—the voters of Oregon. They contend that the act treats the terminally ill with compassion and dignity by allowing them the right to end their lives hu-manely. As of mid-2005, the U.S. Supreme Court had not ruled on the issue of assisted suicide in Oregon.

As of 2005, barbiturates were used primarily for presurgical and surgical anesthesia. They were being administered to patients in operating rooms under an anesthetist's care. They also continued to be used in the treatment of certain types of epilepsy.

Usage Trends

Reactions to barbiturates range from mild sedation to coma and even death. Doctors may prescribe barbiturates as sedatives to calm patients' nerves, reduce tension, or help them sleep. The drugs are also used as an anticonvulsant to control epileptic seizures. The sleep-producing action of barbiturates is used to relax and partially anesthetize patients before some surgical procedures.

At the close of the twentieth century, the DEA reported that barbiturates represented about 20 percent of all depressant prescrip-tions in the United States.

Barbiturate Use Down Since the Mid-1980s, Says SAMHSA

Recent surveys of ILLICIT drug abuse showed a sharp decline in barbiturate abuse since the mid-1980s. The National Survey on Drug

illicit: unlawful

In 1997 Oregon became the only state in the nation to allow assisted suicide. Under the Death with Dignity Act, terminally ill people with less than six months to live can choose to end their lives. During his stint as attorney general of the United States, John Ashcroft challenged the Oregon law in court, but lost. *AP/Wide World Photos.*

Use and Health (NSDUH), formerly known as the National Household Survey on Drug Abuse, is a carefully calculated assessment of American drug use. It is conducted by the Substance Abuse and Mental Health Services Administration (SAMHSA) and obtains information on nine different categories of illicit drug use. As of 2005, the latest results available were from the 2003 survey. All of the respondents to the survey were over the age of twelve. They were asked to report "only uses of drugs that were not prescribed for them or drugs they took only for the experience or feeling they caused." Over-the-counter drugs and legitimate uses of prescription drugs were not included.

According to the 2003 NSDUH summary, prescription-type sedatives were placed in a category called "psychotherapeutic drugs." This category also included TRANQUILIZERS, pain relievers, and stimulants. About 300,000 Americans over the age of twelve reported

tranquilizers: drugs such as Valium and Librium that treat anxiety; also called benzodiazepines (pronounced ben-zoh-die-AZ-uh-peens)

using sedatives without a prescription. The authors of the survey noted that "the number of *first-time* sedative users rose steadily during the late 1960s and early 1970s, and then declined during the early 1980s, remaining below 250,000 per year since 1984." The 2003 estimates were all similar to the corresponding estimates for 2002.

Monitoring the Future Results

The results of the 2004 Monitoring the Future (MTF) study were released to the public on December 21, 2004. Conducted by the University of Michigan (U of M), it was sponsored by research grants from the National Institute on Drug Abuse (NIDA). Like the NSDUH results regarding sedative use from 2002 and 2003, the MTF survey results indicate that barbiturate use among twelfth-grade students held steady between 2003 and 2004.

Effects on the Body

Barbiturates are classified as ultrashort-, short-, intermediate-, and long-acting, depending on how quickly they act and how long their effects last. Ultrashort barbiturates such as thiopental (Pentothal) produce unconsciousness within about a minute of INTRAVENOUS (IV) INJECTION. These drugs are used to prepare patients for surgery; other general ANESTHETICS like nitrous oxide are then used to keep the patient from waking up before the surgery is complete. Because Pentothal and other ultrashort-acting barbiturates are typically used in hospital settings, they are not very likely to be abused, noted the DEA.

Abusers tend to prefer short-acting and intermediate-acting barbiturates. The most commonly abused are amobarbital (Amytal), pentobarbital (Nembutal), and secobarbital (Seconal). A combination of amobarbital and secobarbital (called Tuinal) is also highly abused. Short-acting and intermediate-acting barbiturates are usually prescribed as sedatives and sleeping pills. These pills begin acting fifteen to forty minutes after they are swallowed, and their effects last from five to six hours. Veterinarians use pentobarbital to anesthetize animals before surgery; in large doses, it can be used to euthanize animals.

Long-acting barbiturates such as phenobarbital (Luminal) and mephobarbital (Mebaral) are prescribed for two main reasons. When taken at bedtime, they help treat INSOMNIA. When taken during the day, they have sedative effects that can aid in the treatment of tension and anxiety. These same effects have been found helpful in the treatment of convulsive conditions like epilepsy. Long-acting

intravenous (IV) injection: injection of a liquid form of a drug directly into the bloodstream

anesthetics: substances used to deaden pain

insomnia: difficulty falling asleep or an inability to sleep

Truth Serum

Thiopental is a barbiturate that is marketed under the name Sodium Pentothal, but it is probably best known as "truth serum." When dissolved in water, it can be swallowed or administered by intravenous injection. In large doses, it is one of three drugs used in the United States to execute prisoners on death row. In lower doses, it is sometimes used as a truth serum.

Drug experts claim that truth serum does not force people to tell the truth. It merely decreases their inhibitions, making them more likely to be "caught off guard" when questioned by authorities. People being questioned may slip up and expose a lie or give more information on a subject or event than they intended.

barbiturates take effect within one to two hours and last twelve hours or longer.

Similar to Alcohol

RECREATIONAL USERS report that a barbiturate high makes them feel "relaxed, sociable, and good-humored," according to an *Independent* article. Users typically describe feelings of decreased anxiety, a loss of inhibitions, and an increased sense of confidence. Physical effects include slowed breathing and a lowering of both blood pressure and heart rate.

Like alcohol, barbiturates are intoxicating. During the stage after mild INTOXICATION, the user's speech may be slurred and a loss of coordination may become noticeable. Stumbling and staggering are common. Other symptoms include shallow breathing, fatigue, frequent yawning, and irritability.

When taken in high doses, barbiturates can cause serious side effects, including "unpredictable emotional reactions and mental confusion," noted the *Independent*. Judgment becomes severely impaired and the user may experience mood swings.

The mental effects of barbiturates generally depend on the amount of the drug taken and the strength of the dosage. Generally, a person falls asleep when taking a prescribed dosage at bedtime. But barbiturates remain in the system for a long time. "At normal doses," explained Cynthia Kuhn and her coauthors in *Buzzed: The Straight Facts about the Most Used and Abused Drugs from Alcohol to Ecstasy*, "the major concern is that they can have sedative effects that outlast their sleep-inducing properties.... Driving, flying an airplane, or other activities requiring muscle coordination can be impaired for up to a day after a single dose." Some barbiturates can be detected in a user's urine sample days or even weeks after the drug was consumed.

Dependence, Tolerance, and Overdose

Barbiturate use can lead to both psychological and physical dependence. Psychological addiction can occur quickly. Signs of drug dependence include relying on a drug regularly for a desired effect. The addicted abuser believes he or she must take a barbiturate to sleep, relax, or just get through the day. Continued use of barbiturates leads to physical dependence.

recreational users: people who use drugs solely to achieve a high, not to treat a medical condition

intoxication: drunkenness

As people develop a TOLERANCE for barbiturates, they may need more of the drug or a higher dosage to get the desired effect. This can lead to an overdose, which results when a person takes a larger-than-prescribed dose of a drug. "People who get in the habit of taking sleeping pills every night to fall sleep," noted Andrew Weil and Winifred Rosen in *From Chocolate to Morphine*, "might start out with one a night, progress to two, then graduate to four to get the same effect. One night the dose they need to fall asleep might also be the dose that stops their breathing." Generally, barbiturate overdoses "occur because the effective dose of the drug is not too far away from the LETHAL dose," explained Dr. Eric H. Chudler on the *Neuroscience for Kids* Web site.

Symptoms of an overdose typically include severe weakness, confusion, shortness of breath, extreme drowsiness, an unusually slow heartbeat, and darting eye movements. The amount of a fatal dosage of barbiturate varies from one individual to another. However, the lethal dose is usually ten to fifteen times as large as a usual dose. An overdose affects the heart and the respiratory system. The user then falls into a coma and dies.

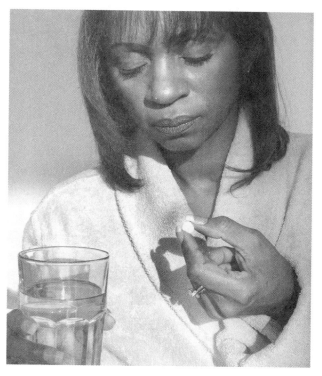

Short-acting and intermediate-acting barbiturates are usually prescribed as sedatives and sleeping pills. *Photo by Dan Newell.*

Clayton pointed out that barbiturates "can have a 'multiplying' effect when taken with other depressants. For example, if someone drinks alcohol and takes a barbiturate, the effect may be ten times stronger than either one taken separately." According to Weil, "many people have died because they were ignorant of this fact."

Older adults and pregnant women should consider the risks associated with barbiturate use. When a person ages, the body becomes less able to rid itself of barbiturates. As a result, people over the age of sixty-five are at higher risk of experiencing the harmful effects of barbiturates, including drug dependence and accidental overdose. When barbiturates are taken during pregnancy, the drug passes through the mother's bloodstream to her fetus. After the baby is born, it may experience WITHDRAWAL symptoms and have trouble breathing. In addition, nursing mothers who take barbiturates may transmit the drug to their babies through breast milk.

tolerance: a condition in which higher and higher doses of a drug are needed to produce the original effect or high experienced

lethal: deadly

withdrawal: the process of gradually cutting back on the amount of a drug being taken until it is discontinued entirely; also the accompanying physiological effects of terminating use of an addictive drug

Dream Time

Barbiturates bring on sleep in people who take them. This slumber, however, differs from normal sleep. Barbiturate use decreases the amount of dream time during sleep known as the rapid eye movement (REM) stage. This phase of sleep is necessary for maintaining good health.

Reactions with Other Drugs or Substances

People who abuse inhalants run a very high risk of overdose if they consume barbiturates while on an inhalant high. OPIATES are also especially dangerous when combined with barbiturates. Barbiturates should not be mixed with alcohol or other drugs, including tranquilizers, muscle relaxants, antihistamines, cold medicines, allergy medicines, and certain pain relievers. The use of barbiturates by people suffering from depression may pose an increased risk of suicide. Children or adults diagnosed with ATTENTION-DEFICIT/HYPERACTIVITY DISORDER (ADHD) may experience increased excitability rather than a calming effect when given barbiturates. In addition, these drugs may lower the effectiveness of birth control pills that contain estrogen. Unless they use a barrier-type form of birth control, women taking oral contraceptives may become pregnant while taking barbiturates.

Treatment for Habitual Users

When addicted users stop taking barbiturates, their bodies must adapt to the lack of drugs in their systems. This process is known as withdrawal. If the users have taken barbiturates in large doses or for an extended period of time, a physician should be consulted about the withdrawal process. An attempt to withdraw abruptly from barbiturates can be fatal.

Withdrawal symptoms usually begin eight to sixteen hours after the last pill was taken. Symptoms in users with a long history of barbiturate use may last up to fifteen days, but the severity of the symptoms decreases as the body rids itself of the drug. During withdrawal, users feel anxious, weak, dizzy, and nauseated. They may also experience shakes, tremors, and even seizures. In addition, users could possibly have HALLUCINATIONS and become violent or hostile.

In some cases, withdrawal symptoms can be deadly. A physician must establish a plan of gradual withdrawal from this type of drug, usually decreasing the dosage by about 10 percent each day over a ten-day to two-week period. The withdrawal process may occur in a hospital, or treatment may be given on an outpatient basis. Either way, counseling is vital. Users who are treated successfully for their physical addiction must follow through with psychological rehabilitation. Behavioral treatment helps former users avoid barbiturates so

opiates: drugs derived from the opium poppy or synthetically produced to mimic the effects of the opium poppy; opiates tend to decrease restlessness, bring on sleep, and relieve pain

attention-deficit/hyperactivity disorder (ADHD): a disorder characterized by impulsive behavior, difficulty concentrating, and hyperactivity that interferes with social and academic functioning

hallucinations: visions or other perceptions of things that are not really present

In a scene from the movie *Valley of the Dolls* (1967), a young woman in a mental institution reaches for a bottle of sleeping pills. The movie follows the lives of three women trying to make it big in New York City and deals with drug addiction. The "dolls" in the movie title refer to drugs.
© 20th Century Fox/ The Kobal Collection.

they can remain drug free even when faced with cravings. Long-term support can be found in twelve-step programs and other support groups that meet regularly.

Consequences

Barbiturates are used to treat anxiety, sleeplessness, muscular tension, and pain. Their calming effect has a serious downside, though. Barbiturates lessen the brain's control over breathing.

Respiratory failure is the primary cause of death in cases of barbiturate overdose. Gahlinger pointed out that "since barbiturates reduce the amount of oxygen reaching the brain, the overdosing person who survives may be left with permanent brain damage."

Barbiturate users can develop a tolerance for the drug. As the body becomes used to the presence of barbiturates in the system, the prescribed dose of the drug may lose its effectiveness. Habitual users may find themselves taking more and more pills in stronger and stronger dosages to achieve the effect they once attained on a low dosage of the drug. This cycle often leads to accidental overdose.

Prolonged barbiturate use can shorten a person's attention span and result in memory loss. Both conditions would make it difficult for a person to do well in school or perform on a job. In addition, barbiturates affect the judgment of those who use them, increasing the likelihood of risky behavior. Users of barbiturates are sometimes tempted to drive while drunk because they know that police will not smell alcohol on their breath.

Taking barbiturates to ease depression "is probably the riskiest way of using them," cautioned Weil. Although these drugs may improve the user's mood temporarily, "over time they often increase anxiety and depression, encouraging further drug-taking in a downward spiral that can end in suicide."

The Law

When barbiturates first became available in the United States, they could be purchased without a prescription. It did not take long, however, for lawmakers to realize that barbiturates were addictive. On their own, some state governments adopted laws in the mid-1930s that banned the sale of nonprescription barbiturates. In 1938, the U.S. government stepped in, passing the U.S. Food, Drug, and Cosmetics Act. This act gave the FDA regulatory power over new drugs, including barbiturates. This means that drug companies would have to apply to the FDA for approval to manufacture such drugs. Once approved, the FDA would determine whether a new drug would require a medical doctor's prescription.

For more than thirty years, until the passage of the Controlled Substances Act (CSA) of 1970, barbiturates were still widely abused. Under the stiffer terms of the CSA, barbiturates became controlled substances. In other words, their use is regulated by certain federal laws. The CSA called for the assignment of all controlled drug substances into one of five categories called schedules. These schedules are based on a substance's medicinal value, possible harmfulness, and potential for abuse and addiction. Schedule I is reserved for the most dangerous drugs that have no recognized medical use.

Various barbiturates fall into three different schedules: Schedule II, Schedule III, and Schedule IV. Drugs in all of these categories cannot be obtained legally without a medical doctor's prescription. Schedule II drugs are dangerous substances with genuine medical uses that also have a high potential for abuse and addiction. They are accepted for medical use with restrictions. These drugs may lead to severe psychological or physical dependence. Barbiturates in this category include amobarbital (Amytal), pentobarbital (Nembutal), and secobarbital (Seconal and Tuinal).

Schedule III drugs have less of a potential for abuse than drugs placed in Schedules I and II. The drugs have real medical uses, but their abuse can still lead to PSYCHOLOGICAL ADDICTION OR PSYCHOLOGICAL DEPENDENCE in those who take them. Barbiturates in this category include aprobarbital (Alurate), butabarbital (Butisol), and butalbital (Fiorinal and Fioricet).

Schedule IV drugs have a low abuse potential when compared to Schedule III drugs. These substances have an accepted medical use, but some patients risk developing a psychological dependence on them. Schedule IV barbiturates include barbital (Veronal), mephobarbital (Mebaral), and phenobarbital (Luminal).

Fines and Jail Time

Possessing barbiturates without a prescription is against the law and can result in up to a year's imprisonment and/or thousands of dollars in fines. The length of the jail sentence and the amount of the fine are increased when a person is convicted of a second or third offense of barbiturate possession. People convicted of distributing or selling barbiturates face lengthy prison terms and fines in the millions of dollars. Selling drugs is a dangerous business for both the buyer and the seller. Illegally distributed Schedule II drugs can kill or seriously injure a user. In cases such as these, the distributor or seller of the substance is considered partially responsible for the user's death and could end up with a lifetime jail sentence.

In the United Kingdom, drugs are regulated by the 1971 Misuse of Drugs Act and the 1986 Medicines Act. The 1971 act placed drugs in three classes: A, B, or C. The most dangerous drugs are called Class A drugs; the least dangerous drugs are in the C category.

Most barbiturates are considered Class B drugs throughout the United Kingdom. If they are used in an injectable form, however, they

psychological addiction or psychological dependence: the belief that a person needs to take a certain substance in order to function

jump to a Class A rating. The maximum penalty for possession of a Class B drug under UK law is five years of prison, an unlimited fine, or a combination of jail time and a fine. Penalties for supplying or distributing Class B drugs are higher. For Class A drugs, the penalty for possession is seven years in prison, an unlimited fine, or both. The supply penalty for this class could land a seller in jail for life.

For More Information

Books

Brecher, Edward M., and others. *The Consumers Union Report on Licit and Illicit Drugs.* Boston: Little Brown & Co., 1972.

Clayton, Lawrence. *Barbiturates and Other Depressants.* New York: Rosen Publishing Group, 1994.

Escohotado, Antonio. *A Brief History of Drugs: From the Stone Age to the Stoned Age.* Rochester, VT: Park Street Press, 1999.

Gahlinger, Paul M. *Illegal Drugs: A Complete Guide to Their History, Chemistry, Use, and Abuse.* Las Vegas, NV: Sagebrush Press, 2001.

Hughes, Richard, and Robert Brewin. *The Tranquilizing of America.* New York: Harcourt, 1979.

Hyde, Margaret O., and John F. Setaro. *Drugs 101: An Overview for Teens.* Brookfield, CT: Twenty-first Century Books, 2003.

Kuhn, Cynthia, Scott Swartzwelder, Wilkie Wilson, and others. *Buzzed: The Straight Facts about the Most Used and Abused Drugs from Alcohol to Ecstasy,* 2nd ed. New York: W.W. Norton, 2003.

Schull, Patricia Dwyer. *Nursing Spectrum Drug Handbook.* King of Prussia, PA: Nursing Spectrum, 2005.

Silverman, Harold M. *The Pill Book,* 11th ed. New York: Bantam, 2004.

Weil, Andrew, and Winifred Rosen. *From Chocolate to Morphine.* New York: Houghton Mifflin, 1993, rev. 2004.

Wolfe, Sidney. *Worst Pills, Best Pills.* New York: Pocket Books, 1999.

Periodicals

Barnett, Jim. "Feds Push Challenge to Assisted Suicide Law." *Oregonian* (November 10, 2004).

Johnson, Kevin, and Richard Willing. "Ex-CIA Chief Revitalizes 'Truth Serum' Debate." *USA Today* (April 26, 2002).

Schodolski, Vincent J. "U.S. Seeks to Bury Oregon Suicide Law." *Knight Ridder/Tribune News Service* (November 27, 2004): p. K6995.

"Sex, Drugs, and Rock 'n' Roll." *Independent* (January 28, 1996): p. 8.

Weathermon, Ron, and David W. Crabb. "Alcohol and Medication Interactions." *Alcohol Research & Health,* vol. 23, no. 1 (1999): pp. 40-54.

Web Sites

"2003 National Survey on Drug Use and Health (NSDUH)." *U.S. Department of Health and Human Services, Substance Abuse and Mental Health Services Administration.* http://www.oas.samhsa.gov/nhsda.htm (accessed June 30, 2005).

"Barbiturates." *Neuroscience for Kids.* http://faculty.washington.edu/chudler/barb.html and http://faculty.washington.edu/chudler/neurok.html (both accessed June 30, 2005).

"Barbiturates." *U.S. Department of Justice, Drug Enforcement Administration.* http://www.usdoj.gov/dea/concern/barbiturates.html (accessed June 30, 2005).

Fort, Joel. "The Problem of Barbiturates in the United States of America." *United Nations Office on Drugs and Crime.* http://www.unodc.org/unodc/bulletin/bulletin_1964-01-01_1_page004.html (accessed June 30, 2005).

Glatt, M. M. "The Abuse of Barbiturates in the United Kingdom." *United Nations Office on Drugs and Crime.* http://www.unodc.org/unodc/bulletin/bulletin_1962-01-01_2_page004.html (accessed June 30, 2005).

Monitoring the Future. http://www.monitoringthefuture.org/ and http://www.nida.nih.gov/Newsroom/04/2004MTFDrug.pdf (both accessed June 30, 2005).

"Prescription Drugs: Abuse and Addiction." *National Institute on Drug Abuse (NIDA) Research Report Series.* http://www.drugabuse.gov/ResearchReports/Prescription/ (accessed June 30, 2005).

See also: Alcohol; Benzodiazepine; Tranquilizers

Benzodiazepine

Official Drug Name: Alprazolam (al-PRAZZ-oh-lam; Xanax), chlordiaze-poxide (klor-dye-az-uh-POKS-ide; Librium), clonazepam (kloh-NAZZ-uh-pam; Klonopin), clorazepate (klor-AZZ-uh-pate; Tranxene), diazepam (dye-AZZ-uh-pam; Valium), flurazepam (flor-AZZ-uh-pam; Dalmane), flunitrazepam (Rohypnol), halazepam (huh-LAZZ-uh-pam; Paxipam), lorazepam (lorr-AZZ-uh-pam; Ativan), midazolam (Versed), oxazepam (oks-AZZ-uh-pam; Serax), prazepam (PRAZZ-uh-pam; Centrax), quazepam (KWAY-zuh-pam; Doral), temazepam (tuh-MAZZ-uh-pam; Restoril), triazolam (try-AY-zoe-lam; Halcion)

Also Known As: Benzos, tranks, downers

Drug Classifications: Schedule IV, except for flunitrazepam (Rohypnol), which is a Schedule III drug; depressant

barbiturates: pronounced bar-BIH-chuh-rits; drugs that act as depressants and are used as sedatives or sleeping pills; also referred to as "downers"

sedative-hypnotic agents: drugs that depress or slow down the body

anxiety disorders: a group of mental disorders or conditions characterized in part by extreme restlessness, uncontrollable feelings of fear, excessive worrying, and panic attacks

What Kind of Drug Is It?

Benzodiazepines (pronounced ben-zoh-die-AZ-uh-peens) are depressants that relieve anxiety. Their names are easy to recognize because many of them end in the suffix "-am." Some common benzodiazepines are alprazolam, diazepam, and lorazepam. Benzodiazepines are only available legally with a doctor's prescription.

A number of medical terms apply to benzodiazepines. Just like alcohol and BARBITURATES, benzodiazepines are classified as depressants because they slow down both the mind and the body. They are also considered SEDATIVE-HYPNOTIC AGENTS and tranquilizers because they reduce anxiety and promote sleep. Benzodiazepines can be addicting.

Overview

Benzodiazepines are widely prescribed in the treatment of ANXIETY DISORDERS, sleep disorders, and seizure conditions. They calm down users by acting on the brain to lower anxiety levels, relax muscles, and bring on sleep. Benzodiazepines were first used in the late 1950s. By the 1960s, physicians were regularly prescribing them to patients in place of barbiturates. Barbiturates, another class of depressants, can slow the breathing center of the brain to dangerously low levels. Benzodiazepines have less of an effect on breathing than barbiturates and are therefore considered safer. In addition, benzodiazepines are less likely to lead to death in cases of overdose.

The likelihood of addiction among benzodiazepine users did not become an issue until several years after their introduction. When taken for a limited amount of time in doctor-prescribed doses, benzodiazepines are generally quite safe. Problems develop when they are taken for more than several months or in larger-than-recommended doses. Psychological and physical dependence on benzodiazepines can actually occur within a matter of weeks. It has also been reported that benzodiazepine abusers usually combine their "benzos" with other drugs or alcohol. These combinations can lead to very serious physical consequences, including slowed breathing, coma, and even death.

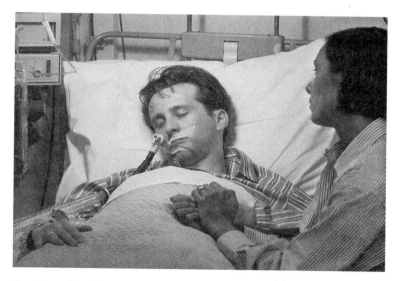

A variety of health conditions can lead to a coma, including head trauma, drinking too much alcohol, and a drug overdose, among other things. A coma is a state of unconsciousness from which a person cannot be awakened by noise or other stimuli. © *Mike Laye/Corbis.*

About fifty different kinds of benzodiazepines were being used throughout the world in 2005. However, only fifteen of these have been approved for use in the United States by the Food and Drug Administration (FDA). According to *The Pill Book,* four of the top seventy-five prescriptions written by U.S. doctors in 2003 were for benzodiazepines:

- alprazolam (Xanax) ranked 12th
- lorazepam (Ativan) ranked 32nd
- clonazepam (Klonopin) ranked 52nd
- diazepam (Valium) ranked 68th

Of these benzodiazepines, alprazolam was the most frequently abused in the United States in the early 2000s. This likely occurs because it acts so quickly—within twenty to thirty minutes. As Lance P. Longo and Brian Johnson, writing in *American Family Physician,* put it, "drugs that work immediately tend to be addictive."

Drug companies classify benzodiazepines according to the length of time it takes for them to begin working. The ultra-short acting benzodiazepines kick in almost immediately and are mainly used in a hospital setting as a form of anesthesia. Two common

---

"Mother's Little Helper"

Historically, tranquilizers were not the drug of choice among the biggest drug users of the 1960s. College students, hippies, and concert-going youths of that decade were more likely to experiment with hallucinogenic drugs. Benzodiazepines and minor tranquilizers were associated more with stay-at-home moms. Their practice of taking Valium—the "little yellow pill"—was widespread in the United States and the United Kingdom during this time. The Rolling Stones recorded a song in 1966 called "Mother's Little Helper" about this trend. As noted on *CNN.com,* the Stones sang: "Mother needs something today to calm her down / And though she's not really ill, There's a little yellow pill / She goes running for the shelter of a mother's little helper. . . ."

It is estimated that in the 1970s, as many as 30 million women were taking minor tranquilizers. "In promoting these drugs, the manufacturers portrayed stresses of everyday life as disease states treatable by prescribing their products," explained Andrew Weil and Winifred Rosen in *From Chocolate to Morphine.* Some advertisements "suggested giving tranquilizers to harried mothers and bored housewives." One particular ad aimed at physicians suggested they carry syringes of injectable diazepam "ready to use, when something must be done to calm the patient in emotional crisis." As Weil pointed out, ads like these always seemed to feature pictures of women as emotionally distressed patients in need of help. Psychiatrists were freely prescribing these minor tranquilizers to women with little regard of their potential for addiction.

---

ultra-short acting benzodiazepines are midazolam (Versed) and triazolam (Halcion). The short-acting benzodiazepines typically begin working in less than half an hour. These are among the most commonly abused drugs and include alprazolam (Xanax) and lorazepam (Ativan). The long-acting benzodiazepines, such as chlordiazepoxide (Librium) and diazepam (Valium), take a longer time to produce effects.

The strongest benzodiazepines, known as high-potency benzodiazepines, include alprazolam, lorazepam, triazolam, and clonazepam. Among the less powerful, or low-potency, benzodiazepines are chlordiazepoxide, clorazepate, diazepam, and flurazepam.

What Is It Made Of?

amines: organic (or carbon-containing) chemical substances made from ammonia

Benzodiazepines consist of chemical substances known as AMINES. All benzodiazepines are produced in laboratories. Like the other amines, they are derived from ammonia, a gas that consists of one molecule of nitrogen and three molecules of hydrogen.

How Is It Taken?

Benzodiazepines are usually taken in capsule or tablet form, but some are available as an injectable solution. The tablets are typically pastel shades of yellow, green, or blue. Some users dissolve the pills in water, mix them with other drugs, and then inject them directly into a vein.

Are There Any Medical Reasons for Taking This Substance?

Physicians use benzodiazepines in the treatment of many anxiety disorders. For example, they are used to treat panic attacks, which are unexpected episodes of severe anxiety that can cause physical symptoms such as shortness of breath, dizziness, sweating, and shaking. The drugs also help people suffering from post-traumatic stress disorder (PTSD), an illness that can occur after someone experiences or witnesses a life-threatening event such as a serious accident, violent assault, or terrorist attack. PTSD symptoms include reliving the experience through nightmares and flashbacks, having problems sleeping, and feeling detached from reality.

Benzodiazepines also help with obsessive-compulsive disorder (OCD), an anxiety disorder that causes people to dwell on unwanted thoughts, act on unusual urges, and perform repetitive rituals such as frequent hand washing. Benzodiazepines may also be used to relieve tension, agitation, insomnia, muscles spasms, and EPILEPTIC seizures.

Patients undergoing surgery, dental procedures, diagnostic studies, and cancer treatments are sometimes given benzodiazepines to help reduce their fear and anxiety. In addition, benzodiazepines may be prescribed for alcoholics and addicts undergoing the DETOXIFICATION process. When used under strict medical supervision, these drugs can lessen the symptoms of withdrawal that occur as the user cuts back on the amount of a drug being taken until use can be discontinued entirely.

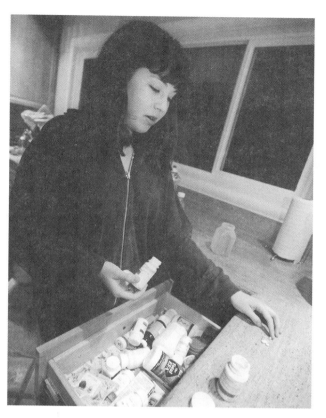

People using prescription drugs must be careful about taking additional medications, even those sold over the counter. Mixing prescribed drugs with alcohol can also lead to serious health problems. For example, combining benzodiazepine with other drugs or alcohol can lead to slowed breathing, coma, and even death. *AP/Wide World Photos.*

epilepsy: a disorder involving the misfiring of electrical impulses in the brain, sometimes resulting in seizures and loss of consciousness

detoxification: a difficult process by which substance abusers stop taking those substances and rid their bodies of accumulated toxins

Usage Trends

Benzodiazepines are very commonly prescribed, but they are supposed to be used *only* for brief periods of time. Benzodiazepine drugs have a number of genuine medical uses, but they are most frequently prescribed to relieve anxiety and fear. According to the American Psychiatric Association (APA), approximately "8 percent of all adults have suffered from a PHOBIA, panic disorder or other anxiety disorder" during any given six-month period. "For millions of Americans, anxiety disorders are disruptive, debilitating and often the reason for loss of job and serious problems in family relationships."

Treating Anxiety

Anxiety disorders are sometimes controllable without drugs. Patients are often able to reduce their anxiety to manageable levels through weekly "talk therapy" sessions with trained psychotherapists. One type of PSYCHOTHERAPY, called COGNITIVE-BEHAVIORAL THERAPY (CBT), has a very high success rate. Cognitive-behavioral therapy helps patients change their outlook on life and recast their negative feelings into positive ones.

In certain cases, however, therapy is not enough. Patients may require medication to control their symptoms. Psychiatrists often prescribe benzodiazepines to such patients. According to the APA, these drugs "relieve the fear, help end the physical symptoms such as pounding heart and shortness of breath, and give people a greater sense of control." Along with that greater sense of control comes the ability to recognize and "reduce the stress that can trigger anxiety."

Benzodiazepines are most commonly prescribed for women and elderly patients. Four out of five people who experience panic attacks are female. Elderly patients are commonly diagnosed with conditions such as insomnia and DEPRESSION. These conditions respond well to treatment with certain benzodiazepines. But long-term use of these drugs among the elderly increases the likelihood of these patients developing a physical dependence on benzodiazepines.

In one study cited by *Mental Health Weekly,* 60 percent of older women taking benzodiazepines by prescription were on the drugs for more than four months. That time period is longer than recommended. In addition, the National Institute on Drug Abuse (NIDA) reported in its "Prescription Drugs: Abuse and Addiction" that "elderly persons who take benzodiazepines are at increased risk for falls that cause hip and thigh fractures, as well as for vehicle accidents."

phobia: an extreme and often unexplainable fear of a certain object or situation

psychotherapy: the treatment of emotional problems by a trained therapist using a variety of techniques to improve a patient's outlook on life

cognitive behavioral therapy (CBT): a type of therapy that helps people recognize and change negative patterns of thinking and behavior

depression: a mood disorder that causes people to have feelings of hopelessness, loss of pleasure, self-blame, and sometimes suicidal thoughts

Benzodiazepines are prescribed to treat anxiety as well as to relieve tension, agitation, insomnia, muscle spasms, and epileptic seizures.
Photo by Erlie E. Pruitt Jr. Courtesy of Lance Logan Sims.

Part of the Multi-Drug Mix

Among drug abusers, benzodiazepines are hardly ever used alone. The White House's drug policy publication *"Pulse Check"* revealed that multi-drug use "increased steadily" between 1993 and 2003. About 80 percent of benzodiazepine abuse occurs in people who regularly abuse other drugs. This has led to "increased complications for drug treatment," noted the *"Pulse Check"* report, because "it is hard to determine what clients are using."

Reading up on Rohypnol

Flunitrazepam (Rohypnol) is an extremely powerful and fast-acting benzodiazepine. The drug began receiving a lot of attention in the mid-1990s, especially on college campuses because of its use as a "date rape" drug. Flunitrazepam is one of the drugs, along with ecstasy (MDMA), used by teens and young adults as part of the nightclub, bar, or "rave" scene. Raves are wild overnight dance parties that usually involve huge crowds of people, loud techno music, and illegal drug use.

Flunitrazepam is also known by the brand name Rohypnol and the street names roofies, R2, Roche, roofinol, rope, rophies, forget-me pill, and Mexican valium. It comes in the form of a small, white tablet with "Roche" on one side and a "1" or "2" in a circle on the other side. The numbers indicate a 1-milligram or 2-milligram dosage. It is usually taken by mouth, often combined with alcohol. Or, it is sometimes snorted after the user crushes the tablets.

The effects of Rohypnol include sedation, muscle relaxation, and anxiety reduction. Its sedative effects are said to be seven to ten times stronger than diazepam (Valium). Because it is tasteless and odorless, flunitrazepam is hard to detect in beverages. After taking this drug, users begin to feel intoxicated rather quickly. The "drunken" feelings soon turn to extreme sleepiness. Speech becomes slurred, and judgment is most definitely impaired. Partial amnesia is a common effect, as well. For this reason, flunitrazepam has been used in date rape.

Victims of date rape are usually unable to remember the assault or identify their attacker because Rohypnol affects one's memory. Rohypnol begins working within minutes of being consumed. Its effects can last up to eight hours. Deep sedation, respiratory distress, and daylong blackouts are some of the more serious possible effects of Rohypnol. In high doses, flunitrazepam can kill.

Rohypnol has never been approved for use in the United States. It is smuggled in from other countries in Europe, Central America, and South America. The U.S. Congress passed the Drug-Induced Rape Prevention and Punishment Act of 1996. This legislation increased the federal penalties for individuals using any controlled substance to aid them in sexual assault. The law makes it a crime to give others a controlled substance without their knowledge or with the intent to commit a violent crime against them. (A separate entry on Rohypnol is available in this encyclopedia.)

ILLICIT drug users report that benzodiazepines increase and lengthen the HIGH they get with other drugs. Heavy drinkers have reported that benzodiazepines enhance the effects of alcohol. These drugs can also ease the process of "coming down" from a stimulant high. So, many multi-drug abusers use it as part of their regular drug mix.

Abuse of benzodiazepines is especially high among heroin, cocaine, and methadone abusers. (A separate entry on each of these drugs is available in this encyclopedia.) According to S. Pirzada Sattar

illicit: unlawful

high: drug-induced feelings ranging from excitement and joy to extreme grogginess

and Subhash Bhatia in an article for *Current Psychiatry Online,* nearly half of all INTRAVENOUS (IV) DRUG ABUSERS also take benzodiazepines. However, "even patients who begin taking benzodiazepines for legitimate reasons may end up abusing them."

Who's Using Benzodiazepines?

Patterns of benzodiazepine use in America have been documented in two long-term surveys. One is the Monitoring the Future (MTF) study conducted by the University of Michigan (U of M) and sponsored by research grants from NIDA. The second is the National Survey on Drug Use and Health (NSDUH), previously called the National Household Survey on Drug Abuse or NHSDA. It is conducted by the Substance Abuse and Mental Health Services Administration (SAMHSA), a division of the U.S. Department of Health and Human Services.

The results of the 2004 MTF study were released to the public on December 21, 2004. Since 1991, U of M has tracked patterns of drug use and attitudes toward drugs among students in the eighth, tenth, and twelfth grades. (Prior to that, from 1975 to 1990, the MTF survey was limited to twelfth graders.) The 2004 MTF survey revealed that the use of tranquilizers and sedatives remained relatively "stable among all grades." About 2.5 percent of eighth graders, 5.1 percent of tenth graders, and 7.3 percent of high school seniors reported using drugs like Xanax between 2003 and 2004.

SAMHSA's 2003 NSDUH was broader than the MTF survey. The NSDUH traces drug use in the United States among people of all ages, not just among eighth, tenth, and twelfth graders. The NSDUH obtains information about nine different categories of illicit drug use. One of those categories includes the nonmedical use of prescription-type pain relievers, tranquilizers, STIMULANTS, and sedatives.

NSDUH reports combine the four prescription-type drug groups into a category referred to as "any psychotherapeutics" (SY-koh-ther-uh-PYOO-tiks). Numerous drugs are covered by this category. All of them are available through prescriptions and sometimes illegally "on the street." Over-the-counter drugs and legitimate uses of prescription drugs are not included in the NSDUH report. Respondents are asked to report only uses of drugs that were not prescribed for them or drugs they took only for the experience or feeling they caused.

Typical Users

Benzodiazepine users can be young or old, male or female. Illicit users—individuals who were not prescribed the drug for a medical reason—typically range in age from their late teens to early thirties. About two-thirds of these users are male.

---

intravenous (IV) drug abusers: abusers who inject the liquid form of a drug directly into their bloodstream

stimulants: substances that increase the activity of a living organism or one of its parts

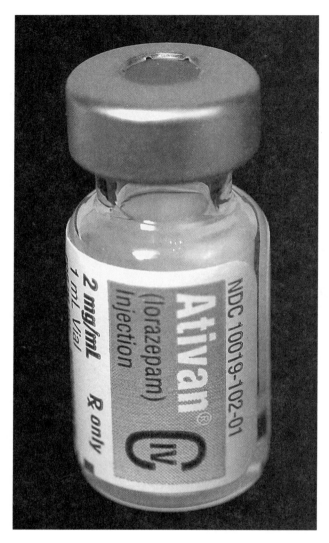

The short-acting benzodiazepines, such as Ativan, typically begin working in less than a half hour and are among the most commonly abused drugs. *Scott Camazine/ Photo Researchers, Inc.*

The results show that a number of Americans became "new users" of psychotherapeutic drugs in 2002. Roughly 1.2 million people began using tranquilizers, and 225,000 began using sedatives. Among fifteen benzodiazepines, the nonmedical use of two specific drugs—alprazolam (Xanax) and lorazepam (Ativan)—rose the most between 2002 and 2003, from 3.5 percent to 4 percent of those surveyed. Use among twelve to seventeen year olds was unchanged, reflecting the same trend as the MTF survey. The biggest jump was seen in users who were slightly older, age eighteen to twenty-five. From 2002 to 2003, usage in that particular age group increased from 6.7 to 7.5 percent.

In Canada, benzodiazepine use is tracked by the Centre for Addiction and Mental Health (CAMH). The CAMH publishes a series of leaflets on drugs under the title "Do You Know . . . . " The "Do You Know ... Benzodiazepines" leaflet states that "approximately 10 percent of Canadians report using a benzodiazepine at least once a year, with one in ten of these people continuing use regularly for more than a year."

Effects on the Body

Benzodiazepines act on the area of the brain that controls emotions. They do this by boosting the effects of a NEUROTRANSMITTER called gamma-aminobutyric acid (GABA). GABA receptor sites are especially numerous on cells in the part of the brain responsible for fear and worrying. Benzodiazepines work by increasing GABA activity. Higher levels of GABA activity help block feelings of tension and anxiety. The result is a calming effect. Some benzodiazepines bind more tightly to GABA receptors than others, causing more intense sedation.

neurotransmitter: a substance that helps spread nerve impulses from one nerve cell to another

Benzodiazepines are designed to produce feelings of relaxation and an increased sense of well-being in the user. But, along with reducing anxiety, these drugs decrease emotional reactions, mental

alertness, and attention span. Common side effects of benzodiazepine use include confusion, drowsiness, loss of coordination, dizziness, and light-headedness. More serious side effects caused by these drugs are rare but can occur. They include outbursts of anger, severe depression, hallucinations, muscle weakness, extreme tiredness, loss of memory, skin rashes, itching, fever and chills, and sores in the throat or mouth.

High doses of benzodiazepines lead to symptoms similar to those caused by excessive use of barbiturates or alcohol. These include slurred speech, impaired memory, slowed breathing, and lowered blood pressure. Although overdosing on benzodiazepines alone is not likely, it has occurred. In these cases, the patients' rate of breathing and blood pressure dropped so low that they went into a coma and eventually died.

Use Interferes with Learning and Memory

Benzodiazepines seem to interfere with memory formation and learning. They "can prevent the brain from recording and adapting to new information," explained Cynthia Kuhn and her coauthors in *Buzzed: The Straight Facts about the Most Used and Abused Drugs from Alcohol to Ecstasy.* "Someone who needs to learn new information should never use these drugs and expect to do so to their full potential."

For example, college students might take benzodiazepines while studying. They might use the drugs in an attempt to relax or to get a good night's sleep. However, such drugs can make it difficult for students to recall the information they need on exam day. Impaired memory is limited to events that occur during the time the drugs are being used. When the dosage wears off, new learning and memory formation become possible again.

Because they decrease mental alertness, benzodiazepines should never be used when driving or operating heavy machinery. "Benzodiazepines slow reaction time and impair driving skills, increasing the risk of motor vehicles crashes in patients who are taking [them]," explained Longo and Johnson. In addition, benzodiazepines should not be taken by pregnant women or by people suffering from lung, kidney, or liver disease.

Addiction and Withdrawal

Benzodiazepines are addictive substances. Regular use of any benzodiazepine can lead to physical and psychological dependence in as little as four to six weeks. According to a 2002 *Mental Health Weekly* article, taking Xanax "for more than eight weeks carries a high

To perform well on school assignments and tests, many students study for long hours. There have been reports of students using benzodiazepines in order to relax or to get a good night's sleep. However, such drugs can make it difficult for students to recall information on exam day. Instead of using drugs, many students opt to study in a group or with a friend to help them stay motivated. © *Jose Luis Pelaez, Inc./Corbis.*

risk of dependency." Both psychologically and physically addicted users may experience cravings for the drug, but those with physical addictions will actually experience withdrawal symptoms if they suddenly stop taking benzodiazepines. In other words, they will become ill if they don't get the drug into their systems. Withdrawal symptoms can be quite serious and range from insomnia, nervousness, irritability, and nausea, to tremors, seizures, and even hallucinations.

Reactions with Other Drugs or Substances

When taken with other depressants such as alcohol or barbiturates, benzodiazepines can be extremely dangerous. The combined effects of two or more depressants can greatly lower blood pressure and reduce a user's ability to breathe. This, in turn, can lead to coma and death. Use of benzodiazepines with meperidine, oxycodone, codeine, or morphine can be deadly as well. (Entries on each of these drugs are available in this encyclopedia).

Treatment for Habitual Users

The potential for addiction to benzodiazepines is very real. That potential is even greater among certain segments of the population, especially those undergoing treatment for substance abuse. "Among psychiatric patients," wrote Sattar and Bhatia, "substance abusers are most likely to abuse benzodiazepines and become addicted to them." Multiple addictions are complicated. Users should seek professional help when trying to stop using the drug.

The withdrawal process can take weeks or even months and requires a combination of physical and psychological care. Benzodiazepine abusers must undergo the process of detoxification under strict medical supervision. During this time, the dosage of the drug is lowered gradually, and eventually use is phased out completely. Cognitive-behavioral therapy helps provide habitual users with the support they need to kick their habit. This type of psychotherapy focuses on increasing a patient's skills for coping with the everyday stresses in life.

Consequences

"It is dangerous to combine any sedative, including benzodiazepines, with anything else that makes a person sleepy," stated Kuhn. *Mental Health Weekly* reported that in 2001, bad reactions to Xanax and other benzodiazepines were responsible for a high percentage of prescription drug-related emergency room visits. The use and abuse of benzodiazepines can impair decision-making, decrease learning skills, and bring on aggression. Each of these factors can have a significant effect on an individual's educational, social, and workplace environments.

Unwanted Side Effects

Interesting evidence has surfaced about the effects of benzodiazepines on some patients. Although such drugs are routinely prescribed to treat the anxiety that comes with depression, benzodiazepines—especially when taken in high doses—may actually *increase* the risk of depression. This theory was reinforced in 2004, when a study was conducted on soldiers returning home from war. War, terrorist attacks, and other life-threatening events can trigger post-traumatic stress disorder (PTSD) in people who have experienced these events firsthand. A Harvard Medical School doctor noted in *Newsweek* that "anxiety-muting benzodiazepines such as lorazepam and clonazepam may actually raise the risk of chronic PTSD if taken continuously." The reasons for this unwanted side effect were still being studied in 2005.

ER Visits

The Drug Abuse Warning Network (DAWN) collects data on drug-related hospital emergency room (ER) visits throughout the United States. ER trips resulting from benzodiazepine abuse numbered more than 100,000 in 2002, an increase of 41 percent since 1995. Complete results of the DAWN report can be found at http://www.oas.samhsa.gov.

The Law

"The nonmedical use or abuse of prescription drugs remains a serious public health concern," wrote the NIDA director in his introduction to "Prescription Drugs: Abuse and Addiction." Medical prescriptions are the primary source of benzodiazepines for abusers, but some of these prescriptions are obtained illegally. Benzodiazepine addicts often use a practice known as "DOCTOR SHOPPING" to keep up with their addiction. They switch doctors and visit emergency rooms regularly in the hopes of getting multiple prescriptions for benzodiazepines. The doctors used in this scheme are usually unaware that another physician has already prescribed the same drugs for the patient.

Writing fake prescriptions on stolen prescription pads is a common practice used to obtain prescription drugs. Another means of getting prescription drugs such as benzodiazepines is by buying the drug from a patient who was legitimately prescribed the medication. These "legitimate" patients can be friends, parents, relatives, or even people on the street offering their pills in exchange for money.

Regardless of how the drugs are obtained, it is against the law to possess or use controlled substances such as benzodiazepines without a doctor's prescription. Selling or distributing benzodiazepines to others is a more serious offense. Physicians who write fraudulent prescriptions are also subject to various legal consequences. These include felony convictions and the possible loss of their medical licenses.

For More Information

Books

Gahlinger, Paul M. *Illegal Drugs: A Complete Guide to Their History, Chemistry, Use, and Abuse.* Las Vegas, NV: Sagebrush Press, 2001.

Kuhn, Cynthia, Scott Swartzwelder, Wilkie Wilson, and others. *Buzzed: The Straight Facts about the Most Used and Abused Drugs from Alcohol to Ecstasy,* 2nd ed. New York: W.W. Norton, 2003.

Preston, John D., John H. O'Neal, and Mary C. Talaga. *Consumer Guide to Psychiatric Drugs.* New York: New Harbinger Publishers, 1998.

Schull, Patricia Dwyer. *Nursing Spectrum Drug Handbook.* King of Prussia, PA: Nursing Spectrum, 2005.

Silverman, Harold M. *The Pill Book,* 11th ed. New York: Bantam, 2004.

Weil, Andrew, and Winifred Rosen. *From Chocolate to Morphine.* New York: Houghton Mifflin, 1993, rev. 2004.

doctor shopping: a practice in which an individual continually switches physicians so that he or she can get enough of a prescription drug to feed an addiction; this makes it difficult for physicians to track whether the patient has already been prescribed the same drug by another physician

Periodicals

"Anti-Anxiety Drugs Being Overprescribed for Medicaid SA Patients." *Mental Health Weekly* (January 19, 2004): p. 3.

"ER Visits Involving Anti-Anxiety Drugs Increase." *Mental Health Weekly* (August 30, 2004): p. 5.

Longo, Lance P., and Brian Johnson. "Addiction: Part I. Benzodiazepines—Side Effects, Abuse Risk, and Alternatives." *American Family Physician* (April 1, 2000): pp. 2121-2131.

Shalev, Arieh Y., and Michael Craig Miller. "To Heal a Shattered Soul." *Newsweek* (December 6, 2004): p. 70.

"Xanax May Be Addictive at Prescribed Doses." *Mental Health Weekly* (October 28, 2002): p. 8.

Web Sites

"2003 National Survey on Drug Use and Health (NSDUH)." *U.S. Department of Health and Human Services, Substance Abuse and Mental Health Services Administration.* http://www.oas.samhsa.gov/nhsda.htm (accessed June 30, 2005).

"Do You Know . . . Benzodiazepines." *Centre for Addiction and Mental Health.* http://www.camh.net/pdf/benzodiazepines_dyk.pdf (accessed June 30, 2005).

Kennedy, Bruce. "The Tranquilizing of America." *CNN.com.* http://www.cnn.com/SPECIALS/1999/century/episodes/06/currents (accessed August 8, 2005).

Monitoring the Future. http://www.monitoringthefuture.org/ and http://www.nida.nih.gov/Newsroom/04/2004MTFDrug.pdf (both accessed June 30, 2005).

"Prescription Drugs: Abuse and Addiction." *National Institute on Drug Abuse (NIDA) Research Report Series.* http://www.drugabuse.gov/ResearchReports/Prescription/ (accessed June 30, 2005).

"Psychiatric Medications." *American Psychiatric Association (APA).* http://www.psych.org/public_info/medication.cfm (accessed June 30, 2005).

"Pulse Check: Drug Markets and Chronic Users in 25 of America's Largest Cities." *Executive Office of the President, Office of National Drug Control Policy.* http://www.whitehousedrugpolicy.gov/publications/drugfact/pulsechk/january04/january2004.pdf (accessed June 30, 2005).

Sattar, S. Pirzada, and Subhash Bhatia. "Benzodiazepines for Substance Abusers: Yes or No?" *Current Psychiatry Online.* http://www.currentpsychiatry.com (accessed February 25, 2005).

See also: Alcohol; Antidepressants; Barbiturates; Ecstasy (MDMA); Rohypnol

Benzylpiperazine/Trifluoromethyl-phenylpiperazine

Official Drug Name: Benzylpiperazine (BENZ-ull-pih-PAIR-uh-zeen; BZP), trifluoromethyl-phenylpiperazine (try-FLU-roh METH-ull FENN-ull-pih-PAIR-uh-zeen; TFMPP)
Also Known As: A2, BZP, legal E, legal X, herbal ecstasy, herbal speed, the party pill, piperazine, and TFMPP
Drug Classifications: Schedule I, stimulant, hallucinogen

intermediaries: chemical compounds that are intended for use in the manufacture of more complex substances

piperazines: pronounced pih-PAIR-uh-zeens; chemical compounds made of carbon, hydrogen, and nitrogen that are used medically to destroy worms and other parasites in humans and animals

hallucinogen: a substance that brings on hallucinations, which alter the user's perception of reality

amphetamines: pronounced am-FETT-uh-meens; stimulant drugs that increase mental alertness, reduce appetite, and help keep users awake

What Kind of Drug Is It?

Benzylpiperazine (BZP) and trifluoromethyl-phenylpiperazine (TFMPP) are both stimulants—substances that increase the activity of a living organism or one of its parts. Neither one of these compounds has any known medical use for humans, at least not in their existing chemical forms. BZP and TFMPP are substances known as INTERMEDIARIES, meaning they are at a middle stage in chemical production. Because PIPERAZINES can dissolve fats, they are often used as cleaning solutions. Usually, piperazines are made into detergents or medicines.

Overview

Chemicals known as piperazines are used for industrial purposes worldwide. A basic piperazine can be changed into a variety of different substances simply by adding different chemical groups to the original compound. For instance, a drug called piperazine citrate destroys intestinal worms, making it useful in the treatment of parasitic infections in both humans and animals. Parasites are organisms that must live with, in, or on other organisms to survive.

Other medicinal and mind-altering qualities of piperazines are being studied as possible treatments for:

- Depression, a mood disorder that causes people to have feelings of hopelessness, loss of pleasure, self-blame, and sometimes suicidal thoughts.
- Psychosis (pronounced sy-KOH-sis), a severe mental disorder that often causes hallucinations and makes it difficult for people to distinguish what is real from what is imagined.
- Alzheimer's disease, a brain disease that usually strikes older individuals and results in memory loss, impaired thinking, and personality changes; symptoms worsen over time.
- Tumors.

BZP and TFMPP are piperazine stimulants. They stimulate the brain, creating HALLUCINOGENIC experiences in some users. Both drugs have been compared to AMPHETAMINES. According to the U.S. Department of Justice, "the amphetamine-like stimulant

124

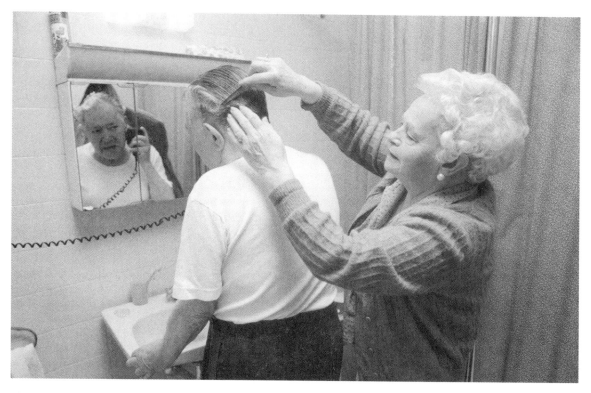

Piperazines are being studied as a possible treatment for Alzheimer's disease—a disease that affects the brain and leads to memory loss, impaired thinking, and personality changes. As these symptoms worsen over time, Alzheimer patients need help taking care of themselves.
© *Stephanie Maze/ Corbis.*

effects of BZP" seem to "attract the attention of drug abusers." The effects of piperazine abuse can be unpredictable. Some users report feelings of relaxation, happiness, and increased closeness with others after taking BZP and TFMPP. However, others describe their experiences with these drugs as frightening and extremely unpleasant. BZP seems to be more commonly abused than TFMPP, probably because there is a greater supply of it available for purchase. Most users of TFMPP prefer to combine it with the club drug ecstasy (MDMA).

Until March of 2004, piperazines were considered legal in the United States. Piperazines sold in bulk over the Internet made their way to the club and RAVE scene. They grew in popularity among adolescents and young adults, sometimes being sold as the

rave: a wild overnight dance party that typically involves huge crowds of people, loud techno music, and illegal drug use

Mystery Ingredients

Most industrial sources supply a BZP preparation that is 97 percent pure, but manufacturers often do not list the ingredients used to prepare the other 3 percent of the compound. Many additives found in industrial chemicals may be toxic or even fatal if consumed. BZP poses a big enough threat to human health on its own. The "mystery ingredients" that are mixed in with it may add to that risk.

dangerous and often-abused drug ecstasy but usually as "BZP," "legal E," "legal X," or "A2." The dangers of BZP and TFMPP stem from their stimulant effects. Rapid heart rhythms, tremors, and convulsions have been reported in some cases.

What Is It Made Of?

BZP and TFMPP are chemical compounds of carbon, hydrogen, and nitrogen. Piperazines are synthetic drugs. They cannot be grown in a garden or dug up from the ground. BZP, the more common of the two abused piperazines, is an odorless, colorless, or faintly yellow oily liquid at room temperature. Like water, it freezes at 32°F (0°C). If consumed by humans or animals in this form, it can cause burns to the skin, lungs, or intestinal tract.

How Is It Taken?

Legal piperazine preparations available in the United States and Canada are listed in the Micromedex Healthtouch prescription database "to treat common roundworms and pinworms." A drug called piperazine citrate comes in various forms, including granules (to be mixed with water), an oral suspension (a liquid medication), or tablets. It can only be obtained with a doctor's prescription. As of 2005, use among humans was limited to the treatment of parasitic worm infections.

Most ILLICIT piperazines are sold in tablet form and contain both BZP and TFMPP. Sometimes, BZP tablets are sold as ecstasy. There is no sure way of knowing the exact dose of BZP and/or TFMPP in tablet form because all of the pills are made in illegal labs. Frequent users usually take anywhere from 35 milligrams to 150 milligrams at a time.

Illegal piperazine tablets are sometimes packaged in vitamin containers. The pills may be white, off-white, tan, or bright shades of green, orange, pink, purple, or yellow. Like ecstasy tablets, piperazine tablets resemble sweet-and-sour candies. They often feature tiny logos—a heart, a fly, a butterfly, a crown, a smiley face, a bull's head, or a squirrel, for example—etched in them. Some users have reported snorting or smoking BZP preparations. This particular method of ingestion irritates the lining of the nose, mouth, and breathing tubes.

illicit: unlawful

Piperazine citrate is used by doctors to destroy intestinal worms, like these roundworms, in humans and animals. It is often used in the treatment of parasitic infections. © *Sinclair Stammers/Science Photo Library/Photo Researchers, Inc.*

Are There Any Medical Reasons for Taking This Substance?

Since the early 1950s, piperazines have been used widely by veterinarians as an ANTHELMINTIC drug. Anthelmintics are used to treat parasitic infections. In other words, they destroy worms. In humans, piperazine citrate serves a similar function and is used to treat pinworm and roundworm infestations in adults and children. The drug acts by paralyzing the muscles of mature worms and dislodging them from the walls of the intestines. The worms are then eliminated as part of a bowel movement.

In 1999, drug researchers in Japan found that a particular form of benzylpiperazine stimulates a brain chemical called ACETYLCHOLINE. A NEUROTRANSMITTER, acetycholine is involved in learning and memory. This led to the discovery of donepezil (Aricept), which helps ward off memory loss in patients with Alzheimer's and other brain diseases.

As of early 2005, other chemical substances related to BZP were being investigated for possible uses in the treatment of depression, psychosis, EPILEPSY, and severe pain. In addition, phenylpiperazine derivatives (substances similar to TFMPP) were being tested for their ability to kill certain types of cancerous tumors.

anthelmintic: pronounced ant-hel-MINN-tick; a substance that helps destroy and expel parasitic worms, especially worms located in the intestines

acetylcholine: pronounced ah-settle-KOH-leen; a neurotransmitter that forms from a substance called choline, which is released by the liver

neurotransmitter: a substance that helps spread nerve impulses from one nerve cell to another

epilepsy: a disorder involving the misfiring of electrical impulses in the brain, sometimes resulting in seizures and loss of consciousness

Typical Users

The U.S. Drug Enforcement Administration reported that the typical abusers of BZP and TFMPP are "adolescents and young adults involved with the current rave culture." Of particular concern is the fact that many of its users do not even know they are taking it. Some dealers do not realize they are selling it. Not only have BZP and TFMPP tablets been found among bags of ecstasy (MDMA) tablets, the powders of all three drugs have been found mixed together in drugs being passed off as pure ecstasy.

BZP is not considered a controlled substance worldwide. In late 2004 and early 2005, it was being sold over-the-counter in New Zealand as an herbal party pill. (Oddly enough, the pills contain no herbs.) The staff of New Zealand's Christchurch Hospital, according to a *New Zealand Press* article, said that piperazine users admitted for emergency treatment "were usually young women in their late teens or early twenties."

Usage Trends

Use of BZP was first reported in the United States and Switzerland in 2000. According to the U.S. Drug Enforcement Administration (DEA), seizure of BZP and TFMPP tablets, capsules, and powders increased steadily through 2004.

Teenagers and young adults who attend raves on a regular basis are the most frequent users of both BZP and TFMPP. Like ecstasy, piperazine has spread from the club scene to high schools and college campuses.

In the United States, BZP is usually imported in powder form and then manufactured into pills. Several hundred pounds of powdered BZP have been seized from India. Busts have been made for possession and use of piperazines throughout the United States, especially in California, Connecticut, and Texas.

In Europe, BZP—which is known there as A2—is marketed "as a cheap and safe alternative compared to illicit amphetamines," stated a DEA "Drug Intelligence Brief" released in December of 2001. As late as 2005, the drug was being sold over-the-counter in New Zealand as a legal stimulant under the brand name Nemesis. "The pills . . . are advertised as safe, legal alternatives to illegal HIGHS. There is no age restriction on sales," according to a drug authority interviewed in the *Ashburton Guardian*.

Louise Bleakley reported in the *New Zealand Press* that benzylpiperazine tablets, commonly referred to there as "party pills," are "neither classified as a drug nor a dietary supplement so there is no requirement for them to be labeled." Casual drug users in New Zealand seemed "less cautious" about taking BZP, noted Bleakley, "because of the commonly used 'herbal' label" on their packaging. "In fact, herbal party pills [are] synthetic compounds."

According to the *New Zealand Press* in late 2004, hospital emergency departments in urban New Zealand reported seeing "at least six patients a weekend suffering severe PARANOIA and dehydration" after taking the so-called herbal drugs. "Party-goers were arriving at the hospital hysterical and requiring sedation." At that time, New Zealand's associate health minister, Jim Anderton, proposed that a new classification be added to the A, B, and C ratings given to drugs

highs: drug-induced feelings ranging from excitement and joy to extreme grogginess

paranoia: abnormal feelings of suspicion and fear

Benzylpiperazine, or BZP, is the active ingredient in some forms of herbal ecstasy. Used as party drugs, they were once legal in the United States.
© James Leynse/Corbis.

there by law. These letter ratings are somewhat similar to the scheduling of drugs by number in the United States. Anderton's idea for a "D" rating, which would include party pills, has received considerable support.

Effects on the Body

Piperazines like BZP and TFMPP are PSYCHOSTIMULANTS. Because they affect the brain, the drugs cause a wide range of sensations and experiences. Sometimes these effects are considered pleasant by the user. Sometimes they are frightening. They can even be life threatening. Piperazines vary in their mind-altering properties. The drugs influence brain function by acting on chemicals called neurotransmitters, which can have profound effects on mood, learning, perceptions, and movement.

psychostimulants: pronounced SY-koh-STIM-yew-lents; stimulants that act on the brain

Animal research has shown that BZP triggers the release of neurotransmitters called DOPAMINE and NOREPINEPHRINE, two natural stimulants that the body produces on its own. TFMPP acts by stimulating nerve receptors sensitive to SEROTONIN, another neurotransmitter.

At doses of 20 milligrams to 100 milligrams, BZP and TFMPP reportedly produce a range of mental experiences lasting six to eight hours. Amphetamine-like effects include euphoria, alertness, a reduced need for both food and sleep, a heightened sense of touch and other pleasurable sensations, and a sense of emotional closeness with others. At higher doses, though, users have reported stomach pain, vomiting, and feelings of extreme anxiety and paranoia. A tingling feeling on the surface of the skin may make users feel as if insects are crawling all over them. Some users end up in emergency rooms panic-stricken, screaming, and suffering from extreme dehydration.

BZP acts very much like amphetamines or speed. Amphetamines are illegal without a prescription from a medical doctor. They can make users jumpy, irritable, and even violent. According to the U.S. Department of Justice, "BZP is about 10 to 20 times less potent than amphetamine." However, just one or two BZP tablets can have extreme negative effects on the people who take them.

Like amphetamines, piperazines increase the heart rate, blood pressure, and body temperature, which can be dangerous or even fatal. At high doses, piperazines may produce HALLUCINATIONS, convulsions, and slowed breathing that can result in death. The physical effects of piperazine use include nausea, vomiting, redness of the skin, stomach pains, thirst, dry mouth, frequent urination, bladder infection or irritation, severe headaches, and "hangover" feelings lasting up to two days. BZP and TFMPP also affect brain centers that control movement. Muscle stiffness, uncontrollable shaking, jaw clenching, and nervous tics may occur in users.

If BZP comes in contact with the eyes or skin, it can cause severe inflammation and burns. When inhaled, it irritates the respiratory tract, leaving the user with a sore throat, coughing fits, and difficulty breathing. Prolonged inhalation can cause chemical burns to the breathing tubes and the buildup of fluid in the lungs. When swallowed, piperazines are absorbed quickly through the linings of the stomach and intestines. Part of the drug is broken down by the actions of the liver and kidneys, and the rest is released from the body as urine.

Because piperazine abuse is relatively new among drug users, the harmful effects of BZP and TFMPP have not been fully determined. According to the Health and Safety Executive of the United Kingdom, piperazines are thought to have the potential to cause

dopamine: pronounced DOPE-uh-meen; a combination of carbon, hydrogen, nitrogen, and oxygen that acts as a neurotransmitter in the brain

norepinephrine: pronounced nor-epp-ih-NEFF-run; a natural stimulant produced by the human body

serotonin: a combination of carbon, hydrogen, nitrogen, and oxygen; it is found in the brain, blood, and stomach lining and acts as a neurotransmitter and blood vessel regulator

hallucinations: visions or other perceptions of things that are not really present

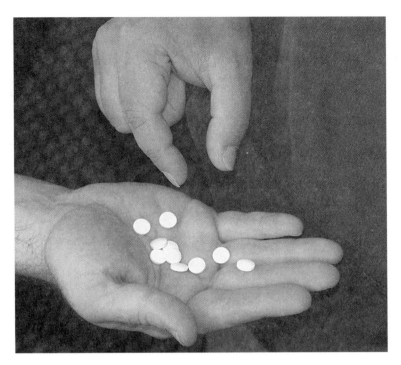

Mixing drugs is very dangerous. Obtaining them illegally is also very risky. The quality and content of illegal drugs are not checked by any government or medical agency, so users never know what they are getting. *Photo by Leitha Etheridge-Sims. Courtesy of Dan Newell.*

asthma, although how this occurs is still unknown. The effects in children and pregnant women also remain unknown.

Former speed addicts who took BZP experienced an increase in blood pressure and short-term mental experiences similar to those brought on by amphetamines. These data suggested that BZP was likely to be addictive and abused. Results of experiments conducted on rhesus monkeys, published in *Drug and Alcohol Dependence* in 2005, confirmed that BZP is as addicting as amphetamines. TFMPP taken alone, however, was not considered likely to be abused. Other animal experiments suggest that the use of piperazines can actually inhibit learning.

Reactions with Other Drugs or Substances

The DEA reports that BZP and TFMPP are sometimes deliberately mixed with ecstasy by drug dealers and then sold as ecstasy. Some users hoping for an extended or intensified high from ecstasy will

Weighty Issues

People who use BZP or TFMPP usually lose interest in food and may stop eating altogether. After about two weeks on the drug, however, the effects on food intake and weight loss level off. When the drug is stopped altogether, a "rebound effect" on the appetite center of the brain may occur, leading to excessive eating and weight gain.

knowingly combine these drugs. A DEA "Drug Intelligence Brief" described the drug-related death of a 23-year-old woman in Zurich, Switzerland, after she had consumed both BZP and ecstasy. Medical evidence suggests that the drug combination made her extremely thirsty. Before going into a coma, she consumed 10 liters of water in just 15 hours. The young woman experienced high blood pressure and brain swelling prior to her death.

Users have reported combining BZP with alcohol, Xanax (a benzodiazepine), dextromethorphan, marijuana, and hydrocodone (a steroid). They have described many of their experiences as frightening or unpleasant. A New Zealand alcohol and drug service expert was quoted in the *Ashburton Guardian* as saying that the "herbal highs" associated with BZP use are intensified by alcohol.

Warnings are given against combining prescription piperazines, used to treat parasitic infections, with certain psychiatric medications. The combination may cause violent seizures or convulsions. Piperazines are especially dangerous when used by people with kidney disease, liver disease, or a history of epilepsy.

Treatment for Habitual Users

The need for emergency room treatment rose considerably by 2004 among users of BZP and TFMPP. Both drugs are produced illegally. In many cases, users are unaware of the dosage of the tablets they take, which increases the risk of overdose and even death. Because piperazine abuse has been recognized only recently, specific programs for rehabilitation have not yet been developed. Treatment will most likely include psychological counseling.

Consequences

Piperazines are capable of disrupting a person's ability to think, communicate, and act sensibly. As with other mind-altering substances, use of BZP or TFMPP may jeopardize work or school performance, ruin relationships, and increase the likelihood of involvements in accidents. Loss of control or inappropriate behavior may cause other people to view the user with suspicion. Addiction can lead the user to abandon educational goals and engage in criminal activity.

The Law

In the United States, the Controlled Substances Act (CSA) of 1970 called for the assignment of all controlled drug substances into one of five categories called schedules. These schedules are based on a substance's medicinal value, possible harmfulness, and potential for abuse and addiction. Schedule I is reserved for the most dangerous drugs that have no recognized medical use.

In 2003, *Drug Topics* reported that the DEA was working to have both BZP and TFMPP added to the list of Schedule I drugs under the CSA. The reasoning behind these actions was that the drugs "have hallucinogenic or amphetamine-like activity and have been abused by individuals who have bought them through Internet companies." Until they were scheduled, BZP and TFMPP could be purchased legally from chemical supply houses. However, they were not intended for human consumption. Buyers got around this specification by lying about the intended use of the drug.

On March 18, 2004, the DEA officially classified BZP as a Schedule I drug, so its use in the United States is now regulated by federal law. Any person convicted of possessing and/or selling a Schedule I drug can face a lengthy prison term and hundreds of thousands of dollars in fines. Repeat offenders receive even harsher punishment.

For More Information

Periodicals

Bleakley, Louise. "Party Pill Labelling Frustrates." *New Zealand Press* (December 28, 2004).

De Boer, D., and others. "Piperazine-Like Compounds: A New Group of Designer Drugs-of-Abuse on the European Market." *Forensic Science International* (September, 2001): pp. 47-56.

"Doctors Warn of Dangers of 'Herbal High' Pills." *New Zealand Press* (November 15, 2004).

Fantegrossi, W. E., and others. "Reinforcing and Discriminative Stimulus Effects of 1-Benzylpiperazine and Trifluoro methyl-phenylpiperazine in Rhesus Monkeys." *Drug and Alcohol Dependence* (February 14, 2005): pp. 161-168.

"Three Substances Shift to Schedule I." *Drug Topics* (August 5, 2002): p. 12.

"Warning over Herbal Highs." *Ashburton Guardian* (February 4, 2005).

"What's Being Added to, Dropped from CS List." *Drug Topics* (October 6, 2003): p. 7.

Web Sites

"BZP and TFMPP: Chemicals Used to Mimic MDMA's Effects. Drug Intelligence Brief, December 2001." *U.S. Department of Justice, Drug Enforcement Administration, Intelligence Division.* http://www.usdoj.gov/dea/pubs/intel/02005/02005.pdf (accessed June 30, 2005).

"Drugs and Chemicals of Concern: N-Benzylpiperazine." *U.S. Department of Justice, Drug Enforcement Administration: Diversion Control Program.* http://www.deadiversion.usdoj.gov/drugs_concern/ (accessed June 30, 2005).

"Manufacture and Distribution of Unapproved Piperazine Products." *U.S. Food and Drug Administration, Center for Veterinary Medicine.* (Guideline No. 102). http://www.fda.gov/cvm/guidance/pipera.html (accessed June 30, 2005).

Pendleton, Robert. "BZP (1 Benzylpiperazine): Frequently Asked Questions." *The Lycaeum Drug Archives.* http://www.lycaeum.org/ (accessed June 30, 2005).

"Piperazine (Systemic)." *Healthtouch Online.* http://www.healthtouch.com/ (accessed June 30, 2005).

"Piperazine Citrate." *Nurses PDR.* http://www.nursespdr.com/ (accessed June 30, 2005).

"Proposed Maximum Exposure Limit for Piperazine and Piperazine Dihydrochloride." *Health & Safety Executive Regulatory Impact Assessment.* http://www.hse.gov.uk/ria/chemical/piperaz.htm (accessed June 30, 2005).

See also: Amphetamines; Designer Drugs; Ecstasy (MDMA)

Where to Learn More

Books

Balkin, Karen F. *Tobacco and Smoking.* San Diego, CA: Greenhaven Press, 2005.

Beers, Mark H., and others. *The Merck Manual of Medical Information,* 2nd ed. New York: Pocket Books, 2003.

Brecher, Edward M., and others. *The Consumers Union Report on Licit and Illicit Drugs.* Boston: Little Brown & Co., 1972. http://www.druglibrary.org/schaffer/library/studies/cu/cumenu.htm (accessed September 12, 2005).

Connelly, Elizabeth Russell. *Psychological Disorders Related to Designer Drugs.* Philadelphia, PA: Chelsea House, 2000.

Drug Enforcement Administration, U.S. Department of Justice. *Drugs of Abuse: 2005 Edition.* Washington, DC: Government Printing Office, 2005. http://www.usdoj.gov/dea/pubs/abuse/index.htm (accessed September 12, 2005).

Drummond, Edward H. *The Complete Guide to Psychiatric Drugs: Straight Talk for Best Results.* New York: Wiley, 2000.

Fenster, Julie M. *Ether Day: The Strange Tale of America's Greatest Medical Discovery and the Haunted Men Who Made It.* New York: HarperCollins, 2001.

Gahlinger, Paul M. *Illegal Drugs: A Complete Guide to Their History, Chemistry, Use and Abuse.* Las Vegas, NV: Sagebrush Press, 2001.

Gorman, Jack M. *The Essential Guide to Psychiatric Drugs,* 3rd ed. New York: St. Martin's Griffin, 1997.

Hyde, Margaret O., and John F. Setaro. *Drugs 101: An Overview for Teens.* Brookfield, CT: Twenty-first Century Books, 2003.

Keltner, Norman L., and David G. Folks. *Psychotropic Drugs.* Philadelphia: Mosby, 2001.

Kuhn, Cynthia, Scott Swartzwelder, and Wilkie Wilson. *Buzzed: The Straight Facts about the Most Used and Abused Drugs from Alcohol to Ecstasy,* 2nd ed. New York: W.W. Norton, 2003.

McCay, William. *The Truth about Smoking.* New York: Facts on File, 2005.

Olive, M. Foster. *Designer Drugs.* Philadelphia: Chelsea House, 2004.

Physicians' Desk Reference, 59th ed. Montvale, NJ: Thomson PDR, 2004.

Physicians' Desk Reference for Nonprescription Drugs and Dietary Supplements, 25th ed. Montvale, NJ: Thomson Healthcare, 2004.

lxxiii

Preston, John D., John H. O'Neal, and Mary C. Talaga. *Consumer's Guide to Psychiatric Drugs.* Oakland, CA: New Harbinger Publications, 1998.

Silverman, Harold M. *The Pill Book,* 11th ed. New York: Bantam Books, 2004.

Sonder, Ben. *All about Heroin.* New York: Franklin Watts, 2002.

Wagner, Heather Lehr. *Cocaine.* Philadelphia: Chelsea House, 2003.

Weatherly, Myra. *Ecstasy and Other Designer Drug Dangers.* Berkeley Heights, NJ: Enslow Publishers, 2000.

Weil, Andrew, and Winifred Rosen. *From Chocolate to Morphine.* Boston: Houghton Mifflin, 1993, rev. 2004.

Wolfe, Sidney M. *Worst Pills, Best Pills: A Consumer's Guide to Avoiding Drug-Induced Death or Illness.* New York: Pocket Books, 2005.

Periodicals

Hargreaves, Guy. "Clandestine Drug Labs: Chemical Time Bombs." *FBI Law Enforcement Bulletin* (April, 2000): pp. 1-9. http://www.fbi.gov/publications/leb/2000/apr00leb.pdf (accessed September 13, 2005).

Jefferson, David J. "America's Most Dangerous Drug." *Newsweek* (August 8, 2005).

Reid, T.R. "Caffeine." *National Geographic* (January, 2005): pp. 3-33.

Web Sites

"2003 National Survey on Drug Use and Health (NSDUH)." *Substance Abuse and Mental Health Services Administration (SAMHSA).* http://www.drugabusestatistics.samhsa.gov (accessed September 13, 2005).

"A to Z of Drugs." *British Broadcasting Corporation (BBC).* http://www.bbc.co.uk/crime/drugs (accessed September 13, 2005).

"Cigarette Smoking among American Teens Continues to Decline, but More Slowly than in the Past." *National Institute of Drug Abuse.* http://www.nida.nih.gov/Newsroom/04/2004MTFTobacco.pdf (accessed September 13, 2005).

"Club Drugs—An Update: Drug Intelligence Brief" (September 2001). *U.S. Department of Justice, Drug Enforcement Administration, Intelligence Division.* http://www.usdoj.gov/dea/pubs/intel/01026 (accessed September 13, 2005).

"Consumer Education: Over-the-Counter Medicine." *Center for Drug Evaluation and Research, U.S. Food and Drug Administration.* http://www.fda.gov/cder/consumerinfo/otc_text.htm (accessed September 13, 2005).

"DEA Briefs & Background: Drug Descriptions." *U.S. Drug Enforcement Administration.* http://www.dea.gov/concern/concern.htm (accessed September 13, 2005).

Natural Sources of Drugs

Left: Wild ephedra is shown growing in a canyon in Utah. *See* Ephedra, Vol. 3. *(© Scott T. Smith/Corbis)*

Above right: The sap of the opium poppy is used to make a variety of prescription and illegal painkillers. See Codeine, Vol. 2; Heroin, Vol. 3; Morphine, Vol. 4; and Opium, Vol. 5. *(© Vo Trung Dung/Corbis)*

Natural Sources of Drugs

Right: Some Native Americans use the hallucinogenic peyote cactus in religious rituals. *See* Mescaline, Vol. 4. *(AP/Wide World Photos)*

Below left: Tobacco is one of the most widely abused, mind-altering drugs in the world. See Nicotine, Vol. 4. *(© Kevin Fleming/Corbis)*

Natural Sources of Drugs

Top: Marijuana is the most widely used illegal controlled substance in the world. *See* Marijuana, Vol. 4. *(AP/Wide World Photos)*

Middle: Coffee is a major source of caffeine. *See* Caffeine, Vol. 2. *(© Renée Comet/PictureArts/Corbis)*

Bottom: DMT is found in the poisonous venom of the cane toad. *See* Dimethyl-tryptamine (DMT), Vol. 2. *(© Wayne Lawler; Ecoscene/Corbis)*

Herbal Drugs and Dietary Supplements

Top: Wild echinacea is shown growing near Mount Adams in Washington. *See* Herbal Drugs, Vol. 3. *(© Steve Terrill/Corbis)*

Middle: St. John's Wort is used to treat depression and anxiety. *See* Antidepressants, Vol. 1, and Herbal Drugs, Vol. 3. *(© Clay Perry/Corbis)*

Bottom: The bulking supplement creatine is used by weight lifters, bodybuilders, and other athletes. *See* Creatine, Vol. 2. *(© Najlah Feanny/Corbis)*

Older Illicit Drugs

Top: When snorted, cocaine reaches the brain in less than one minute. *See* Cocaine, Vol. 2. *(Photo by Lezlie Light)*

Middle: Putting tiny amounts of LSD on blotter papers is a common way to take a dose. *See* LSD (Lysergic Acid Diethylamide), Vol. 3. *(Sinclair Stammers/Photo Researchers, Inc.)*

Bottom: Heroin is a Schedule 1 drug, meaning that it has no medical value but a high potential for abuse. *See* Heroin, Vol. 3. *(Garry Watson/Science Photo Library)*

Prescription Drugs

Top row, left: Adderall®, 5 mg. *See* Adderall, Vol. 1.

Top row, middle: Darvocet-N®, 100 mg. *See* Opium, Vol. 5.

Top row, right: Demerol®, 100 mg. *See* Meperidine, Vol. 4.

2nd row, left: Dexedrine®, 5 mg. *See* Dextroamphetamine, Vol. 2.

2nd row, middle: Dilaudid®, 4 mg. *See* Hydromorphone, Vol. 3.

2nd row, right: Halcion®, 0.25 mg. *See* Benzodiazepine, Vol. 1.

3rd row, left: Lasix®, 40 mg. *See* Diuretics, Vol. 2.

3rd row, middle: MS Contin®, 15 mg. *See* Morphine, Vol. 4.

3rd row, right: Nitroglycerin, 6.5 mg. *See* Amyl Nitrite, Vol. 1.

4th row, left: OxyContin®, 40 mg. *See* Oxycodone, Vol. 5.

4th row, middle: Paxil®, 40 mg. *See* Antidepressants, Vol. 1.

4th row, right: Restoril®, 7.5 mg. *See* Benzodiazepine, Vol. 1.

5th row, left: Ritalin®, 20 mg. *See* Ritalin and Other Methylphenidates, Vol. 5.

5th row, middle: Valium®, 5 mg. *See* Tranquilizers, Vol. 5.

5th row, right: Vicodin ES®, 7.5 mg. *See* Meperidine, Vol. 4.

Bottom row, left: Wellbutrin®, 100 mg. *See* Antidepressants, Vol. 1.

Bottom row, middle: Xanax®, 2 mg. *See* Benzodiazepine, Vol. 1.

Bottom row, right: Xenical®, 120 mg. *See* Diet Pills, Vol. 2.

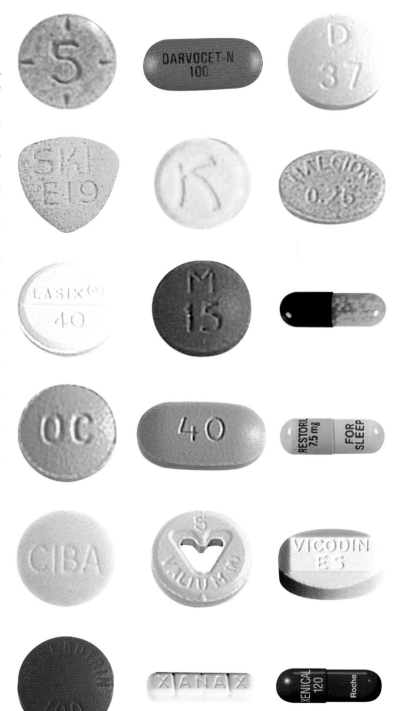

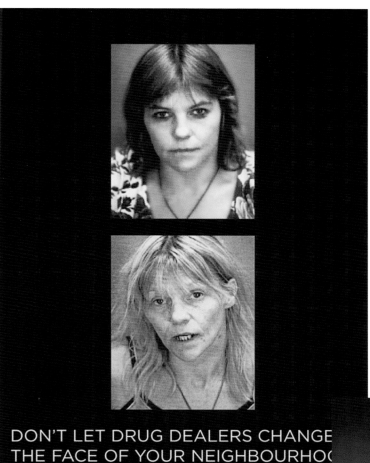

DON'T LET DRUG DEALERS CHANGE
THE FACE OF YOUR NEIGHBOURHOO
Call Crimestoppers anonymously on 0800 555 111.

**Public Service
Announcements (PSAs)
Warning Against Drug Use**

Left: Anti-methamphetamine public service announcement. See Methamphetamine, Vol. 4. (© Handout/Reuters/Corbis)

Below right: Anti-inhalant public service announcement. *See* Inhalants, Vol. 3. (National Institute on Drug Abuse)

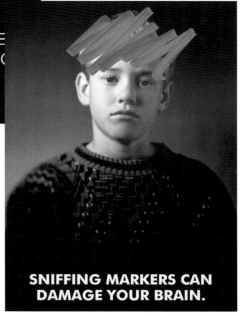

**SNIFFING MARKERS CAN
DAMAGE YOUR BRAIN.**

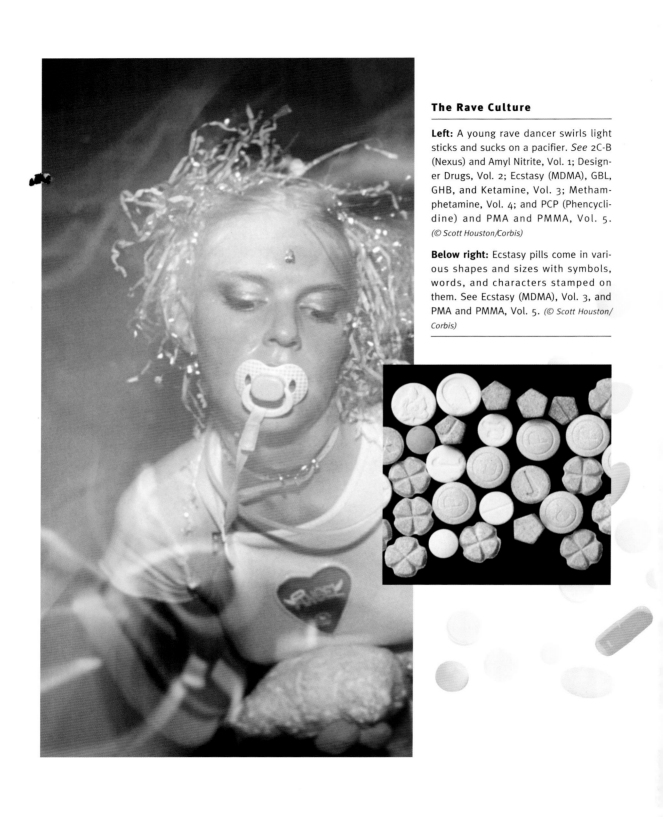

The Rave Culture

Left: A young rave dancer swirls light sticks and sucks on a pacifier. *See* 2C-B (Nexus) and Amyl Nitrite, Vol. 1; Designer Drugs, Vol. 2; Ecstasy (MDMA), GBL, GHB, and Ketamine, Vol. 3; Methamphetamine, Vol. 4; and PCP (Phencyclidine) and PMA and PMMA, Vol. 5. *(© Scott Houston/Corbis)*

Below right: Ecstasy pills come in various shapes and sizes with symbols, words, and characters stamped on them. See Ecstasy (MDMA), Vol. 3, and PMA and PMMA, Vol. 5. *(© Scott Houston/ Corbis)*

"Drug Abuse Warning Network, 2003: Interim National Estimates of Drug-Related Emergency Department Visits." *U.S. Department of Health and Human Services, Substance Abuse and Mental Health Services Administration.* http://dawninfo.samhsa.gov/files/DAWN_ED_Interim2003.pdf (accessed September 13, 2005).

"Drug Facts." *Office of National Drug Control Policy.* http://www.whitehousedrugpolicy.gov/drugfact/ (accessed September 13, 2005).

Drug Free AZ. http://www.drugfreeaz.com/ (accessed September 13, 2005).

"Drug Guide by Name." *Partnership for a Drug-Free America.* http://www.drugfree.org/Portal/Drug_Guide (accessed September 13, 2005).

"Drug Information." *CESAR: Center for Substance Abuse Research at the University of Maryland.* http://www.cesar.umd.edu/cesar/drug_info.asp (accessed September 13, 2005).

"Drug Information." *MedlinePlus.* http://www.nlm.nih.gov/medlineplus/druginformation.html (accessed September 13, 2005).

"Drugs and Chemicals of Concern." *U.S. Department of Justice, Drug Enforcement Administration, Office of Diversion Control.* http://www.deadiversion.usdoj.gov/drugs_concern (accessed September 13, 2005).

"Drugs and Human Performance Fact Sheets." *National Highway Traffic Safety Administration.* http://www.nhtsa.dot.gov/people/injury/research/job185drugs/technical-page.htm (accessed September 13, 2005).

"Drugs of Abuse: Uses and Effects Chart." *U.S. Department of Justice, Drug Enforcement Administration.* http://www.usdoj.gov/dea/pubs/abuse/chart.htm (accessed September 13, 2005).

"Eating Disorders Information Index." *National Eating Disorders Association.* http://www.nationaleatingdisorders.org/p.asp?WebPage_ID=294. (accessed September 13, 2005).

"Educating Students about Drug Use and Mental Health." *Centre for Addiction and Mental Health.* http://www.camh.net/education/curriculum_gr1to8intro.html (accessed September 13, 2005).

"The Faces of Meth." *Multnomah County Sheriff's Office.* http://www.facesofmeth.us/main.htm (accessed September 13, 2005).

"Generation Rx: National Study Reveals New Category of Substance Abuse Emerging: Teens Abusing Rx and OTC Medications Intentionally to Get High" (April 21, 2005). *Partnership for a Drug-Free America.* http://www.drugfree.org/Portal/About/NewsReleases/Generation_Rx_Teens_Abusing_Rx_and_OTC_Medications (accessed September 13, 2005).

"Health Channel—Drugs." *How Stuff Works.* http://health.howstuffworks.com/drugs-channel.htm (accessed September 13, 2005).

"Health Information from the Office of Dietary Supplements." *National Institutes of Health, Office of Dietary Supplements.* http://ods.od.nih.gov/Health_Information/Health_Information.aspx (accessed September 13, 2005).

"Herbal Supplements: Consider Safety, Too." *National Institutes of Health, National Center for Complementary and Alternative Medicine.* http://nccam.nih.gov/health/supplement-safety/ (accessed September 13, 2005).

"In the Spotlight: Club Drugs" (updated September 1, 2005). *National Criminal Justice Reference Service.* http://www.ncjrs.gov/spotlight/club_drugs/summary.html (accessed September 13, 2005).

"Index to Drug-Specific Information." *Center for Drug Evaluation and Research, U.S. Food and Drug Administration.* http://www.fda.gov/cder/drug/DrugSafety/DrugIndex.htm (accessed September 13, 2005).

Kyle, Angelo D., and Bill Hansell. "The Meth Epidemic in America—Two Surveys of U.S. Counties: The Criminal Effect of Meth on Communities and The Impact of Meth on Children" (July 5, 2005). *National Association of Counties (NACo).* http://www.naco.org/Content/ContentGroups/Publications1/Press_Releases/Documents/NACoMethSurvey.pdf (accessed September 13, 2005).

Monitoring the Future. http://www.monitoringthefuture.org/ and http://www.nida.nih.gov/Newsroom/04/2004MTFDrug.pdf (both accessed September 13, 2005).

"National Drug Intelligence Center (NDIC) Fast Facts Page." *National Drug Intelligence Center.* http://www.usdoj.gov/ndic/topics/ffacts.htm (accessed September 13, 2005).

"National Drug Threat Assessment: 2005" (February 2005). *U.S. Department of Justice, National Drug Intelligence Center.* http://www.usdoj.gov/ndic/pubs11/12620/index.htm (accessed September 13, 2005).

National Institute on Drug Abuse. http://www.nida.nih.gov/ and http://www.drugabuse.gov/ (both accessed September 13, 2005).

Neuroscience for Kids. http://faculty.washington.edu/chudler/neurok.html (accessed September 13, 2005).

"NIDA for Teens: The Science behind Drug Abuse: Mind over Matter." *National Institute on Drug Abuse.* http://teens.drugabuse.gov/mom/ (accessed September 13, 2005).

"NIDA InfoFacts: Science-Based Facts on Drug Abuse and Addiction." *National Institutes of Health, National Institute on Drug Abuse.* http://www.nida.nih.gov/infofacts/ (accessed September 13, 2005).

"NIDA Research Reports Index." *National Institutes of Health, National Institute on Drug Abuse.* http://www.nida.nih.gov/ResearchReports (accessed September 13, 2005).

"Partnership Attitude Tracking Study (PATS): Teens, 2004." *Partnership for a Drug-Free America.* http://www.drugfree.org/Files/Full_Report_

PATS_TEENS_7th-12th_grades_2004 (accessed September 13, 2005).

"Pulse Check: Drug Markets and Chronic Users in 25 of America's Largest Cities." *Executive Office of the President, Office of National Drug Control Policy.* http://www.whitehousedrugpolicy.gov/publications/drugfact/pulsechk/january04/january2004.pdf (accessed on September 13, 2005).

"Tobacco Information and Prevention Source (TIPS)." *Centers for Disease Control, National Center for Chronic Disease Prevention and Health Promotion.* http://www.cdc.gov/tobacco/issue.htm (accessed September 13, 2005).

"Under the Counter: The Diversion and Abuse of Controlled Prescription Drugs in the U.S." (July 2005). *National Center on Addiction and Substance Abuse at Columbia University.* http://www.casacolumbia.org/Absolutenm/articlefiles/380-final_report.pdf (accessed September 13, 2005).

Organizations

Al-Anon/Alateen (Canada)
Capital Corporate Centre, 9 Antares Dr., Suite 245
Ottawa, ON K2E 7V5
Canada
(613) 723-8484
(613) 723-0151 (fax)
wso@al-anon.org
http://www.al-anon.alateen.org/

Al-Anon/Alateen (United States)
1600 Corporate Landing Pkwy.
Virginia Beach, VA 23454-5617
USA
(757) 563-1600
(757) 563-1655 (fax)
wso@al-anon.org
http://www.al-anon.alateen.org/

Alcoholics Anonymous (AA)
475 Riverside Dr., 11th Floor
New York, NY 10115
USA
In the U.S./Canada: Look for "Alcoholics Anonymous" in any telephone directory.
http://www.aa.org/

American Botanical Council
6200 Manor Rd.
Austin, TX 78723
USA

(512) 926-4900
(800) 373-7105
(512) 926-2345 (fax)
abc@herbalgram.org
http://www.herbalgram.org

American Council for Drug Education (ACDE; a Phoenix House agency)
164 West 74th St.
New York, NY 10023
USA
(800) 488-DRUG
acde@phoenixhouse.org
http://www.acde.org

American Society of Addiction Medicine (ASAM)
4601 N. Park Ave., Upper Arcade #101
Chevy Chase, MD 20815
USA
(301) 656-3920
(301) 656-3815 (fax)
email@asam.org
http://www.asam.org/

Attention Deficit Disorder Association (ADDA)
P.O. Box 543
Pottstown, PA 19464
USA
(484) 945-2101
(610) 970-7520 (fax)
http://www.add.org/

Canadian Centre on Substance Abuse (CCSA)
75 Albert St., Suite 300
Ottawa, ON K1P 5E7
Canada
(613) 235-4048
(613) 235-8101 (fax)
info@ccsa.ca
www.ccsa.ca

Center for Substance Abuse Research (CESAR)
4321 Hartwick Rd., Suite 501
College Park, MD 20740
USA
(301) 405-9770
(301) 403-8342 (fax)
CESAR@cesar.umd.edu
www.cesar.umd.edu

Center for Substance Abuse Treatment (CSAT; a division of the Substance Abuse and Mental Health Services Administration)
1 Choke Cherry Rd., Room 8-1036
Rockville, MD 20857
USA
(800) 662-HELP(4357) or (877) 767-8432 (Spanish)
http://csat.samhsa.gov or http://findtreatment.samhsa.gov

Centers for Disease Control and Prevention (CDC; a division of the U.S. Department of Health and Human Services)
1600 Clifton Rd.
Atlanta, GA 30333
USA
(404) 639-3311
(800) 311-3435
http://www.cdc.gov/

Cocaine Anonymous World Services (CAWS)
3740 Overland Ave., Suite C
Los Angeles, CA 90034
USA
(310) 559-5833
(310) 559-2554 (fax)
cawso@ca.org
http://www.ca.org/

DARE America
P.O. Box 512090
Los Angeles, CA 90051-0090
USA
(800) 223-DARE
webmaster@dare.com
http://www.dare.com

Do It Now Foundation
Box 27568
Tempe, AZ 85285-7568
USA
(480) 736-0599
(480) 736-0771 (fax)
e-mail@doitnow
http://www.doitnow.org

Europe Against Drugs (EURAD)
8 Waltersland Rd.
Stillorgan, Dublin
Ireland
01-2756766/7
01-2756768 (fax)

eurad@iol.ie
www.eurad.net

Institute for Traditional Medicine (ITM)
2017 SE Hawthorne Blvd.
Portland, OR 97214
USA
(503) 233-4907
(503) 233-1017 (fax)
itm@itmonline.org
http://www.itmonline.org

Join Together (a project of the Boston University School of Public Health)
One Appleton St., 4th Floor
Boston, MA 02116-5223
USA
(617) 437-1500
(617) 437-9394 (fax)
info@jointogether.org
http://www.jointogether.org

Marijuana Anonymous World Services
P.O. Box 2912
Van Nuys, CA 91404
USA
(800) 766-6779
office@marijuana-anonymous.org
http://www.marijuana-anonymous.org

Methamphetamine Treatment Project, University of California at
Los Angeles, Integrated Substance Abuse Programs (ISAP)
11050 Santa Monica Blvd., Suite 100
Los Angeles, CA 90025
USA
(310) 312-0500
(310) 312-0538 (fax)
http://www.methamphetamine.org/mtcc.htm or www.uclaisap.org

Narconon International
7060 Hollywood Blvd., Suite 220
Hollywood, CA 90028
USA
(323) 962-2404
(323) 962-6872 (fax)
info@narconon.org or rehab@narconon.org
http://www.narconon.org

Narcotics Anonymous (NA)
P.O. Box 9999
Van Nuys, CA 91409

USA
(818) 773-9999
(818) 700-0700 (fax)
www.na.org

Narcotics Anonymous World Services Office (WSO)—Europe
48 Rue de l'Été/Zomerstraat
B-1050 Brussels
Belgium
32-2-646-6012
32-2-649-9239 (fax)
http://www.na.org

National Association for Children of Alcoholics (NACoA)
11426 Rockville Pike, Suite 100
Rockville, MD 20852
USA
(301) 468-0985
(888) 55-4COAS
(301) 468-0987 (fax)
nacoa@nacoa.org
http://www.nacoa.org/

National Cancer Institute, Tobacco Control Research Branch (TCRB)
Executive Plaza North, Room 4039B
6130 Executive Blvd. MSC 7337
Rockville, MD 20852
USA
(301) 594-6776
(301) 594-6787 (fax)
blakek@mail.nih.gov
www.tobaccocontrol.cancer.gov or http://dccps.nci.nih.gov/tcrb

National Capital Poison Center—Poison Help
3201 New Mexico Ave., NW Suite 310
Washington, DC 20016
USA
(202) 362-3867
(800) 222-1222
(202) 362-8377 (fax)
pc@poison.org
www.poison.org or www.1-800-222-1222.info

National Center for Complementary and Alternative Medicine Clearing-house (NCCAM; a division of the National Institutes of Health)
P.O. Box 7923
Gaithersburg, MD 20898
USA
(888) 644-6226

info@nccam.nih.gov
http://nccam.nih.gov/

National Center for Drug Free Sport, Inc.
810 Baltimore
Kansas City, MO 64105
USA
(816) 474-8655
(816) 474-7329 (fax)
info@drugfreesport.com
http://www.drugfreesport.com

National Center on Addiction and Substance Abuse at Columbia University (CASA)
633 Third Ave., 19th Floor
New York, NY 10017-6706
USA
(212) 841-5200
(212) 956-8020 (fax)
www.casacolumbia.org

National Council on Alcohol and Drug Dependence, Inc. (NCADD)
22 Cortlandt St., Suite 801
New York, NY 10007-3128
USA
(212) 269-7797
(800) 622-2255
(212) 269-7510 (fax)
national@ncadd.org
http://www.ncadd.org

National Eating Disorders Association
603 Stewart St., Suite 803
Seattle, WA 98101
USA
(206) 382-3587
(800) 931-2237
info@NationalEatingDisorders.org
http://www.nationaleatingdisorders.org

National Families in Action
2957 Clairmont Road NE, Suite 150
Atlanta, GA 30329
USA
(404) 248-9676
(404) 248-1312 (fax)
nfia@nationalfamilies.org
http://www.nationalfamilies.org/

National Inhalant Prevention Coalition (NIPC)
332 - A Thompson St.
Chattanooga, TN 37405
USA
(423) 265-4662
(800) 269-4237
nipc@io.com
http://www.inhalants.org

National Institute of Mental Health (NIMH; a division of the National
Institutes of Health)
6001 Executive Boulevard, Room 8184, MSC 9663
Bethesda, MD 20892-9663
USA
(301) 443-4513
(866) 615-6464
(301) 443-4279 (fax)
nimhinfo@nih.gov
http://www.nimh.nih.gov/

National Institute on Drug Abuse (NIDA; a division of the National
Institutes of Health)
6001 Executive Blvd., Room 5213
Bethesda, MD 20892-9561
USA
(301) 443-1124
(888) 644-6432
information@nida.nih.gov
http://www.drugabuse.gov or http://www.nida.nih.gov

National Institutes of Health (NIH)
9000 Rockville Pike
Bethesda, MD 20892
USA
(301) 496-4000
NIHinfo@od.nih.gov
http://www.nih.gov/

Nicotine Anonymous
419 Main St., PMB #370
Huntington Beach, CA 92648
USA
(415) 750-0328
info@nicotine-anonymous.org
http://www.nicotine-anonymous.org

Office of Dietary Supplements (ODS; a division of the National Institutes
of Health)
6100 Executive Blvd., Room 3B01, MSC 7517
Bethesda, MD 20892-7517

USA
(301) 435-2920
(301) 480-1845 (fax)
ods@nih.gov
http://ods.od.nih.gov/

Office of National Drug Control Policy (ONDCP; a division of the Executive Office of the President of the United States)
c/o Drug Policy Information Clearinghouse
P.O. Box 6000
Rockville, MD 20849-6000
USA
(800) 666-3332
(301) 519-5212 (fax)
ondcp@ncjrs.gov
http://www.whitehousedrugpolicy.gov/

Oregon Health & Science University, Department of Medicine, Division of Health Promotion and Sports Medicine
3181 S.W. Sam Jackson Park Rd., CR110
Portland, OR 97239-3098
USA
(503) 494-8051
(503) 494-1310 (fax)
hpsm@ohsu.edu
http://www.ohsu.edu/hpsm

SAMHSA's National Clearinghouse for Alcohol and Drug Information (NCADI)
P.O. Box 2345
Rockville, MD 20847-2345
USA
(301) 468-2600
(800) 729-6686
http://www.health.org

Students Against Destructive Decisions (SADD) National
Box 800
Marlborough, MA 01752
USA
(877) SADD-INC
(508) 481-5759 (fax)
info@sadd.org
http://www.sadd.org/

Substance Abuse and Mental Health Services Administration (SAMHSA; a division of the U.S. Department of Health and Human Services)
1 Choke Cherry Rd., Room 8-1036
Rockville, MD 20857

USA
(301) 443-8956
info@samsha.hhs.gov
http://www.samhsa.gov

U.S. Anti-Doping Agency
1330 Quail Lake Loop., Suite 260
Colorado Springs, CO 80906-4651
USA
(719) 785-2000
(866) 601-2632; (800) 233-0393 (drug reference line);
or (877) PLAY-CLEAN (877-752-9253)
(719) 785-2001 (fax)
drugreference@usantidoping.org
http://www.usantidoping.org/

U.S. Drug Enforcement Administration (DEA)
Mailstop: AXS, 2401 Jefferson Davis Hwy.
Alexandria, VA 22301
USA
(202) 307-1000
http://www.dea.gov

U.S. Food and Drug Administration (FDA)
5600 Fishers Ln.
Rockville, MD 20857
USA
(888) INFO-FDA (888-463-6332)
http://www.fda.gov

World Anti-Doping Agency (WADA)
Stock Exchange Tower, 800 Place Victoria, Suite 1700
P.O. Box 120
Montreal, PQ H4Z 1B7
Canada
(514) 904-9232
(514) 904-8650 (fax)
info@wada-ama.org
www.wada-ama.org/

Volume numbers are in *italic*.

Boldface indicates main entries and their page numbers.

Illustrations are marked by (ill.).

E